CW00432101

French Glossary of Tourism

French-English
English-French

EuroLexus series

i

impact books

First published in Great Britain in 1994 by
Impact Books
151 Dulwich Road, London SE24 0NG

© Lexus Ltd 1994

ISBN 1 874687 40 4

Printed and bound by The Guernsey Press, Guernsey

ont contribué/contributors

Patricia Clarke   Céline Haddad
Con Ring   Ronnie Smith

TABLE DES MATIÈRES
CONTENTS

PREFACE
PRÉFACE

This glossary contains a wide range of vocabulary relevant to the tourist industry. Particular attention has been focused on the vocabulary used and encountered by those who are service providers in the tourist industry: the vocabulary of hoteliers, hotel staff, travel agents, tour operators, airlines, airport personnel, restaurateurs, tourist information personnel, leisure specialists and others. With an appendix containing typical tourism-related letters in both French and English, useful phrases, conversion tables and geographical names, this is a highly practical bilingual reference tool for practitioners or students of the tourist trade.

Ce lexique contient une grande variété de termes relatifs à l'industrie du tourisme. Il rend compte, avec un intérêt particulier, du vocabulaire utilisé et rencontré par les prestataires de services touristiques : le vocabulaire des voyagistes et des agents de voyages, des professionnels de l'hôtellerie et de la restauration, des transporteurs et du personnel aéroportuaire, des agents d'information touristique et des spécialistes du loisir. En annexe vous trouverez des exemples de lettres usuelles dans l'industrie touristique en anglais et en français, des phrases et expressions utiles, des tables de conversion et une liste bilingue de noms géographiques, ce qui fait de cet ouvrage un outil de référence fort pratique pour les étudiants et les professionnels du marché du tourisme.

abréviations/**abbreviations**

adj	*adjectif*/adjective
Am	American English/*anglais américain*
Br	British English/*anglais britannique*
f	*féminin*/feminine
qch	*quelque chose*/something
qn	*quelqu'un*/somebody
m	*masculin*/masculine
pl	*pluriel*/plural
sb	somebody/*quelqu'un*
sth	something/*quelque chose*
vi	*verbe intransitif*/intransitive verb
vt	*verbe transitif*/transitive verb
≈	*équivalent culturel*/cultural equivalent

A

à [*destination*] to
Abacus *m* Abacus
abats *mpl* offal; [*de volaille*] giblets
abbaye *f* abbey
abonnement saisonnier *m* season ticket
Académie internationale du tourisme *f* International Academy of Tourism
accident *m* accident
accompagnateur *m* courier, tour conductor *Am*, tour leader *Am*
accompagnatrice *f* courier, tour conductor *Am*, tour leader *Am*
accord bilatéral *m* bilateral agreement
accord inter-compagnie *m* interlining agreement
accord de franchise *m* franchise agreement
accords d'Helsinki *mpl* Helsinki Agreement, Helsinki Accord
accréditation *f* accreditation
accréditif *m* [*lettre de crédit*] letter of credit
accueil *m* reception
accueil handicapés *m* services for the disabled
accueillir to greet
acculturation *f* acculturation
ACECI = Association des Compagnies Européennes des Charters Indépendants *f*

achat *m* purchase
achat de bloc-sièges *m* advance booking charter
achats hors taxes *mpl* tax-free shopping
acheter to purchase
acheteur *m* purchaser, buyer
acompte *m* down payment
actif circulant *m* current assets
actionnaire *mf* shareholder
activité aquatique *f* water fun
activité sportive *f* sport, sporting activity
activité de plein air *f* outdoor activity
adaptateur *m* adaptor
addition *f* bill, check *Am*
administration *f* administration
ADONET = Association Des Offices Nationaux Étrangers de Tourisme *f*
ADP = Aéroports De Paris
AEA *f* AEA
AEHT = Association Européenne des écoles d'Hôtellerie et du Tourisme *f*
aérogare *m* terminal building
aéroglisseur *m* hovercraft
aéronef *m* aircraft
Aéropoint *m* ≈ airmile; *accumuler des Aéropoints* to collect airmiles
aéroport *m* airport
aéroport "hub" *m* hub airport

aéroport régional *m* regional airport

aéroport d'apport extérieur *m* feeder airport; [*pour "hub"*] spoke

aéroport de déroutement *m* diverting airport

aéroport de remplacement *m* alternative airport

Aéroports de Paris *m* body which controls Paris airports

aéroportuaire airport

AFAT = Association Française d'Action Touristique *f*

affectation des places *f* seating plan

affichage *m* display

afficher complet to be sold out

afficher les prix to display prices

afficheur *m* visual display unit

affrètement *m* chartering

affréter to charter

affréteur *m* charterer

AFPTA = Association Française des Professionnels du Tourisme d'Affaires *f*

âge *m* age

agence *f* agency

agence commerciale *f* public sales office

agence distributrice *f* retail travel agency

Agence nationale d'information touristique *f* national body which deals with tourism information

agence réceptive *f* ground handling agency

Agence régionale de tourisme et loisirs *f* name given to the "Comités régionaux du tourisme" in French overseas territories

agence spécialisée dans le tourisme d'affaires *f* business house agency

agence spécialisée dans le voyage de stimulation *f* incentive company

agence de réceptif *f* ground handling agency, ground operator

agence de réservation *f* booking agency

agence de voyages *f* travel agency

agence de voyages de discompte *f* discount travel agency, bucket shop

agenda *m* diary

agenda de réservation *m* book register, reservations book, hotel register

agent commercial *m* sales representative

agent exclusif *m* sole agent

agent général *m* general sales agent

agent de réceptif *m* ground handling agent

agent de réservation *m* reservation agent

agent de sécurité *m* security officer

agent de voyages *m* travel agent

agneau *m* lamb

agrément *m* agency appointment; [*garantie financière*] bonding scheme

agrément ATAF *m* ATAF bonding scheme

agrément IATA *m* IATA bonding scheme

aide-cuisinier *m* kitchen assistant

aide-gouvernante *f* assistant housekeeper

aide-serveur *m* busboy *Am*,

waiter's assistant
aide de cuisine *mf* kitchen hand
AIDT = Association Interparlementaire Du Tourisme *f*
AIEST = Association Internationale d'Experts Scientifiques du Tourisme *f*
aiglefin *m* haddock
AIH = Association Internationale de l'Hôtellerie *f*
ail *m* garlic
aile *f* wing
air conditionné *m* air conditioning
air/mer air/sea
Airbus *m* Airbus
aire naturelle *f* small, informal campsite
aire de jeux *f* play area
aire de pique-nique *f* picnic site, picnic area
aire de stationnement *f* [*des avions*] apron
AIT = Académie Internationale du Tourisme *f*
alarme incendie *f* fire alarm
alerte à la bombe *f* bomb scare
alèse *f* undersheet
aller à bicyclette to cycle
aller-retour *m* return ticket, round-trip ticket *Am*
aller simple *m* single ticket, one-way ticket
allotement *m* allotment
allumettes *fpl* matches
aloyau *m* sirloin
alphapage *m* bleeper
alpinisme *m* mountaineering
altitude *f* altitude
Amadeus *m* Amadeus
améliorer to upgrade
aménagement du territoire *m* physical planning

ameublement *m* furnishings, furniture
ampoule *f* (light) bulb
amuse-gueule *m* appetizer
ananas *m* pineapple
anchois *m* anchovy
Ancien Monde *m* Old World
ANCV = Association Nationale pour les Chèques Vacances *f*
anguille *f* eel
animal domestique *m* pet
animateur *m* entertainments officer, animator, social officer
animateur de croisière *m* cruise director
animateur de réception *m* toast master
animation *f* [*actif*] activities; [*passif*] entertainment
ANIT = Agence Nationale d'Information Touristique *f*
anniversaire *f* birthday; [*commémoration*] anniversary
annuaire téléphonique *m* telephone directory
annulation *f* cancellation
annulation de dernière minute *f* late cancellation
annuler to cancel
apéritif *m* aperitif
APEX *m* APEX
APGI = Association Professionel des Guides-Interprètes *f*
Apollo *m* Apollo
appareil automatique de paiement de parking *m* parking ticket machine
appartement *m* apartment
appartement en multipropriété *m* timeshare
appel *m* [*téléphonique*] telephone call
appel interurbain *m* trunk call

appel matinal *m* early morning call

appel de réveil *m* wake-up call, alarm call

appeler to call; [*client qui n'est pas dans sa chambre*] to page

apport de devises étrangères *m* foreign currency earnings

apprenti *m* trainee

approvisionnement *m* supplies

après-ski *m* après-ski

APSAV = Association Professionnelle de Solidarité des Agences de Voyages *f*

AR (= Aller-Retour) *m* RT

architecte paysagiste *m* landscape gardener

argent *m* money

argent comptant *m* cash

argent liquide *m* cash

argenterie *f* silverware

armateur *m* shipowner

armoire *f* wardrobe, clothes closet *Am*

arrhes *fpl* deposit

arrivée *f* arrival

arrivée anticipée *f* early arrival

arrivée matinale *f* early morning arrival

arrivée tardive *f* late arrival

arrivée de touristes *f* tourist arrival

arriver [*dans un hôtel*] to arrive, to check in

artichaut *m* artichoke

articles divers *mpl* sundries

artisanat *m* craftwork

ARTL = Agence Régionale de Tourisme et Loisirs *f*

AS (= Aller Simple) OW

ascenseur *m* lift, elevator *Am*

ascenseur à bagages *m* baggage lift

ascenseur de service *m* service lift

asperges *fpl* asparagus

assaisonner to season

assiette *f* plate

assistance juridique *f* legal aid

assistance sanitaire *f* medical care

assistance technique aux véhicules *f* roadside assistance

assistant de direction *m* deputy manager, assistant manager

assistant du chef de cuisine *m* sous chef

assistante gouvernante *f* assistant housekeeper

association commerciale *f* trade association

Association européenne des compagnies aériennes *f* Association of European Airlines

Association européenne des compagnies d'aviation régionales *f* European Regional Airlines Association

Association européenne des écoles d'hôtellerie et du tourisme *f* European Association of Hotel and Tourism Schools

Association française d'action touristique *f* French tourism body which welcomes foreign journalists and people in the tourism industry

Association française des professionnels du tourisme d'affaires *f* association of agencies which specialize in business travel

Association internationale d'experts scientifiques du tourisme *f* International Association of Scientific Experts in Tourism

Association internationale de

charter aérien *f* International Air Carrier Association

Association internationale de tour managers *f* International Association of Tour Managers

Association internationale de l'hôtellerie *f* International Hotel Association

Association internationale des bureaux de congrès et de tourisme *f* International Association of Convention and Visitor Bureaux

Association internationale des transporteurs aériens *f* International Air Transport Association

Association interparlementaire du tourisme *f* Interparliamentary Association for Tourism

Association mondiale des agences de voyages *f* World Association of Travel Agencies

Association Nationale pour les Chèques Vacances *f* association that runs holiday savings scheme for workers with contributions from employers

Association professionnelle de solidarité des agences de voyages *f* professional association for travel agencies

Association professionnelle des guides-interprètes *f* professional association of bilingual tour guides

association d'automobilistes *f* motoring organization

association de tourisme *f* tourism association

Association des compagnies européennes des charters indépendants *f* association of independent European charterers

Association des offices nationaux étrangers de tourisme *f* association of foreign national tourist offices based in France

Association des transporteurs aériens de la zone franc *f* air transport association of French-speaking countries

assurance *f* insurance

assurance bagage(s) *f* baggage insurance

assurance dépannage *f* car breakdown and recovery insurance

assurance médicale *f* medical insurance

assurance médicale de voyage *f* travel medical insurance

assurance responsabilité civile *f* public liability insurance

assurance vacances *f* holiday insurance

assurance pour les personnes transportées *f* personal accident insurance

assurance sur les objets personnels *f* personal property insurance

ATAF = **Association des Transporteurs Aériens de la zone Franc** *f*

atelier *m* [*de maintenance*] workshop

ATH = **Attaché Tourisme-Hôtellerie** *m*

attaché commercial *m* sales representative

attaché tourisme-hôtellerie *m* Chamber of Commerce and Industry employee in charge of tourism

atterrir to land

atterrissage *m* landing

attraction touristique *f* tourist attraction, visitor attraction

attractions *fpl* attractions; [*touristiques*] sights

attrait touristique *m* tourist attraction; [*charme*] tourist appeal

attribuer [*chambre*] to allocate

auberge *f* hostel, inn

auberge rurale *f* country inn

auberge de campagne *f* country inn

auberge de jeunesse *f* youth hostel, cotel *Am*

aubergine *f* aubergine, egg plant *Am*

audit marketing *m* marketing audit

auditeur *m* auditor

auditorium *m* auditorium

autobus *m* bus

autocar *m* coach

autocariste *m* coach tour operator

autochtone *m* non-alien, native

autocollant F *m* F sticker (*for French cars*)

automatisation *f* automation

automne *m* autumn, fall *Am*

autoroute *f* motorway, highway *Am*

auto-stop *m* hitch-hiking; *faire de l'auto-stop* to hitch-hike

avance: à l'avance in advance; *d'avance* in advance

aviation *f* aviation

avion *m* aircraft, airplane, plane

avion charter *m* charter plane

avion gros porteur *m* jumbo jet, wide bodied aircraft

avion moyen porteur *m* regular bodied aircraft

avion petit porteur *m* narrow bodied aircraft

avion supersonique *m* supersonic aircraft

avion-taxi *m* taxiplane

avion à hélices *m* prop jet

avion à réaction *m* jet

avion de ligne *m* passenger aircraft

avis de billet payé d'avance *m* prepaid ticket advice

avis de délogement *m* room change notice

avis de réception *m* message from reception

avocat *m* avocado

axe routier *m* trunk road

B

babyphone *m* baby-listening microphone

baby-sitting *m* baby-sitting

bac *m* [*pour factures, etc.*] tray

bac restauration *m* "baccalauréat" in restaurant work

bac technologique hôtelier *m* "baccalauréat" of vocational training in hotel work

BAFA = Brevet d'Aptitude à la Fonction d'Animateur *m*

BAFD = Brevet d'Aptitude à la Fonction de Directeur *m*

bagage *m* piece of luggage

bagages *mpl* luggage, baggage; *faire ses bagages* to pack

bagages accompagnés *mpl* accompanied baggage

bagages enregistrés *mpl* checked baggage

bagages non-accompagnés *mpl* unaccompanied baggage

bagages non-enregistrés *mpl* unchecked baggage

bagage(s) à main *m(pl)* hand baggage, hand luggage, cabin baggage, carry-on baggage

bagages de soute *mpl* hold baggage

bagagiste *m* luggage porter, porter; [*à aéroport*] baggage handler

baignoire *f* bath, tub *Am*

bain *m* bath

bain bouillonnant *m* spa bath

bain de vapeur *m* steam bath

bains *mpl* baths

baisser les prix to cut prices

balance touristique *f* tourism balance

balance du main courantier de nuit *f* night auditor's report

balcon *m* balcony

banane *f* banana

banque *f* bank

banquet *m* banquet

bar *m* bar

bar à vin *m* wine bar

barmaid *f* barmaid

barman *m* barman

barbecue *m* barbecue

barre de soutien *f* [*de baignoire*] bath rail

base de données *f* database

base de loisirs *f* country park

base de plein air et loisirs *f* country park

basse saison *f* low season

bateau *m* ship, boat

bateau-hôtel *m* botel

bateau à fond de verre *m* glass-bottomed boat

bateau d'excursion *m* pleasure boat

bateau de croisière *m* cruise ship

bavette *f* skirt (of beef)

bébé *m* baby, infant

bed and breakfast *m* bed and breakfast, B & B

bénéfice *m* profit

bénéfice d'exploitation *f* operating profit

BEP = Brevet d'Enseignement Professionnel *m*

BEP hôtellerie *m* certificate of vocational training in hotel work

betterave *f* beetroot

beurre *m* butter

bible *f* bible

bicyclette *f* bicycle

bidet *m* bidet

bien-aménagé well-appointed

bien cuit well done

biens d'équipement *mpl* capital goods

bienvenue: *bienvenue en France* welcome to France; *bienvenue à Glasgow* welcome to Glasgow

bière *f* beer

bière blonde *f* lager

bière brune *f* ≈ brown ale

bière rousse *f* bitter

bifteck *m* steak

bilan de la disponibilité des chambres *m* room availability report

bilingue bilingual

billet *m* ticket

billet aller *m* single ticket, one-way ticket

billet aller-retour *m* return ticket, round-trip ticket *Am*

billet bradé *m* discounted ticket

billet "congés payés" *m* SNCF rate for workers allowing discount once a year for holiday travel purposes

billet demi-tarif *m* half-fare ticket

billet "famille nombreuse" *m* special SNCF rates for families with 3 children or more

billet Joker *m* saver rail ticket

billet neutre *m* blank ticket

billet open *m* open(-date) ticket

billet simple *m* single ticket

billet souple *m* flexible ticket

billet d'avion *m* plane ticket, airline ticket, air ticket

billet d'avion à tarif réduit *m* discounted air ticket

billet de première *m* first class ticket

billet de seconde *m* second class ticket

billet de tour du monde *m* round-the-world ticket

billet de transport *m* ticket

billet sans condition *m* flexible ticket

billets complémentaires *mpl* conjunction tickets

billetterie *f* ticket office; [*délivrance de titres de transport*] ticketing

billetterie automatique *f* automatic ticket machine

billettiste ticketing clerk

bip *m* bleeper

biscuit *m* biscuit

bistro(t) *m* bistro

BITEJ = Bureau International pour le Tourisme et les Échanges de la Jeunesse *m*

BITS = Bureau Internationale du Tourisme Social *m*

blanc *m* [*de poulet*] chicken breast, breast of chicken

blanc white

blanchir to blanche

blanchisserie *f* laundry

bleu [*viande*] very rare

bloc-notes memo pad, note pad

bloc sanitaire *m* toilet block

bloc-sièges *m* allotment, block of seats

bloquer [*chambres*] to block
bœuf *m* beef
bois *m* wood
boisson *f* drink, beverage
boisson chaude *f* hot drink
boisson fraîche *f* cold drink
boîte *f* (night)club
boîte aux lettres *f* post box, mail box *Am*
bon *m* slip; [*avoir*] coupon, voucher
bon plein crédit *m* full credit voucher, unlimited value coupon
bon vacances *m* voucher supplied by holiday associations to less well-off families to help cover holiday expenses
bon d'agence *m* travel agent's voucher
bon d'annulation *m* cancellation form
bon d'échange *m* travel agent's voucher, voucher
bon d'échange "crédit illimité" *m* unlimited value voucher, full credit voucher
bon d'hébergement *m* accommodation voucher
bon d'hôtel *m* hotel voucher
bon de caisse *m* petty cash voucher
bon de commande *m* purchase order
bon de débours *m* [*pour services aux clients*] visitors paid out voucher, VPO voucher
bon de décaissement *m* disbursement voucher, paid out voucher
bon de réduction *m* discount voucher
bon de réservation *m* reservation form
bon de transfert débit *m* transfer debit voucher
bonnet de bain *m* shower cap
bord: à bord on board
bord de mer *m* seaside
bordereau d'encaissement *m* pay-in slip
bordereau de change *m* change form
bordereau de réservations *m* reservation sheet
borne incendie *f* fire hydrant
bouche d'incendie *f* fire hydrant
bouchon *m* cork; *droit de bouchon* *m* corkage
bouchonné corked
bouilli boiled
bouillir to boil
boulangerie *f* bakery
bouquet *m* bouquet
bouquet d'accueil *m* welcome bouquet
bourbon *m* bourbon
bouteille *f* bottle
boutiquaire *m* shopping area
boutique *f* shop
boutique d'aéroport *f* airport shop
boutique de cadeaux *f* gift shop
boutique de souvenirs *f* souvenir shop
boutique de souvenirs-cadeaux *f* souvenir and gift shop
boutique hors taxes *f* duty-free shop, tax-free shop
BP = Brevet Professionnel *m*
BP restaurant *m* vocational qualification in restaurant work
BP de barman *m* vocational qualification in barwork
BP de cuisinier *m* vocational qualification in catering
BP de sommelier *m* vocational qualification in wine-waiting
BPAL = Base de Plein Air et

9

Loisirs *f*

bradé cut-price

braisage *m* braising

braisé braised

brasserie *f* brasserie

brevet professionnel *m* vocational qualification

Brevet d'aptitude à la fonction d'animateur *m* professional qualification for entertainments organizers

Brevet d'aptitude à la fonction de directeur *m* professional qualification for entertainments directors

Brevet d'enseignement professionnel *m* vocational qualification

Brevet de technicien hôtelier *m* professional qualification in hotelkeeping

Brevet de technicien supérieur *m* advanced vocational qualification

Brevet de technicien supérieur de tourisme-loisirs *m* advanced professional qualification in tourism and leisure

broche *f* spit

brochette *f* kebab; [*broche*] skewer

brochure *f* leaflet, brochure

brocoli *m* broccoli

broyeur d'ordures *m* waste disposal unit

brunch *m* brunch

BSP *m* BSP

BTH = Brevet de Technicien Hôtelier *m*

BTS = Brevet de Technicien Supérieur *m*

BTS gestion en hôtellerie et restauration *f* advanced vocational course in hotel management and catering

BTS hôtellerie-restauration *m* advanced vocational qualification in hotelkeeping

BTSTL = Brevet de Technicien Supérieur de Tourisme-Loisirs *m*

buanderie *f* laundry, laundry room, in-house laundry

budget *m* budget

buffet *m* buffet

buffet froid *m* cold buffet

buffet à volonté *m* unlimited buffet

buffet de salades *m* salad bar

buffet du petit déjeuner *m* breakfast buffet

bulletin d'annulation *m* cancellation form

bulletin d'inscription *m* registration form

bulletin de changement de tarif *m* tariff change notification form

bulletin de délogement *m* room change notification form

bulletin de dépôt *m* safe deposit receipt

bumping *m* bumping

bungalow *m* bungalow

bureau *m* office

bureau central *m* central office

Bureau international du tourisme social *m* International Bureau of Social Tourism

Bureau international pour le tourisme et les échanges de la jeunesse *m* International Bureau for Youth Tourism and Exchanges

bureau d'émission *m* issuing office

bureau d'information *m* information office

bureau d'inscriptions *m*

registration desk
bureau de change *m* bureau de change
bureau de contrôle *m* control office
bureau de facturation *m* billing office
bureau de main-courante *m* book-keeper's office

bureau de poste *m* post office
bureau de renseignements *m* enquiry desk, information desk; [*pièce*] information office
bureau de réservations *m* reservations bureau, booking office
bureau de tabac *m* tobacconist
bureautique *f* office automation

C

cabaret *m* cabaret
cabillaud *m* cod
cabine *f* cabin, berth
cabine téléphonique *f* telephone box, telephone booth *Am*
cabine de bain *f* changing cubicle
cabine de luxe *f* de-luxe cabin, stateroom
cabinet de toilettes *m* toilet, washroom *Am*
câble *m* wire, cable
cabotage *m* cabotage
cacher kosher
cachet *m* validator, stamp
cadeau *m* gift
cadeau publicitaire *m* freebie, giveaway
cadre *m* executive
café *m* coffee, black coffee; [*bar*] café

café complet *m* café complet
café crème *m* white coffee
café décaféiné *m* decaffeinated coffee
café au lait *m* white coffee, coffee with milk *Am*
cafétéria *m* cafeteria
cafetier *m* breakfast cook, café-owner
cafetier-limonadier *m* café-owner
cafetière *f* coffee pot
cage d'escalier *f* stairwell
cahier de bord *m* logbook, memorandum
cahier de consignes *m* logbook
cahier de réclamations *m* complaints book
cahier des prix *m* price manual
cahier des tarifs *m* tariff manual
caille *f* quail

caisse *f* cash desk; [*enregistreuse*] cash register

caisse électronique *f* electronic billing machine

Caisse nationale des Monuments historiques et des sites *f* ≈ National Trust

caissier *m* cashier, auditor

caissier de nuit *m* night auditor

caissier de la réception *m* front office cashier

calamar *m* squid

cale *f* hold

calèche *m* hansom

camp *m* camp

camp d'adolescents *m* holiday camp for teenagers, camp *Am*

camp de loisirs *m* holiday camp

camp de tourisme *m* holiday camp; [*terrain de camping aménagé*] camp site (with facilities)

campage-caravanage *m* camping-caravanning

campagne *f* [*paysage*] countryside

campagne publicitaire *f* advertising campaign

campagne de marketing *f* marketing campaign

campagne de publicité *f* advertising campaign

camper to camp

campeur *m* camper

camping *m* [*activité*] camping; [*lieu*] camping site, camp site

camping aménagé *m* camp site (with facilities)

camping-car *m* camper, mobile home, motor-home *Am*, recreational vehicle *Am*

camping-caravaning *m* camping-caravanning

camping libre *m* non-site camping

in suitable spots with permission if required

camping sauvage *m* wild camping

camping à la ferme *m* farm camping

canal *m* canal

canapé *m* sofa

canapé-lit sofa bed, studio bed

canard *m* duck

canoë-kayac *m* canoeing

canyoning *m* canyoning

CAP = Certificat d'Aptitude Professionnelle *m*

CAP café-brasserie *m* certificate of vocational training in café and bar work

CAP hébergement *m* certificate of vocational training in accommodation

CAP restaurant *m* certificate of vocational training in restaurant work

CAP de cuisine *m* certificate of vocational training in catering

capacité *f* capacity

capacité d'accueil *f* accommodation capacity, available bed capacity; [*en sièges*] seating capacity, carrying capacity

capitaine *m* captain

capitale *f* capital

captif captive

car *m* coach

car-ferry *m* car ferry

caractéristiques du comportement *fpl* behaviour characteristics

carafe *f* carafe

caravanage *m* caravanning

caravane *f* caravan, trailer *Am*

caravane de tourisme *f* touring caravan

caravaning *m* caravanning
carnaval *m* carnival
carnet de bord *m* memorandum
carnet de passage en douanes *m*
  carnet
carnet de voyage *m* travel
  documents
carotte *f* carrot
carré *m* best end of neck
carré Jeunes *m* reduced-rate rail
  travel card for young people
  within France
carré d'agneau *m* rack of lamb
carrelet *m* plaice
**carrousel de livraison des
  bagages** *m* baggage carousel
carte *f* card; [*de pays, etc.*] map;
  [*menu*] menu; *à la carte* à la
  carte
carte accréditive *f* charge card
carte American Express *f*
  American Express (card)
carte Amex *f* Amex (card)
carte Amtrak *f* Amtrak Rail Pass
carte bancaire *f* cheque card,
  banker's card
carte Bleue *f* Visa (card)
carte-clé *f* key card
carte-clé électronique *f* electronic
  key card
carte couple-famille *f* reduced-
  rate rail travel card for families
  that do not qualify for the "carte
  famille nombreuse"
carte Eurocard Mastercard *f*
  Mastercard, Access
carte famille nombreuse *f*
  reduced-rate card for families
  with three or more children
carte grise *f* log book
carte internationale d'étudiant *f*
  International Student Identity
  Card

carte Inter-rail *f* Inter-Rail Card
carte Jeunes *f* reduced-rate rail
  travel card for young people
  within France
carte Kiwi *f* ≈ Family Railcard
carte magnétique *f* [*clé*] magnetic
  card
carte magnétique d'accès à bord
  f magnetic boarding pass
carte marque-place *f* place name
carte orange *f* RATP pass
carte postale *f* postcard
carte Train Évasion Randonnée *f*
  [*forfait SNCF train + vélo*]
  cycling by train
carte Vermeil *f* ≈ Senior Citizen's
  Railcard
carte Visa *f* Visa (card)
**carte d'abonnement de transport
  aérien** *f* airpass
carte d'accès à bord *f* boarding
  pass
carte d'adhérent *f* membership
  card
carte d'embarquement *f*
  embarkation card, boarding card
carte d'identité *f* identity card
carte de crédit *f* credit card
carte de débarquement *f* landing
  card
carte de fidélité *f* frequent user
  card, valued customer card
carte de paiement *f* payment card
**carte de réduction dans les
  transports** *f* discount travel card
carte de train *f* railcard;
  [*abonnement, forfait*] rail pass
carte de visite *f* business card
carte des vins *f* wine list
cas litigieux *m* dispute
cascade *f* waterfall
case *f* pigeonhole; [*paillote*] cabin
casier *m* rack

13

casier à clés et à courrier *m* key and mail rack

casier à skis *m* ski rack

casino *m* casino

cassis *m* blackcurrant; [*liqueur*] blackcurrant liqueur

catalogue *m* catalogue

catalogue de vacances *m* holiday brochure

catégorie *f* category

catégorie d'hébergement *f* accommodation category

cathédrale *f* cathedral

caution *f* deposit, surety

cave *f* cellar

cave à vin *f* wine cellar

caviar *m* caviar

CDAT = Commission Départementale d'Action Touristique *f*

CDD = Contrat à Durée Déterminée *m*

CDI = Contrat à Durée Indeterminée *m*

CDT = Comité Départemental du Tourisme *m*

CE (=Communauté Européenne) *f* EC

CEAC (= Commission Européenne de l'Aviation Civile) *f* ECAC

CEE (= Communauté Économique Européenne) *f* EEC

CEH = Conférence Européenne des Horaires des trains de voyageurs *f*

céleri *m* celery

cellier *m* cellar

Celsius centigrade

cendrier *m* ashtray

centrale d'achat(s) *f* central purchasing group, central buying group

centrale de réservations *f* central reservations unit, central reservations office

centre commercial *m* shopping centre, shopping mall *Am*

centre médical d'urgence *m* emergency medical service

centre sportif *m* sports centre

centre ville *m* city centre

centre d'accueil *m* visitor centre

centre d'affaires *m* business centre; [*dans aéroport, hôtel*] business lounge

centre d'artisanat *m* craft centre

centre d'information *m* information centre

centre d'intérêt touristique *m* tourist attraction, visitor attraction

centre de conférences *m* conference centre

centre de loisirs *m* leisure centre, recreation centre

centre de réservation *m* reservation centre

centre de sport et de remise en forme *m* health and fitness centre

centre de thalassothérapie *m* thalassotherapy centre

centre de vacances *m* holiday centre

céréales *fpl* cereals

cérémonie d'ouverture *f* opening ceremony

cerise *f* cherry

certificat de navigabilité aérienne *m* certificate of airworthiness

certificat de vaccination *m* vaccination certificate

CET (= Commission Européenne de Tourisme) *f* ETC

CFHRCD = Confédération Française des Hôteliers, Restaurateurs, Cafetiers et Discothèques f
chaîne f chain
chaîne franchisée f franchised chain
chaîne hôtelière f hotel chain
chaîne intégrée f corporate-operated group
chaîne volontaire f consortium
chaîne de charters f back-to-back
chaise f chair
chaise longue f deckchair
chalet m chalet, lodge
chaloupe f [*bateau*] tender
chambre f room
chambre catégorie "luxe" f deluxe room
chambre double f double room
chambre individuelle f single room
chambre libre f vacancy
chambre triple f triple room
chambre à deux lits simples f twin(-bedded) room
chambre à lits jumeaux f twin(-bedded) room
chambre avec petit déjeuner f [*with continental breakfast*] continental plan; [*with English breakfast*] Bermuda Plan
chambre d'hôte f bed and breakfast
chambre de Commerce f Chamber of Commerce
chambre de vapeur f steam room
chambre en recouche f stay-over
chambré [*vin*] at room temperature
chambres attenantes fpl adjoining rooms
chambres communicantes fpl connecting rooms

champagne m champagne
champignon m mushroom
changer de l'argent to change money
charcuterie f butcher selling meat that has been treated; [*viande*] cooked meats
chargé [*période*] busy
charges fpl costs
chariot m trolley; [*à bagages*] luggage trolley
chariot de desserts m dessert trolley
charter partiel m partial charter
chartérisation f chartering
chasse f hunting, shooting
chasser to hunt
chasseur m bellboy, porter
chasseur-bagagiste m luggage porter, porter
château m castle; [*demeure de famille aristocratique*] stately home
chauffage f heating
chauffage central m central heating
chauffé heated
chauffeur m chauffeur; *avec chauffeur* chauffeur-driven; *sans chauffeur* self-drive
chef m chef
chef barman m head barman
chef caissier m head cashier
chef chasseur m head porter, bell captain *Am*
chef comptable m head accountant
chef concierge m head hall porter, head porter
chef hôtesse f senior stewardess
chef main-courantier m head book-keeper
chef pâtissier m chef patissier, pastry chef

chef serveur *m* waiting chef

chef standardiste *m* head switchboard operator

chef de cuisine *m* chef de cuisine, head chef

chef de groupe *m* group leader

chef de partie *m* [*poissonnier, boucher, etc.*] chef de partie

chef de partie boucher *m* larder chef

chef de partie poissonnier *m* fish cook

chef de petit déjeuner *m* breakfast chef

chef de rang *m* head waiter, chef de rang, captain *Am*, station waiter

chef de réception *m* reception manager, front office manager

chef de service *m* head of department, department head, head of section

chef de l'animation *m* entertainments director

chef des ventes *m* sales manager

chemin de randonnée *m* footpath, hiking trail, nature trail

cheminée *f* [*intérieure*] fireplace

chenil *m* kennel

chèque *m* cheque, check *Am*

chèque bancaire *m* bank cheque

chèque certifié *m* certified cheque

chèque postal *m* post office cheque

chèque-restaurant *m* luncheon voucher

chèque stimulation-voyage *m* incentive travel cheque issued by companies

chèque de voyage *m* traveller's cheque, traveler's check *Am*

chevalet *m* easel

chevreuil *m* venison

chien *m* dog

chien d'aveugle *m* guide dog

chiffre d'affaires *m* sales, turnover

chocolat chaud *m* hot chocolate

chou *m* cabbage

choucroute *f* sauerkraut

chou-fleur *m* cauliflower

CNRH = Confédération Nationale de la Restauration et de l'Hôtellerie *f*

cidre *m* cider

ciel: à ciel ouvert open-air

cigare *m* cigar

cigarette *f* cigarette

cigarillo *m* cigarillo

cinéma *m* cinema

cintre *m* hanger

circuit *m* touring holiday; [*excursion*] tour

circuit aventure *m* adventure holiday

circuit court *m* direct selling by a tour operator

circuit long *m* indirect selling by a tour operator

circuit mixte fermé *m* direct selling and indirect selling through selected agents by a tour operator

circuit mixte ouvert *m* direct and indirect selling through all travel agencies by a tour operator

circuit mixte sélectionné *m* direct and indirect selling through selected agents by a tour operator

circuit touristique *m* tourist route

circuit de distribution *m* distribution channel

circuit en car *m* coach tour

cité historique *f* historic town

citoyenneté *f* citizenship

citron *m* lemon

citron pressé *m* freshly squeezed lemon juice

citron vert *m* lime

CIWLT = Compagnie Internationale des Wagons-Lits et du Tourisme *f*

classe affaires *f* business class, club class, executive class

classe économique *f* economy class

classe de mer *f* school study trip to the seaside

classe de nature *f* nature study

classe de neige *f* school study trip to the mountains

classé [*monument, etc.*] listed

classement hôtelier *m* hotel classification

classement par étoiles *m* star rating

classer [*hôtel*] to grade, to classify

classeur *m* folder

clé passe-partout *f* passkey, master key

clé à puce *f* computerized key

clé de la chambre *f* room key

clef *f* key

client *m* customer; [*d'hôtel aussi*] guest

client imprévu *m* chance customer

client non venu *m* no-show

client régulier *m* regular client

client de passage *m* passing customer

client sans réservation *m* chance guest, walk-in

clientèle *f* clientele

clientèle de passage *f* over-night clientele

climat *m* climate

climatisation *f* air conditioning

club *m* club

club de compagnie aérienne *m* airline club

club de gymnastique *m* fitness centre, gym

club de loisirs *m* leisure club

club de ski *m* ski club

club de sport *m* sports club

club de vacances *m* holiday club, vacation center *Am*

CNT = Conseil National du Tourisme *m*

cocktail *m* cocktail; [*réception*] cocktail party

cocktail d'accueil *m* welcome drink

CODATEL = COopération pour le Développement et les Aménagements du Tourisme Et des Loisirs *f*

code aéroport *m* airport code

code compagnie aérienne *m* airline code

code couleurs *m* colour coding

code devise *m* currency code

code État *m* state code

code pays *m* country code

code ville *m* city code

code de billetterie *m* ticketing code

code de conduite *m* code of conduct

codification tarifaire *f* fare basis

coefficient de remplissage *m* load factor

cœur *m* [*abats*] heart

coffre(-fort) *m* safety deposit box, safe

coffre à bagages *m* [*dans avion*] baggage compartment

COFIT = Confédération Française des Industries du Tourisme *f*

cognac *m* cognac, brandy

coiffeuse *f* [*meuble*] dressing table;

[*personne*] hairdresser

coin-cuisine *m* kitchenette

coin enfants *m* [*de restaurant*] children's area

collation *f* refreshments, snack, light meal

collectif communal

collet *m* [*de veau*] scrag, neck slice *Am*

colloque *m* seminar

colonie de vacances *f* holiday camp

combinaison *f* combination

Comité départemental du tourisme *m* advisory body which promotes tourism at departmental level

Comité régional du tourisme *m* tourist board which does regional promotion in France and abroad

Comité du tourisme de l'Organisation de coopération et de développement économiques *m* Tourism Committee of the Organisation for Economic Cooperation and Development

commandant de bord *m* [*d'avion*] captain

commander to order

commentaires client *mpl* customer comments

commerce de détail *m* retail trade

commercialisation *f* marketing

commis *m* commis chef, commis waiter

commis de cuisine *m* commis chef

commis de rang *m* trainee chef de rang

commis de salle *m* waiter

commissaire de bord *m* purser

commission *f* commission

Commission départementale d'Action touristique *f* departmental body which advises on tourism accommodation classification

Commission européenne de tourisme *f* European Travel Commission

Commission européenne de l'aviation civile *f* European Civil Aviation Conference

Commission de propagande touristique des pays alpins *f* Alpine Tourist Commission

commissionnaire *m* commissionaire

commode *f* chest of drawers

communicant [*chambres*] connecting

communication interurbaine *f* long-distance call

communications *fpl* communications

commuter *m* [*court-courrier*] commuter plane

compagnie aérienne *f* airline

compagnie aérienne nationale *f* flag airline, national airline

Compagnie internationale des wagons-lits et du tourisme *f* company which operates sleeping coaches on continental trains

compagnie maritime *f* shipping line

compagnie d'aviation *f* airline

compagnie d'aviation civile *f* civil airline

compagnie de transports *f* carrier

compagnie de transports nationale *f* flag carrier

compartiment *m* compartment

compartiment fumeurs *m* smoking compartment

compartiment non-fumeurs *m* no-smoking compartment

complet no vacancies, fully booked; [*théâtre, excursion*] sold out

complexe hôtelier *m* hotel complex

complexe touristique *m* holiday complex, tourism complex

complexe de loisirs *m* leisure complex

comportement du consommateur *m* consumer behaviour

compostage *m* date-stamping

composter to date-stamp

compris included

comptabilité *f* accountancy, accounts; [*service*] accounts

comptable d'hôtel *m* hotel accountant

compte *m* account; *faire les comptes* to cash up

compte accréditif *m* charge account

compte créditeur *m* account payable

compte débiteur *m* account receivable

compte à crédit *m* credit account

compte des clients *m* guest folio

compte en souffrance *m* outstanding account, delinquent account

compteur *m* meter

comptoir-caisse *m* cashier's desk

comptoir d'enregistrement *m* check-in desk

comptoir d'information *m* information desk

comptoir de réception *m* reception desk

comptoir du concierge *m* porter's desk, concierge's desk

concert *m* concert

concierge *mf* concierge, house porter, hall porter

concombre *m* cucumber

concurrence des prix *f* price competition

condiments *mpl* condiments

conditions générales de vente *fpl* general conditions of sale

conditions météorologiques *fpl* weather conditions

conditions particulières *fpl* restrictions

conditions particulières de vente *fpl* special conditions of sale

conditions de réservation *fpl* conditions of reservation

conducteur *m* [*de voiture, de train*] driver

Confédération française des hôteliers, restaurateurs, cafetiers, et discothèques *f* French confederation of hoteliers, restaurateurs, café-keepers and discotheques

Confédération française des industries du tourisme *f* French hospitality industry confederation

Confédération nationale de la restauration et de l'hôtellerie *f* French confederation of hotel and catering

Conférence européenne des horaires des trains de voyageurs *f* European Passenger Train Timetable Conference

conférence maritime *f* shipping conference

conférencier *m* guest speaker

configuration *f* configuration

confirmation *f* confirmation

confirmation écrite *f* written

19

confirmation
confirmation de réservation *f* confirmation of reservation
confirmer to confirm
confiture *f* jam
confort *m* comfort
confortable comfortable
congé *m* holiday
congés payés *mpl* paid holidays
conglomérat *m* conglomerate
congrès *m* congress, convention, conference
consécutif consecutive
Conseil national du tourisme *m* tourism advisory body
Conseil supérieur du Tourisme *m* government body for tourism policy
conseil de surveillance *m* supervisory board
conseiller commercial *m* sales consultant
conserves *fpl* preserves
consigne automatique *f* luggage lockers
consigne (à bagages) *f* baggage room, left luggage (office), check room *Am*
consignes en cas d'incendie *fpl* fire notice, fire regulations
consommé *m* consommé
consommer sur place to eat in
conteneur à bagages *m* baggage container
contingent *m* block, allotment
continuation en vol *f* onward flight
contrat hôtelier *m* contract between a hotel and a travel agent
contrat temporaire *m* temporary contract
contrat à durée déterminée *m* fixed-term contract

contrat à durée indéterminée *m* permanent contract
contrat à plein temps *m* full-time contract
contrat à temps partiel *m* part-time contract
contrat d'allotement *m* allotment contract
contrat d'association *m* joint venture
contrat d'assurance *m* insurance contract
contrat de contingent *m* allotment contract, block booking
contrat de gestion *m* management contract
contrat de transport *m* contract of carriage
contrat de travail *m* contract of employment
contre-filet *m* tenderloin
contremarque *f* ticket voucher
contresigner to countersign
contrôle douanier *m* customs control
contrôle de bagages *m* baggage check
contrôle de l'immigration *m* immigration control
contrôle des bagages à main *m* hand baggage check
contrôle des changes *m* exchange controls
contrôle des passeports *m* passport control
contrôle des stocks *m* stock control
contrôles aux frontières *mpl* border controls
contrôleur *m* controller
contrôleur financier *m* financial controller
contrôleur de gestion *m* controller

contrôleur de trafic aérien *m* air traffic controller

contrôleur (de la) restauration *m* food and beverage manager

convention *f* convention

convention internationale *f* international convention

Convention d'Athènes *f* Athens Convention

Convention de Berne *f* Berne Convention

Convention de Bruxelles *f* Brussels Convention

Convention de Chicago *f* Chicago Convention

Convention de Varsovie *f* Warsaw Convention

Coopération pour le développement et les aménagements du tourisme et des loisirs *f* cooperation for tourism and leisure development

copropriété *f* co-ownership

copropriété différée *f* timeshare taken on a lease basis converting to ownership after 9 years

coq de bruyère *m* grouse

corbeille à papier *f* wastepaper basket, wastebasket *Am*

corbeille de fruits *f* basket of fruit

cornichon gherkin

correspondance *f* connection; [*vol aussi*] connecting flight

correspondant local *m* [*pour les voyagistes*] resort representative

correspondant d'agréments *m* travel agent (for rail and sea) working as such but without having yet obtained qualification

correspondant de licence *m* travel agent (for airlines) working as such but without having yet obtained qualification

côte *f* coast

côte d'agneau *f* lamb cutlet, lamb chop

côte d'Azur *f* French Riviera

côtelette *f* [*de porc*] spare rib

côtelettes *fpl* [*agneau*] riblets; [*lamb, mutton*] breast

côtes découvertes *fpl* middle neck

couchette *f* couchette

couette *f* quilt, duvet

couple *m* couple

coupon hôtel *m* hotel coupon

coupon de réservation *m* reservation ticket

coupon de vol *m* flight coupon

courant électrique *m* power, electricity

courgette *f* courgette, zucchini *Am*

courrier *m* post, mail

courrier interne *m* internal mail

cours de change *m* exchange rate

cours de tennis *m* tennis lesson

courses *fpl* shopping; *faire des courses* to go shopping

court: à court de personnel short-staffed

court-courrier short-haul

court de tennis *m* tennis court

courtage *m* broking

courtier *m* broker

courtier de l'air *m* air broker

coût marginal *m* marginal cost

coût réel d'exploitation *m* actual operating cost

couteau *m* knife

coûts d'exploitation *mpl* operational costs

couvert *m* place setting, cover; *mettre le couvert* to lay the table

couverts *mpl* cutlery

couverture d'assurance *f* insurance cover

crabe *m* crab

crédit *m* credit; ***faire crédit*** to give credit

crème *f* cream

crème *m* [*café*] white coffee

crème fraîche *f* soured cream

créneau horaire *m* slot

crêperie *f* pancake house

creuse [*heure*] off-peak

crevette *f* [*grise*] shrimp; [*rose*] prawn

critique gastronomique *m* food critic

croisière *f* cruise

croisière fluviale *f* river-cruise

croisière lacustre *f* lake-cruise

croisière maritime *f* sea-cruise

croissance du tourisme *f* tourism growth

CRT = Comité Régional du Tourisme *m*

cru *m* [*vin*] vintage

cru raw, uncooked

cruche *f* jug

crustacés *mpl* shellfish

cuillère *f* spoon

cuillère à dessert *f* dessert spoon

cuillère à soupe *f* soup spoon

cuisinette *f* kitchenette

cuisinier *m* cook

cuisinier-pâtissier *m* pastry cook

cuisinier en chef *m* executive chef

cuisse *f* [*de viande*] leg

cuisseau *m* [*de veau*] leg

cuisson à la vapeur *f* steaming

cuisson au grill *f* grilling

cuisson en bain de friture *f* deep-fat frying

cuit: pas assez cuit underdone

cuit à l'étouffée steamed

cuit au four baked

culinaire culinary

culotte *f* [*de bœuf*] rump steak

culture *f* culture

culturel cultural

curry: au curry curried

cuvée de la maison *f* house wine

cuvée du patron *f* house wine

cuvette *f* toilet

cycliste *m* cyclist

cyclotourisme *m* cycling holiday(s)

D

dactylo *mf* typist

Dagober *m* SNCF system for making train reservations by minitel

danse *f* dance

darne *f* (fish) steak

DATAS II *m* DATAS II

date *f* date

date limite d'émission de billet *f* ticketing time limit

date de départ *f* date of departure, departure date

date de naissance *f* date of birth

date de retour *f* date of return

day use *f* [*location de chambres seulement durant la journée*] day let

de [*sur horaire*] from

débarcadère *f* jetty

débarquer to disembark

débiteurs divers *mpl* sundry debtors, city ledger

débours *mpl* [*pour services aux clients*] visitors paid out, VPO

déca *m* decaf

décalage horaire *m* time difference; *souffrir du décalage horaire* to have jet-lag

déclarer to declare

déclasser to downgrade

décliner toute responsabilité to accept no liability

décollage *m* take-off

décoller to take off

décor de table *m* table decoration, table centre

décorateur d'intérieur *m* interior decorator

décoration *f* decor

décoration florale *f* floral arrangement

découper [*viande*] to carve

dédommagement *m* compensation

dédommagement de non accès à bord *m* denied boarding compensation

dédouanement *m* customs clearance

défaire ses bagages to unpack

défection *f* no-show

dégustation *f* tasting

déguster to taste

déjeuner *m* lunch, luncheon

déjeuner to lunch

déjeuner buffet *m* buffet lunch

déjeuner d'affaires *m* business lunch

déjeuner à l'extérieur to eat out

délai de réservation *m* advance booking period

Délégation régionale du Tourisme *f* government body in charge of regional tourism

délégué commercial *m* sales representative

délivrance de billets *f* ticketing

délogement *m* room change

demande *f* query; [*économique*] demand

demande touristique *f* demand for tourism

demande d'intervention de réparation *f* maintenance work request

demi-bouteille *f* half-bottle

demi-pension *f* half board, American plan *Am*

dentifrice *m* toothpaste

dentiste *m* dentist

départ *m* departure; [*de bateau*] sailing

départ anticipé *m* early departure

départ différé *m* delayed departure

départ matinal *m* early morning departure

département *m* department

département des services *m* service department

dépense moyenne journalière par client *f* resident's average daily spend

dépenses *fpl* expenditure

dépenses courantes *fpl* current expenditure

dépenses touristiques internationales *fpl* international tourism expenditure

déplacement *m* trip

déplacements *mpl* travel

dépliant *m* leaflet, brochure

déposer la clé to leave the key

dépôt de clés *m* key depository

déranger: ne pas déranger do not disturb

dératisation pest control

déroutement *m* re-routing

désinsectisation *f* pest control

désistement *m* cancellation; [*sans préavis*] no-show

se **désister** to cancel

dessert *m* dessert, pudding

desserte *f* side table; [*à roulettes*] trolley; [*transport*] serving; [*de table*] clearing

desservir [*transport*] to serve; [*table*] to clear

dessous-de-verre *m* coaster

dessus-de-lit *m* bedspread

destination *f* destination

destination touristique *f* tourism destination, tourist destination

détecteur de fumée *m* smoke detector

détective de l'hôtel *m* house detective, hotel detective

détente *f* recreation

dettes à court terme *fpl* current liabilities

dettes à long terme *fpl* long term liabilities

deux étoiles two-star

deuxième classe *f* second class, standard class

deuxième étage *m* second floor, third floor *Am*

développement régional *m* regional development

développement du tourisme *m* tourism development

devis: faire un devis to quote (a price)

devise *f* currency

devise convertible *f* convertible currency

devise faible *f* soft currency

devise forte *f* hard currency

devise internationale *f* international currency

devises étrangères *fpl* foreign currency

DGAC (= Direction Générale de l'Aviation Civile) *f* [*en GB*] ≈ CAA, [*aux USA*] ≈ CAB

diabétique diabetic

diarrhée du voyageur *f* diarrhoea, holiday tummy

digestif *m* digestif

dinde *f* turkey

dîner *m* dinner, evening meal

dîner dehors to dine out, to eat out

dîner à l'extérieur to dine out, to eat out

dîner dansant *m* dinner dance

dîner de gala *m* gala dinner

direct direct

directeur *m* manager; [*en chef*] director

directeur adjoint *m* deputy manager; [*plus haut dans hiérarchie*] deputy director

directeur administratif *m* executive director

directeur commercial *m* sales manager; [*en chef*] sales director

directeur général *m* managing director

directeur-gérant *m* executive director

directeur hôtelier *m* hotel
manager; [*en chef*] hotel director
directeur local *m* local manager
directeur régional *m* regional
manager; [*en chef*] district
manager
directeur d'exploitation *m*
operations manager; [*en chef*]
operations director
directeur d'hôtel *m* hotel
manager; [*en chef*] hotel director
directeur d'hôtel-restaurant *m*
hotel and restaurant manager
directeur de cafétéria *m* cafeteria
manager
directeur de division *m* [*au siège*]
divisional director
directeur de marketing *m*
marketing manager; [*en chef*]
marketing director
directeur de nuit *m* night manager
directeur de restaurant *m*
restaurant manager
directeur de service *m* head of
department, unit manager
directeur de l'animation *m*
entertainments director, social
director
directeur de l'hébergement *m*
rooms division manager, front of
house manager
directeur de la publicité *m*
advertising manager; [*en chef*]
advertising director
directeur de la restauration *m*
catering manager
directeur des approvisionnements
m food and beverage manager
directeur des banquets *m*
banqueting manager
directeur des exploitations *m*
operations manager; [*en chef*]
operations director

directeur des relations publiques
m public relations manager; [*en
chef*] public relations director
directeur des réservations *m*
reservations manager
**directeur des services de
restauration** *m* catering manager
**directeur des ventes et du
marketing** *m* sales and
marketing manager; [*en chef*]
sales and marketing director
directeur du crédit *m* credit
manager
directeur du personnel *m*
personnel manager; [*en chef*]
personnel director
direction *f* direction; [*de société*]
management
direction générale *f* senior
management
**Direction générale de l'Aviation
civile** *f* [*en GB*] ≈ Civil Aviation
Authority; [*aux USA*] ≈ Civil
Aeronautics Board
**Direction de l'Industrie
touristique** *f* body which
implements government tourism
policy
directive *f* instruction; [*de
gouvernement, CE*] directive
directrice *f* manageress
discothèque *f* disco, discotheque
discrimination par les prix *f* price
discrimination
disponibilité de dernière minute *f*
late availability
disponible available
disposition des sièges *f* seating
plan
dissuasion *f* [*ciblage*] demarketing
distractions *fpl* entertainment
distractions en vol *m* in-flight
entertainment

distributeur automatique de billets *m* ticket machine

distributeur automatique de titres de transport *m* automatic ticket dispenser

distributeur de boissons *m* drinks machine, drinks dispenser, drinks vending machine

distributeur de cigarettes *m* cigarette machine

DIT = Direction de l'Industrie Touristique *f*

divers miscellaneous

divertissement *m* entertainment

dividende *m* dividend

division hôtellerie *f* hotel division

division de formation professionnelle *f* training division

documentaire touristique *m* travelogue

documentaire de voyage *m* travelogue

documentation touristique *f* travel literature, tourist literature

documents de voyage *mpl* travel documents

domaine skiable *m* skiing area

domestique domestic

dommages *mpl* damage

donner sur to face, to overlook

dortoir *m* dormitory

dossier client *m* client file

dossier crédit *m* credit file

dossier de voyage *m* travel documents

douane *f* customs; *sous douane* in the customs zone

double vitrage *m* double glazing

douche *f* shower

doux sweet

drap *m* (bed) sheet

draps et taies d'oreiller *mpl* bed linen

dresser la table to set the table, to lay the table

droit hôtelier *m* hotel law

droit aux vacances *m* holiday entitlement

droit d'entrée *m* admission fee

droit d'escales techniques *m* freedom to land for technical reasons

droit de bouchon *m* corkage, cork charge

droit de survol d'un État *m* freedom to overfly a country without landing

droits acquittés *mpl* duty paid

droits de cabotage *mpl* cabotage rights

droits de douane *mpl* customs duties

droits de trafic *mpl* [*des compagnies aériennes*] traffic rights

DRT = Délégation Régionale du Tourisme *f*

dumping *m* dumping

duplex *m* duplex

durée moyenne de séjour *f* average length of stay

durée de séjour *f* length of stay

durée de vol *f* flight time

durée de voyage *f* journey time

E

eau *f* water

eau gazeuse *f* sparkling water

eau minérale *f* mineral water

eau non potable *f* not drinking water

eau plate *f* still mineral water

eau potable *f* drinking water

eau de toilette *f* toilet water

eau-de-vie *f* brandy

eau du robinet *f* tap water

eau en bouteille *f* bottled water

échange culturel *m* cultural exchange

échange linguistique *m* language exchange holiday

échange d'appartement *m* flat swap

échantillonnage *m* sampling

échine *f* [*porc*] spare rib

échinée *f* [*de porc*] spare rib

éclairage *m* lighting

éclairage de sécurité *m* emergency lighting

école hôtelière *f* hotel school

économie *f* economy

écouteurs *mpl* headphones

écran *m* screen

écran de cinéma *m* cinema screen, movie screen *Am*

écran de projection *m* projection screen

écrémage *m* creaming

écu *m* ECU

édredon *m* eiderdown

éducatif educational

Éductour *m* educational tour

effectuer une réservation to make a reservation

églefin *m* haddock

église *f* church

électricité *f* electricity

embarcadère *f* jetty

embargo *m* embargo

embarquement *m* embarkation

embarquer to board

émetteur de signaux *m* bleeper

émetteur de touristes tourist-generating

emplacement *m* location, site

emploi généré par le tourisme *m* tourism-generated employment

emploi lié au tourisme *m* tourism-related employment

emploi saisonnier *m* seasonal employment

emplois fonctionnels *mpl* back of the house

employé à l'enregistrement des bagages *m* check-in clerk

employé d'hôtel *m* hotel clerk

employé du hall *m* front of house employee

employé du vestiaire *m* cloakroom attendant

emporter to take away; *pizza à emporter* take-away pizza

encaissement *m* paying-in, encashment *Br*

encaisser to cash

enclave touristique *f* tourist enclave

encombrement *m* congestion

endive *f* chicory

endos *m* endorsment

enfant *m* child; *menu enfant* children's menu

enlèvement des ordures *m* garbage disposal

enquête *f* enquiry; [*étude de marché, etc.*] survey

enquête par sondage *f* sample survey

enquête sur l'hébergement *f* accommodation survey

enregistrement *m* [*des bagages*] check-in; [*de données*] recording; [*dans base de données*] record

enregistrement anticipé *m* advanced check-in

enregistrer [*bagages*] to check in; [*données*] to record

enseigne *f* sign

ensoleillement *m* sunshine

entrecôte *f* rib steak

entrée *f* [*d'immeuble*] entrance; [*au restaurant*] starter

entrée principale *f* public entrance

entremets *m* dessert, sweet

entreprise touristique primaire *f* primary tourist enterprise

entreprise touristique secondaire *f* secondary tourist enterprise

entreprise de transport public *f* common carrier

entretien *m* [*réparations*] maintenance; [*ménage*] housekeeping

entretien des chambres *m* room servicing

environnement *m* environment

environnement touristique *m* tourist environment

épaule *f* shoulder

épi de maïs *m* corn on the cob

épinards *mpl* spinach

équipage *m* crew

équipe d'animation *f* entertainments team

équipe d'entretien *f* maintenance team

équipe de nuit *f* night shift

équipement audio-visuel *m* audio-visual equipment

équipement sportif *m* sports facilities

équipements *m* [*service, confort*] amenities

équitation *f* horse riding

escalade *f* rock-climbing

escale *f* stopover, layover

escalier *m* stairs

escalier de secours *m* fire escape

escargot *m* snail

espace aérien *m* air space

espacement des sièges *m* seat pitch

espadon *m* swordfish

espèces *fpl* cash

Estel *m* French computer reservations network for travel agents

Esterel *m* [*pour transport aérien*] main French computer reservations system

établissement *m* establishment

établissement thermal *m* spa

établissement des menus *m* menu planning

établissement des prix *m* price fixing, pricing

étage *m* storey, floor

étape *f* [*de circuit*] leg

état des chambres *m* room status

état et disponibilité d'une chambre *m* room status

été *m* summer

étiquette *f* label; [*de bagages*] baggage tag

étiquette autocollante d'identification de bagage *f* baggage claim sticker

étoile *f* star; *sans étoile* lowest hotel classification for "hôtels de tourisme"; *une étoile* one star; *deux/trois/quatre étoiles* two/three/four stars

étranger *m* alien, foreigner; *à l'étranger* abroad

étrangère *f* alien, foreigner

étude *f* study, survey; *voyage d'études* educational tour, study tour

étude de faisabilité *f* feasibility study

étude de marché *f* market survey

étude de marché standard *f* omnibus survey

étude sur le tourisme de loisir *f* holiday survey

étude sur les destinations *f* destination survey

étude sur les touristes *f* visitor survey

étudiant *m* student

eurailpass *m* Eurailpass

eurobudget *m* Eurobudget

eurochèque *m* Eurocheque

eurodollar *m* Eurodollar

eurotourisme *m* Eurotourism

Eurotunnel *m* Channel tunnel, Chunnel

évaluation des coûts *f* cost analysis

évaluer les coûts de qch to cost sth

événement *m* event

éventail de produits *m* sales mix

évier *m* sink

excédent de bagages *m* excess baggage

excédent de kilométrage *m* excess mileage

excédent de poids *m* excess weight

excédent de valeur *m* excess value

excursion *f* excursion; [*d'une journée*] day trip, day tour; [*lors d'une escale*] shore excursion

excursion en car *f* coach trip

excursionniste *mf* excursionist, same-day visitor

exempt de droits de douane duty-free

exempt de TVA zero-rated

exercice d'évacuation en cas d'incendie *m* fire drill

exportation *f* export

exportations invisibles *fpl* invisible exports

exportations visibles *fpl* visible exports

exposition *f* exhibition

exposition solaire *f* exposure to the sun

express *m* express

extincteur *m* fire extinguisher

extra extra

extrait de compte *m* statement of account

F

facilité d'accès pour fauteuils roulants *f* wheelchair access

facilité d'accès pour personnes handicapées *f* disabled access

FACIT = Fonds d'Aide au Conseil et à l'Innovation Touristique *m*

facteur démographique *m* demographic factor

facteur déterminant *m* determining factor, determinant

facteur socio-économique *m* socio-economic factor

facturation *f* billing, invoicing

facture *f* invoice

facture client *f* guest bill

facture de confirmation *f* confirmation invoice

facture des extras *f* extras bill

facturer to invoice for

facultatif optional

FAGIHT = Fédération Autonome Générale de l'Industrie Hôtelière Touristique *f*

faire du tourisme to do some sightseeing

faire du trekking to trek

faisan *m* pheasant

fait maison home-made

familial [*pension, hôtel*] family-run, owner-managed

famille *f* family

Famtour *m* familiarization tour, familiarization trip, fam trip

Fantasia *m* Fantasia

farce *f* stuffing

farci stuffed

fast-food *m* fast-food bar, fast food restaurant

fauteuil *m* armchair

fauteuil roulant *m* wheelchair

faux-filet *m* tenderloin

fax *m* fax

faxer to fax

fédération *f* federation

Fédération autonome générale de l'industrie hôtelière touristique *f* independent hotel industry federation

Fédération européenne des villes de congrès *f* European Federation of Conference Towns

Fédération française du tourisme populaire *f* organization which arranges holidays for the less well-off

Fédération française des stations vertes de vacances *f* French federation for green tourism

Fédération française des techniciens supérieurs du tourisme *f* association concerned with training in tourism

Fédération internationale de camping et de caravaning *f* International Federation of Camping and Caravanning

Fédération internationale des

auberges de jeunesse *f*
International Youth Hostel
Federation

**Fédération nationale de
l'industrie hôtelière** *f* French
national hotel industry federation

Fédération nationale des CDT *f*
national federation of "Comités
départementaux de tourisme"

**Fédération nationale des gîtes
ruraux** *f* French national
federation for rural gîtes

**Fédération nationale des offices
de tourisme et syndicats
d'initiative** *f* national federation
of tourist offices

**Fédération nationale des services
loisirs-accueil** *f* national
federation of hospitality and
leisure industries

**Fédération unie des auberges de
jeunesse** *f* French federation of
youth hostels

**Fédération universelle des
associations d'agences de
voyages** *f* Universal Federation
of Travel Agents' Associations

femme d'affaires *f* businesswoman

femme de chambre *f* chamber
maid, maid, room attendant

fer à repasser *m* iron

ferroviaire rail

ferry(-boat) *m* ferry

ferry roulier *m* roll-on roll-off
ferry

ferry trans-Manche *m* cross-
Channel car ferry

festival *m* festival

festival culturel *m* arts festival

festival de musique *m* music
festival

fête *f* festival; [*privée*] party

**feuille d'inventaire du linge des
chambres** *f* room linen inventory

feuille d'occupation journalière *f*
daily density chart, daily
forecast chart

feuille de présence *f* work
schedule, time sheet

feuille de réservation *f* reservation
form, booking form

feuille de séjour *f* guest folio

feuille des arrivées et des départs
f arrival and departure list, A&D
list

feuille des mouvements *f* arrival
and departure list, A&D list

feuille des recettes *f* cashier's
record form

**feuille des réservations
journalières** *f* daily density
reservation chart, daily forecast
chart

feuille des réveils *f* call sheet

**FEVC (= Fédération Européenne
des Villes de Congrès)** *f* EFCT

**FFTST = Fédération Française
des Techniciens Supérieurs du
Tourisme** *f*

**FIAJ (= Fédération
Internationale des Auberges de
Jeunesse)** *f* IYHF

**FICC = Fédération
Internationale de Camping et
de Caravaning** *f*

fiche *f* card; [*électrique*] jack plug

fiche client *f* [*carte*] room rack
card; [*sur ordinateur*] guest
folio, guest file

fiche concierge *f* concierge's slip

fiche explicative *f* [*dans les
chambres*] information sheet

fiche Kardex *f* guest history card

fiche-message *f* message form

fiche voyageur *f* registration card
for foreign guests

fiche Whitney *f* Whitney card

fiche d'accueil *f* registration form

fiche d'appréciation *f* customer satisfaction questionnaire

fiche d'arrivée *f* registration form

fiche d'hôtel *f* key card

fiche d'inscription *f* registration form

fiche d'inspection des chambres *f* housekeeper's report

fiche d'observations *f* [*questionnaire d'évaluation*] comment card

fiche d'occupation *f* room rack card

fiche de blocage *f* block card, reservation rack card, room rack card

fiche de compte *f* accounts card

fiche de demande de renseignements *f* enquiry card

fiche de facture *f* account card

fiche de pointage *f* clocking-in card

fiche de police *f* registration card to be filled in by hotel guests from non-EC countries; [*au débarquement*] landing card

fiche de poste *f* [*descriptif des tâches à accomplir*] task sheet

fiche de prévision de réservation *f* advanced reservation card

fiche de réexpédition du courrier *f* mail fowarding slip

fiche de réservation *f* reservation form, reservation card, rack slip

fiche de tableau des réservations *f* reservation rack card

fichette client *f* reservation card

fichette d'arrivée *f* arrival form

fichier *m* card index; [*informatique*] file

fichier Kardex *m* guest history file

fichier (des) clients *f* client file, customer file

file "objets à déclarer" *f* red channel

filer à l'anglaise to walk out, to skip, to leave without paying

filet *m* fillet

filiale *f* subsidiary

financement *m* financing

finances *fpl* finance

FIT = Fonds d'Intervention Touristique *m*

flambé flambé

flanchet *m* [*de bœuf*] flank of beef

flèche lumineuse *f* pointer; [*de sortie de secours, etc.*] luminous arrow

flétan *m* halibut

fleur *f* flower

fleuriste *m* florist

fleuron *m* flagship

flexibilité *f* flexibility

flotte *f* fleet

fluctuation saisonnière *f* seasonal fluctuation

fluctuation des prix *f* price fluctuation

flûte à champagne *f* champagne flute

FNCDT = Fédération Nationale des Comités Départementaux de Tourisme *f*

FNGR = Fédération Nationale des Gîtes Ruraux *f*

FNIH = Fédération Nationale de l'Industrie Hôtelière *f*

FNOTSI = Fédération Nationale des Offices de Tourisme et Syndicats d'Initiative *f*

FNSLA = Fédération Nationale des Services Loisirs-Accueil *f*

foie *m* [*de poulet, de veau*] liver

foie gras *m* foie gras

foire *f* fair
foire commerciale *f* trade fair
folklorique folk
fonds commun *m* common fund
Fonds d'aide au conseil et à l'innovation touristique *m* government funding body for tourism development
Fonds d'intervention touristique *m* government tourism funding body
fonds de caisse *m* float
forfait *m* package, package deal
forfait avion + croisière *m* fly cruise
forfait avion + location de voiture *m* fly drive
forfait avion + train *m* fly rail
forfait week-end *m* weekend package
forfait de remontées mécaniques *m* lift pass
forfait de ski *m* ski pass
formalités douanières *fpl* customs formalities
formalités d'entrée *fpl* entry requirements
formation *f* training
formulaire E111 *m* form E111
formulaire d'appréciation *m* customer satisfaction questionnaire
formulaire d'assurance *m* insurance form
formulaire de confirmation *m* confirmation form
formulaire de détaxe *m* Tax Free Shopping Form
formulaire de réservation de groupe *m* bulk reservation form
formule-club *f* club package
formule-hôtel *f* hotel package
fouiller [*personne*] to frisk;

[*bagages*] to search
fourchette *f* fork
fournisseur *m* supplier
foyer *m* hostel
frais cool; [*rafraîchi*] chilled; [*fruit*] fresh
frais administratifs *mpl* administrative costs
frais généraux *mpl* overheads
frais médicaux *mpl* medical expenses
frais au sol *mpl* ground costs
frais d'adhésion *mpl* membership charge
frais d'agence *mpl* agency fee
frais d'annulation *mpl* cancellation charge
frais d'exploitation *mpl* operational costs
frais d'inscription *mpl* membership fee
frais de réservation *mpl* booking fee, reservation charge
fraise *f* strawberry
framboise *f* raspberry
franchisage *m* franchising
franchise *f* allowance; [*de franchisé*] franchise
franchise douanière *f* customs allowance
franchise (de) bagages *f* baggage allowance
franchisé *m* franchisee
franchiseur *m* franchisor
franchising *m* franchising
Frantour Tourisme *m* indicates travel agency which sells SNCF tickets
frappé iced, well chilled
fréquence touristique *f* tourism frequency
fréquentation *f* [*occupation*] occupancy

frit fried
frites *fpl* French fries, chips
friture *f* frying
fromage *m* cheese
fromage blanc *m* fromage frais
fromage frais *m* fromage frais
fromage de chèvre *m* goat's cheese
frontière *f* border
fruit *m* fruit
fruits de mer *m* seafood

FUAAV (= Fédération Universelle des Associations d'Agences de Voyages) *f* UFTAA
FUAJ = Fédération Unie des Auberges de Jeunesse *f*
fuite *f* leakage
fumé smoked
fumeurs smoking
funiculaire *m* funicular
fuseau horaire *m* time-zone

G

galerie marchande *f* shopping arcade
galerie d'art *f* art gallery
Galileo *m* Galileo
gamme de prix *f* price range, rate spread
gant de toilette *m* facecloth
garage *m* garage
garanti guaranteed
garantie *f* guarantee
garçon *m* [*serveur*] waiter
garçon d'ascenseur *m* lift attendant, bellhop *Am*, bellboy *Am*
garçon d'étage *m* floor waiter
garçon de comptoir *m* barman
garde d'enfants *f* child-minding, baby sitting
garderie *f* creche

gare *f* train station
gare maritime *f* harbour terminal
gare routière *f* coach station, bus depot, bus station
garni garnished
garniture *f* vegetables
gastronomie *f* gastronomy
gâteau *m* cake
Gemini *m* Gemini
gérant *m* house manager, manager
gérant de l'hôtel *m* hotel manager
géré en famille family-run
gésier *m* gizzard
gestion *f* management
gestion hôtelière *f* hotel administration, hotel management, hospitality management
gestion d'hôtel et de restaurant *f*

hotel and catering management

gestion de l'hébergement *f* accommodation management

gestion des ressources humaines *f* human resources management

gestion du tourisme *f* tourism administration

gibier *m* game

gigot *m* [*d'agneau*] leg

gilet de sauvetage *m* life-jacket

gin *m* gin

gin tonic *m* gin and tonic, G and T

gîte *m* gîte

gîte "camping-caravaning" à la ferme *m* campsite in close proximity to a farm

gîte "chambre d'hôte" *m* bed and breakfast

gîte équestre *m* rural gîte with horses for hire

gîte rural *m* holiday cottage; holiday apartment (in the country)

gîte rural communal *m* gîte communally owned by a village or group of villages

gîte rural privé *m* privately owned gîte

gîte à la noix *m* [*bœuf*] silverside

gîte d'enfants *m* holiday placements for children with a rural family

gîte d'étape *m* transit accommodation for hikers, cyclists etc

gîte de derrière *m* [*bœuf*] shank

gîte de devant *m* [*bœuf*] shin, shank *Am*

Gîtes de France *mpl* association which offers various types of rural accommodation

glace *f* ice, ice-cream

glace pilée *f* crushed ice

glaçon *m* ice cube

GM (= Gentil Membre) *m* holiday maker (at Club Med)

GO (= Gentil Organisateur) *m* activity organizer (at Club Med)

golf *m* golf

goûter *m* afternoon tea

gouvernante *f* housekeeper

gouvernante adjointe *f* assistant housekeeper

gouvernante générale *f* executive housekeeper, head housekeeper

gouvernante d'étage *f* floor housekeeper

gouvernante du soir *f* turndown housekeeper

GR (= sentier de Grande Randonnée) *m* long-distance footpath

gracieux complimentary

grand lit *m* double bed

grand livre *m* ledger

grande ligne *f* inter-city line

grandes vacances *fpl* long holidays, long vacation *Am*, main holiday

gratuité *f* [*place gratuite*] free place

grill *m* steakhouse, grill

grillé grilled

grivèlerie *f* offence of ordering food in restaurant etc and being unable to pay

groom *m* page, page boy

gros porteur polyvalent *m* multi-purpose large-capacity jet

groupage *m* consolidation

groupe *m* group, party

groupe électrogène *m* generator

groupe hôtelier *m* hotel group

groupe linguistique *m* language group

groupe scolaire *m* school party

groupe socio-économique *m*
socio-economic group
**Groupe d'action du tourisme
européen** *m* European Tourism
Action Group
groupe d'intérêt commun *m*
common interest group
**Groupement des industries du
tourisme et du transport** *m*
association of tourism and
transport industries
groupeur *m* consolidator
GSA *m* general sales agent
guéridon *m* gueridon, dumb waiter
guichet *m* ticket desk, ticket office
guichet automatique *m* automatic
ticket machine
guide *mf* (tour) guide
guide *m* [*livre*] guide, guide book
guide-conférencier *m* guide
guide gastronomique *m* good

food guide
guide-interprète *mf* bilingual tour
guide
guide interprète auxiliaire *mf*
seasonally employed bilingual
tour guide
guide-interprète local *mf*
bilingual tour guide restricted to
work in one town or department
guide-interprète national *mf* full-
time permanent bilingual tour
guide
guide local *mf* local guide
guide touristique *m* guide book,
tourist guide, travel guide
guide de conversation *m* phrase
book
guide de montagne *m* mountain
guide
guide de voyages *m* travel
directory

H

habitué *m* regular
haddock *m* smoked haddock
hall *m* lobby; [*d'aéroport*] lounge;
[*de gare*] concourse
hall d'accueil *m* reception, lobby
hall d'aéroport *m* airport lounge
hall d'entrée *m* entrance hall
hall d'entrée d'hôtel *m* hotel

lobby
hall de réception *m* foyer, lobby
hall des départs *m* departure
lounge
hampe *f* [*de bœuf*] cut taken
between the flank and the sirloin
handicapé handicapped, disabled
haut-parleur *m* Tannoy, loud-

speaker
haute saison *f* high season
hebdomadaire weekly
hébergement *m* accommodation,
accommodations *Am*
hébergement non marchand *m*
visiting friends and relatives,
VFR
hébergement à titre gracieux *m*
visiting friends and relatives,
VFR
hébergement de courte durée *m*
short-stay accommodation
hébergement de transit *m* transit
accommodation
hébergement de vacances *m*
holiday accommodation
**hébergement en pension
complète** *m* board and lodging
héberger to accommodate
hélicoptère *m* helicopter
héliport *m* heliport
heure *f* time; [*60 minutes*] hour
heure exacte *f* exact time
heure limite d'enregistrement *f*
check-in time
heure d'arrivée *f* arrival time
heure d'arrivée prévue *f*
estimated time of arrival, ETA
heure d'été *f* Summer Time,
daylight saving time
heure de départ *f* [*d'un hôtel*]
check-out time, departure time
heure de départ prévue *f*
estimated time of departure,
ETD
heure de pointe *f* peak time
heure du vol *f* flight time
heures supplémentaires *fpl*
overtime
heures d'ouverture *fpl* opening
hours
hiver *m* winter

homard *m* lobster
homme à tout faire *m* handyman
homme d'affaires *m* businessman
homme d'entretien *m*
maintenance man
honorer [*réservation*] to honour
horaire *m* timetable
horaires *mpl* timetable, schedule
horaires flottants *mpl* fluctuating
timetable
horaires d'été *mpl* summer
timetable
horaires de départ *mpl* departure
schedule; [*de bateau*] sailing
schedule
hors-saison off-season
hors service out of order
hors-taxe duty-free
hors-d'œuvre *m* hors d'œuvre,
starter
hors d'usage out of service
hospitalité *f* hospitality
hôte de marque *m* VIP guest
hôtel *m* hotel
hôtel balnéaire *m* seaside hotel
hôtel classe touriste *m* tourist
class hotel
hôtel-club *m* leisure hotel
hôtel familial *m* family-run hotel
hôtel homologué *m* hotel classified
by the "préfecture de région"
hôtel médicalisé *m* spa hotel
hôtel milieu-de-gamme *m* mid-
category hotel
hôtel non homologué *m* simple,
basic hotel classified by the
"préfectures"
hôtel quatre étoiles luxe *m* five-
star hotel, luxury hotel
hôtel une étoile *m* one-star hotel
hôtel d'aéroport *m* airport hotel
hôtel de congrès *m* hotel with
conference facilities

hôtel de gare *m* railway hotel
hôtel de luxe *m* luxury hotel
hôtel de plage *m* beach hotel
hôtel de préfecture *m* quite small and basic hotel classified by the "préfectures"
hôtel de tourisme *m* hotel classified by the ministry of Tourism
hôtel de vacances *m* holiday hotel
hôtel de ville *m* town hall, city hall
hôtel en ville *m* town hotel
hôtelier *m* hotelier, hotel operator
hôtelier hotel
hôtellerie *f* hotel business, hotelkeeping, hotel industry, hospitality business

hôtellerie de plein air *f* camping and caravaning
hôtesse *f* hostess, stewardess
hôtesse d'accueil *f* hostess
hôtesse de l'air *f* air hostess, cabin attendant, flight attendant
HOTREC *f* HOTREC
"hub" *m* hub
huile *f* oil
huître *f* oyster
hutte *f* cabin
hydravion *m* seaplane
hydrofoil *m* hydrofoil
hydroglisseur *m* hovercraft, jetfoil
hydrominéralisme *m* water cures
hydroptère *m* hydrofoil
hygiène *f* hygiene

I

IATA (= Association Internationale des Transporteurs Aériens) *f* IATA
île *f* island
immigration *f* immigration
immobilier de loisir *m* holiday property
immobilisations *fpl* fixed assets
immunisation *f* immunization
implant *m* in-house travel agency, in-plant agency *Am*
importation *f* import

importations invisibles *fpl* invisible imports
impôt sur l'hôtellerie *m* hotel tax
impression *f* [*document*] printout
imprimante *f* printer
imprimé *f* form
incident technique *m* technical hitch, technical problem
inclus included
inclusive tour *m* inclusive tour
indemnité *f* compensation
indicateur *m* timetable

indicateur horaire *m* timetable
indicateur de l'état des chambres *m* room status indicator
indications spéciales *fpl* special indications
indice de fréquentation *m* visitor index; [*pour hôtel*] room occupancy index
industrie hôtelière *f* hotel industry, hospitality industry
industrie liée au tourisme *f* tourism-related industry
industrie touristique *f* tourist industry
industrie de l'hébergement *f* accommodation industry
industrie de l'hôtellerie *f* hotel industry, professional hospitality industry
industrie de l'hôtellerie et de la restauration *f* hotel and catering industry
industrie de la restauration *f* catering industry
industrie des loisirs *f* leisure industry
industrie des services *f* service industry
informatisation *f* computerization
informatisé computerized
infrastructure *f* infrastructure
infusion *f* herbal tea
ingénieur de vol *m* flight engineer
injection *f* jab
inoculation *f* inoculation
*s'***inscrire** to register
insonorisation *f* soundproofing
inspection *f* inspection
installations *fpl* facilities, fittings
installations sanitaires *fpl* sanitary installations
installations touristiques *fpl* tourist facilities, visitor facilities

installations de loisirs *fpl* recreation facilities
installer [*faire asseoir*] to seat
institut de beauté *m* beauty salon
Institut de formation des agents de voyage *m* training institute for travel agents
intégration horizontale *f* horizontal integration
intégration verticale *f* vertical integration
intégration verticale en amont *f* vertical backward integration
intégration verticale en aval *f* vertical forward integration
intempérie *f* poor weather conditions
inter-compagnie [*aérienne*] interline; ***accord inter-compagnie*** interlining agreement
intercontinental intercontinental
interdiction de vol *f* aircraft grounding
intérêt *m* interest
Intergroupe Tourisme *m* Tourism Intergroup
interne in-house
interprète *mf* interpreter
interrompre un voyage to break a journey
interurbain [*train*] InterCity; [*appel, bus*] long-distance
investissement *m* investment
isolation phonique *f* soundproofing
isolation thermique *f* thermal insulation
issue de secours *f* emergency exit
itinéraire optimal *m* optimal route
itinéraire touristique *m* tourist route
itinéraire sur mesure *m* tailor-made itinerary

J

jacuzzi *m* jacuzzi
jambon *m* ham
jambon blanc *m* boiled ham
jambon cru *m* dried and salted ham eaten raw
jardin *m* garden
jardin botanique *m* botanical gardens
jardin public *m* park
jardinier *m* gardener, groundskeeper
jardinière *f* jardiniere; [*de légumes*] mixed vegetables
jarret *m* [*du veau, du bœuf*] knuckle, shin
jet-ski *m* jet-skiing
jetée *f* jetty
jeu *m* game

Jeune Voyageur Service *m* SNCF service for children travelling unaccompanied
jour: par jour per day; *2/3 jours* [*séjour*] short break
jour férié *m* public holiday
journal *m* newspaper
journaux-tabac *m* newsagent and tobacconist
journée-vacance *f* tourist day
journée d'étude *f* study day
jumbo-jet *m* jumbo jet
jumelage *m* [*de villes*] twinning
jus d'orange *m* orange juice
jus de fruit *m* fruit juice
jus de fruit pressé *m* freshly squeezed fruit juice
JVS = Jeune Voyageur Service *m*

K

kardex *f* guest history card
ketchup *m* tomato ketchup
kilométrage maximal autorisé *m* maximum permitted mileage

kiosque à journaux *m* newspaper stand, newsstand
kitchenette *f* kitchenette

L

lac *m* lake; [*en Écosse*] loch; [*en Irlande*] lough
lacustre [*transport*] lake
lait *m* milk
lait de chèvre *m* goat's milk
laitue *f* lettuce
lampe *f* lamp
lampe de chevet *f* bedside lamp
langouste *f* rock lobster
langoustine *f* Dublin Bay prawn
langue étrangère *f* foreign language
langue officielle *f* official language
lapin *m* rabbit
lard *m* bacon
lardons *mpl* diced bacon fat
lasagnes *fpl* lasagne
latitude *f* latitude
lavabo *m* wash(hand) basin
lecteur de cartes *m* credit card reader
légumes *mpl* vegetables
lentilles *fpl* lentils
lettre *f* letter
lettre de change *f* bill of exchange
lettre de confirmation *f* letter of confirmation
lettre de crédit *f* letter of credit
LFAJ = Ligue Française des Auberges de Jeunesse *f*
liaison *f* link
liaison aérienne *f* airlink, air service
liaison aérienne directe *f* direct

airlink
liaison inter-aéroports *f* airport shuttle link
libérer [*chambre*] to vacate
libertés commerciales *fpl* commercial freedoms
libertés de l'air *fpl* freedoms of the air
librairie *f* bookshop
libre free; [*chambre aussi, toilettes*] vacant
libre circulation de personnes *f* free movement of people
licence *f* licence
licence d'agent des voyages *f* travel agent's licence
licence d'alcool licence (to sell alcohol)
lieu de vacances *m* holiday resort
lièvre *m* hare
liftier *m* lift attendant, elevator attendant *Am*
ligne *f* [*transport*] route; *la compagnie qui assure la ligne Paris-Bordeaux* the carrier which operates Paris-Bordeaux
ligne extérieure *f* [*de téléphone*] outside line
ligne intérieure *f* domestic route; *la compagnie qui assure les lignes intérieures* the carrier which services domestic destinations
ligne internationale *f* international

route

ligne maritime *f* shipping line

ligne radiale *f* minor domestic air route

ligne saisonnière *f* seasonally operated air route

ligne spécifique *f* [*de téléphone*] dedicated line

ligne téléphonique directe *f* direct dial telephone

ligne transversale *f* domestic or international air route but not serving the capital

ligne de banlieue *f* commuter line

ligne de changement de date *f* International Date Line

ligne de changement de jour *f* International Date Line

lignes de chemin de fer interurbaines *fpl* inter-city rail service

Ligue française des auberges de jeunesse *f* French association of youth hostels

limitation de poids *f* weight limit

limonade *f* lemonade

linge *m* linen

lingère *f* linen-keeper

lingerie *f* linen room, linen store

liqueur *f* liqueur

liquide *m* [*monnaie*] cash

liseuse *f* [*en train, en avion*] reading light

liste noire *f* blacklist

liste d'attente *f* waiting list, waitlist

liste d'occupation des chambres *f* reservations chart

liste des arrivées *f* arrivals list

liste des clients *f* guest list

liste des départs *f* departure list

liste des réservations *f* reservation list

liste des tarifs *f* price list, tariff; [*de transport*] fare list

liste des VIP *f* VIP list

lit *m* bed; *faire un lit* to make a bed

lit escamotable *m* Murphy bed

lit pliant *m* foldaway bed, folding bed

lit une place *m* single bed

lit à baldaquin *m* fourposter bed, tester bed

lit d'enfant *m* cot, crib *Am*

lit d'hôtel *m* hotel bed

lit de bébé *m* cot, crib *Am*

lit de camp *m* camp bed, cot *Am*

literie *f* bedding

lits jumeaux *mpl* twin beds

lits superposés *mpl* bunk beds

littérature du tourisme *f* tourist literature

littoral *m* coast

livre d'inventaire *m* stock book

livre de caisse *m* cash book

livre de consignes *m* logbook

livre de réservation *m* reservations book, book register, hotel register

livre de trésorerie générale *m* general cash book

livrée: en livrée liveried

location *f* hiring, renting; [*logement*] rented accommodation; *un appartement en location* a self-catering apartment

location d'avion avec équipage *f* wet lease

location d'avion sans équipage *f* dry lease

location d'avions *f* aircraft leasing

location de bateau avec équipage *m* crewed charter

location de bateau sans équipage *f* bareboat charter

location de matériel de ski *f* hire of ski equipment
location de voitures *f* car rental, car hire
locaux communs *mpl* public areas
locaux de service *mpl* service areas
logement à demeure *m* live-in accommodation
logement sans restauration *m* accommodation only
logis à la ferme *m* farmhouse accommodation
logo *m* [*d'un groupe*] logo
loi de déréglementation des compagnies aériennes *f* Airline Deregulation Act

loisir *m* leisure
loisirs *mpl* leisure activities
long-courrier long-haul
longe *f* [*du veau, du porc*] loin
longitude *f* longitude
louer to rent; [*de propriétaire à client*] to rent out
loueur *m* [*de bateau, d'avion*] charterer; [*de voiture, d'appartement*] lessor
luge *f* sled
lune de miel *f* honeymoon
luxe *m* luxury
luxe de luxe, luxury
luxueux deluxe
lycée technique hôtelier *f* hotel school

machine à cirer les chaussures *f* shoe polishing machine
machine à rayons X *f* X-ray machine
macreuse *f* shoulder (of beef)
magasin *m* shop
magnétophone *m* tape recorder
magnétoscope *m* video recorder
mailing *m* mailshot
main-courante *f* day book
maintenance *f* maintenance
Maison internationale de la jeunesse *f* hostel-style accommodation for young people
maison meublée *f* furnished house
Maison de province *f* regional tourist offices based in Paris
Maisons familiales de vacances *f* government-funded organization offering budget family holiday accommodation
maître-coq *m* executive chef
maître d'hôtel *m* head waiter,

43

maître d' *Am*

maîtrise de sciences-techniques *f* higher vocational qualification

maladie contagieuse *f* contagious disease

malentendu *m* misunderstanding

malle *f* trunk

mallette *f* briefcase

mandat postal *m* money order

manifestation *f* event, event attraction

manifestation culturelle *f* cultural event

manifestation sportive *f* sporting event

manifeste *m* manifest

manoir *m* manor (house)

manutentionnaire *m* storekeeper, storeman

maquereau *m* mackerel

marchandise hors taxes *f* duty-free goods

marche *f* walking, hiking

marché *m* market

marché-cible *m* target market

marché touristique *m* tourist market

marché aux puces *m* flea market

marché des loisirs *m* leisure market

marché du tourisme *m* tourism market, holiday market, travel market

marcher [*en randonnée*] to walk, to hike

marge bénéficiaire *f* profit margin

marina *f* marina

mariné marinated

marketing *m* marketing

marketing ciblé *m* target marketing

marmelade *f* marmalade

masque d'oxygène *m* oxygen mask

matelas *m* mattress

matériel audio-visuel *m* audio-visual equipment

matériel de couchage *m* bedding

mayonnaise *f* mayonnaise

mécanicien *m* mechanic

mécanisme des taux de change *m* Exchange Rate Mechanism

médaillon *m* medallion

médecin *m* doctor

melon *m* melon

membres de l'équipage *mpl* flight personnel, cabin staff

Ménestrel *m* French computer reservations network for travel agents

menu *m* menu

menu déjeuner *m* lunch menu

menu enfant *m* children's menu

menu table d'hôte *m* table d'hôte menu

menu à prix fixe *m* set menu, fixed-price menu

mer *f* sea

mercatique *f* marketing

méridien *m* meridian

meringue *f* meringue

message *m* message

message téléphonique *m* telephone message

mesure: sur mesure tailor-made

météo *f* weather forecast

métro *m* underground, tube, subway *Am*

mettre la table to lay the table, to set the table

mettre le couvert to set the table

mettre qch sur un compte to charge sth to an account, to put sth on a bill

meublé furnished

meublé de tourisme *m* self-catering accommodation

meubles *mpl* furniture

MFV = Maisons Familiales de Vacances *fpl*

micro *m* microphone, mike

migration *f* migration

MIJE = Maison Internationale de la JEunesse *f*

milk-shake *m* milk-shake

mille *m* [*1,609 km*] mile

mille nautique *m* nautical mile

millésime *m* vintage

mini-bar *m* mini bar

minibus *m* minibus

mini-golf *m* crazy-golf

mini-séjour *m* mini-break, short break

ministère du Tourisme *m* Ministry of Tourism

ministre du Tourisme *m* Minister for Tourism

minitel *m* minitel, French national videotex network; *service de réservation par minitel* minitel reservations service

minute: de dernière minute late

miroir *m* mirror

mobil-home *m* mobile home

mobilier *m* furnishings, furniture

mode de paiement *m* method of payment, form of payment

modification *f* alteration, change

modifier [*billet, etc.*] to alter, to change

mois *m* month

monastère *m* monastery

moniteur *m* instructor; [*écran*] VDU, monitor

moniteur de ski *m* ski instructor

monitorat sportif *m* sports instruction

monitrice *f* instructress

mono (= moniteur) *mf* instructor; instructress

montagne *f* mountain

montant *m* amount

monte-charge *m* service lift

monte-plat *m* dumb waiter

monument *m* monument

monument classé *m* listed monument, listed building

monument historique *m* historic(al) monument, ancient monument

monument historique classé *m* listed ancient monument

moquette *f* (fitted) carpet

morue *f* cod

mosquée *f* mosque

motel *m* motel

moto *f* motorbike

motocyclette *f* motorcycle

moules *fpl* mussels

mousseux sparkling

moustique *m* mosquito

mouton *m* mutton

mouvement touristique *m* tourism flow

moyen-courrier medium-haul

moyen de paiement *m* means of payment

moyenne saison *f* shoulder period

MST = Maîtrise de Sciences Techniques *f*

MST hôtellerie-restauration *m* higher vocational qualification in hotel and catering

müesli *m* muesli

multinationale *f* multinational

multipropriété *f* multi-ownership, timesharing; *un appartement en multipropriété* a timeshare

mûre *f* blackberry

musée *m* museum; [*d'art*] art gallery

musée des Arts et traditions populaires *m* folk museum

musée des Transports *m* transport
   museum
musique de fond *f* background
music
musulman Muslim

nager to swim
naissance *f* birth
nappe *f* tablecloth
natation *f* swimming
national national
nationalisé state-owned
nationalité *f* nationality
naturisme *m* naturism
nautisme *m* water sports
navet *m* turnip
navette *f* shuttle; [*autocar*] shuttle
   (bus); *faire la navette entre* to
   shuttle between
navette gratuite *f* courtesy bus
navette de transfert *f* transfer bus
navigation de plaisance *f* pleasure
   cruising, yachting
nécessaire de couture *f* sewing kit
neige *f* snow
neiger to snow
nettoyage *m* cleaning
nettoyage à sec *m* dry cleaning
nettoyer to clean
night-club *m* (night)club
niveau arrivée *m* arrivals level
niveau départ *m* departures level

niveau tarifaire *m* fare level
niveau d'occupation *m* occupancy
   level
nœud (marin) *m* knot
noix *f* walnut; [*de veau*] topside
nolisation *f* chartering
nolisé charter
nom *m* name, surname
nom de famille *m* surname
nom de jeune fille *m* maiden name
nombre de voyages illimité *m*
   unlimited travel
non alcoolisé non-alcoholic
non cessible [*billet, etc.*] not
   transferable
non-confirmé unconfirmed
non fumeurs no-smoking
non modifiable not alterable; *"non
   modifiable"* no change allowed
non-prévu non-scheduled
non remboursable non-refundable
no-show *m* no-show
notation hôtelière *f* hotel grading
note *f* bill, check *Am*
note de débit *f* debit note
note de service *f* memo

nourriture *f* food
Nouveau Monde *m* New World
nouvelle cuisine *f* nouvelle cuisine
nouvelle propriété *f* timeshare taken on a lease basis converting to ownership after 9 years
nudisme *m* nudism, naturism
nuit *f* night
nuit à la belle étoile *f* night in the open, night under the stars
nuit d'hôtel *f* bed-night
nuitée *f* bed-night, overnight stay
numéro vert *m* 0800 telephone number, toll-free number *Am*
numéro d'IT *m* IT number
numéro de carte d'identité *m* ID number
numéro de chambre *m* room number
numéro de passeport *m* passport number
numéro de place *m* [*de place assise*] seat number
numéro de vol *m* flight number
nurserie *m* baby-changing area

O

OACI (= Organisation de l'Aviation Civile Internationale) *f* ICAO
objets trouvés *mpl* lost property, lost and found *Am*
objets de valeur *mpl* valuables
obligation "vacances" *f* holiday bond, vacation bond *Am*
obligation de résidence de tourisme *m* holiday property bond
OCCAJ = Organisation Centrale des Camps et Activités de Jeunesse *f*
occupation double *f* double occupancy
occupation maximale *f* capacity occupancy
occupation des chambres *f* room occupancy
occupation des lits *f* bed occupancy
occupation par une seule personne *f* single occupancy
occupé occupied; [*toilettes*] engaged
OCDE = (Organisation de Coopération et de Développement Économiques) *f* OECD
œnologie: faire un stage d'œnologie to go on a wine

appreciation course

œnologique: croisière œnologique wine-tasting cruise

œuf *m* egg

œuf dur *m* hard-boiled egg

œuf poché *m* poached egg

œuf à la coque *m* boiled egg

œuf au plat *m* fried egg

œufs brouillés *mpl* scrambled egg(s)

Office municipal du tourisme *m* city tourism office

Office national du tourisme *m* National Tourist Office

Office du tourisme *m* tourist information centre, tourist office

office du tourisme-syndicat d'initiative *m* tourist information centre

Office du tourisme universitaire *m* ≈ Campus Travel

Office du tourisme et des congrès de Paris *m* Tourist Office and Conventions Bureau of Paris

Offices nationaux étrangers du tourisme *mpl* Foreign Government Tourist Offices

officiel official

offre promotionnelle *f* promotional offer

offre spéciale *f* special offer

oignon *m* onion

OK OK

olive *f* olive

OMT = Office Municipal du Tourisme *m*

OMT (= Organisation Mondiale du Tourisme) *f* WTO

ONET (= Offices Nationaux Étrangers du Tourisme) *mpl* FGTO

opéra *m* opera

opérateur *m* operator

opératrice *f* operator

option *f* option; *en option* optional; *prendre une option* to take an option

optionnel optional

orange *f* orange

orange pressée *f* freshly squeezed orange juice

orchestre *m* band; [*de musique classique*] orchestra

ordinateur *m* computer

ordinateur portable *m* portable computer

ordre de réparation *m* repair order

oreiller *m* pillow

organisateur de conférences *m* conference organizer

organisateur de congrès *m* conference organizer

organisateur de groupe *m* group organizer

organisateur de voyages *m* tour operator

organisation *f* organization

Organisation centrale des camps et activités de jeunesse *f* organization which arranges holidays for young people

Organisation maritime internationale *f* International Maritime Organisation

Organisation mondiale du tourisme *f* World Tourism Organization

Organisation de Coopération et de développement économiques *f* Organization for Economic Cooperation and Development

organisation de manifestations *f* event management

Organisation de l'aviation civile internationale *f* International

Civil Aviation Organization
origine *f* origin
OT = Office du Tourisme *m*
OTSI (= Office du Tourisme-Syndicat d'Initiative) *m* tourist office

OTU = Office du Tourisme Universitaire *m*
outre-mer: d'outre-mer overseas
ouvre-boîte *m* tin-opener, can-opener
ouvre-bouteille *m* bottle-opener

P

paiement préalable *m* prepayment
pain *m* bread
palace *m* luxury hotel
palais *m* palace
palais des congrès *m* convention centre
paleron *m* neck, chuck *Am*
pamplemousse *m* grapefruit
panaché *m* shandy
panier-repas *m* packed meal, packed lunch
panneau *m* sign
panonceau *m* sign
panoramique scenic
papier hygiénique *m* toilet tissue
papier peint *m* wallpaper
papier à lettres *m* note paper, stationery
papiers *mpl* [*passeport, visa, etc.*] documents
paquebot *m* liner
paquebot de haute mer *m* ocean liner

paquebot de ligne *m* liner
paquet *m* parcel
par: par personne/chambre/nuit per person/room/night; *par avion* by plane
parachute ascensionnel *m* parascending
para-hôtellerie *f* serviced accommodation industry
parallèle de latitude *m* parallel of latitude
parallèle de longitude *m* parallel of longitude
parc *m* [*d'hôtel*] grounds; [*public*] park
parc aquatique *m* water park
parc national *m* National Park
parc naturel *m* nature reserve
parc naturel national *m* national park
parc résidentiel de loisirs *m* chalet park, holiday camp
parc zoologique *m* zoo park

parc à thème *m* theme park
parc de loisirs *m* leisure park
parc de stationnement *m* car park, parking lot *Am*
parc des expositions *m* exhibition centre
parcours *m* leg; [*itinéraire*] route
parcours à vide *m* deadhead flight, empty leg
parcours de golf *m* golf course
parfum *m* perfume; [*de glace*] flavour
parfumerie *f* perfumery
parking *m* car park, parking lot *Am*
parking courte durée *m* short-stay car park
parking longue durée *m* long-stay car park
parking privé *m* private car park; *"parking privé"* private parking
parrainer to sponsor
PARS *m* PARS
part de marché *m* market share
partager to share
particulier private; [*salle de bain*] en-suite
partir to leave; [*bateau*] to sail
passage *m* [*en bateau*] crossing; *de passage* transient
passage de frontière *m* border crossing
passager *m* passenger
passager direct *m* through passenger
passager piéton *m* foot passenger
passager à pied *m* foot passenger
passager en correspondance *m* transfer passenger
passager en transit *m* transit passenger
passe(-partout) *m* [*clé*] master key
passe-plat *m* serving hatch
passeport *m* passport

passer la nuit to spend the night
passer les vacances to holiday, to vacation *Am*
passerelle *f* boarding bridge; [*escalier*] boarding steps; [*de ferry*] linkspan, boarding ramp
pastille pour purifier l'eau *f* water sterilizing tablet
pâté *m* pâté
pâtes *fpl* pasta
pâtisserie *f* cakes, pastries; [*commerce*] cake shop
pâtissier *m* pastry cook
patrimoine *m* heritage
patrimoine culturel *m* cultural heritage
patrimoine naturel *m* natural heritage
pavé *m* [*de bœuf*] thick slice of beef steak
pavillon de complaisance *m* flag of convenience
payé à l'avance pre-paid
payer to pay
pays *m* country
pays émetteur *m* tourism generating country
pays étranger *m* foreign country
pays hôte *m* host country
pays industrialisé *m* industrialized country, developed country
pays riche *m* advanced country
pays d'incoming *m* tourism receiving country
pays d'origine *m* country of origin
pays d'outgoing *m* tourism generating country
pays en (voie de) développement *m* developing country
paysage *m* scenery
PDV (= Point De Vente) *m* POS
péage *m* toll
pêche *f* fishing

pêche à la ligne *f* angling
pêche à la mouche *f* fly fishing
pédalo *m* pedalo, pedal boat
peignoir de bain *m* bathrobe
pèlerin *m* pilgrim
pèlerinage *m* pilgrimage
penderie *f* wardrobe, clothes closet *Am*
péniche *f* barge
péniche-hôtel *f* botel
pension *f* pension, guest house; *en pension* en pension
pension complète *f* full board, American plan *Am*
pension de famille *f* boarding house
pensionnaire *m* paying guest
période blanche *f* moderately busy period on the SNCF calendar
période bleue *f* slackest period on the SNCF calendar
période estivale *f* summer season
période rouge *f* busiest period on the SNCF calendar
période de fêtes *f* holiday period
période de pointe *f* peak period
personnalité *f* VIP, Very Important Person
personne âgée *f* senior citizen
personne handicapée à mobilité réduite *f* disabled person
personne du troisième âge *f* senior citizen
personnel *m* personnel, staff
personnel extra *m* relief staff
personnel qualifié *m* qualified staff
personnel au sol *m* ground staff
personnel d'encadrement *m* management; [*animateurs*] activity organizers; [*moniteurs*] instructors
personnel d'entretien *m* maintenance staff
personnel de bar *m* bar staff
personnel de cabine *m* flight personnel, cabin staff
personnel de nettoyage *m* cleaning staff
personnel de restauration *m* catering staff
personnel en contact avec la clientèle *m* "contact" staff
personnel qualifié *m* qualified staff
perte *f* loss
pétillant lightly sparkling
petit déjeuner américain *m* American breakfast
petit déjeuner continental *m* Continental breakfast
petit déjeuner à l'anglaise *m* English breakfast
petit pain *m* roll, bread roll
petite caisse *f* petty cash
petits fours *mpl* petits fours
petits pois *mpl* peas
pharmacie *f* chemist's, pharmacy *Am*
photo d'identité *f* passport-sized photograph
photocopier to photocopy
photocopieuse *f* photocopier
PIB (= Produit Intérieur Brut) *m* GDP
pichet *m* jug
pictogramme *m* pictogram
pièce d'identité *f* ID, identification, proof of identity
pied *m* [*de porc*] trotter
pied-à-terre *m* pied-à-terre
pigeon *m* pigeon
pilon *m* [*de poulet*] drumstick
piscine *f* swimming pool
piscine couverte *f* indoor pool
piscine intérieure *f* indoor

swimming pool

piscine d'eau douce *f* freshwater swimming pool

piscine d'eau de mer *f* sea-water pool

piscine de plein air *f* open air pool

piste cyclable *f* cycle path

piste d'atterrissage *f* airstrip

piste de luge *f* toboggan run

piste de ski *f* ski slope

pizzeria *f* pizzeria, pizza parlor *Am*

placard *m* cupboard, closet *Am*

place: il y a encore de la place there's still room

place assise *f* seat

place confirmée *f* confirmed seat

place côté couloir *f* aisle seat

place côté fenêtre *f* window seat

place fumeur smoking seat

place non-fumeur *f* no-smoking seat

plage *f* beach

plage privative *f* private beach

plage privée *f* private beach

plage publique *f* public beach

plainte *f* complaint

plan *m* plan; [*de ville*] map

plan d'étage *m* floor plan

plan d'évacuation *m* escape route

planche à repasser *f* ironing board

planche à voile *f* windsurfing; [*matériel*] windsurfer, sailboard

planification *f* planning

planification du marketing *f* marketing planning

planifier to plan

planning Whitney *m* Whitney system

planning d'occupation journalière *m* daily occupancy forecast

planning d'occupation des chambres *m* room letting sheet

planning de disponibilité des chambres *m* room availability chart

planning de réservation de type Whitney *m* Whitney advance booking rack

planning de travail *m* work schedule

plante *f* plant

planter une tente to pitch a tent

plaque GB *f* GB plate

plat *m* [*contenant*] dish; [*contenu*] course

plat principal *m* main course

plat (de service) *m* serving dish

plat du jour *m* today's special

plateau *m* tray

plateau petit déjeuner *m* breakfast tray

plateau repas *m* meal tray

plateau de courtoisie *m* hospitality tray

plateau de fromages *m* cheese board

plateau en argent *m* silver salver

plein tarif *m* full fare; [*à hôtel*] rack rate

plein-temps: à plein-temps full-time

pleine saison *f* high-season

plongée (sous-marine) *f* diving, scuba diving

plonger to dive

plongeur *m* dishwasher

pluvieux wet

PNB (= Produit National Brut) *m* GNP

poids *m* weight

poids au décollage *m* take-off weight

point: à point medium-rare

point de départ *m* point of departure

point de vente m point of sale; [*magasin*] sales outlet

poireau m leek

poisson m fish

poisson d'eau douce m freshwater fish

poisson de mer m seafish

poissonnier m fishmonger

poitrine f [*porc*] belly; [*bœuf*] brisket

poivron m pepper

police d'assurance f insurance policy

police de non-annulation f no-cancellation policy

police de l'immigration f immigration police

politique touristique f tourism policy

politique de crédit f credit policy

politique de vente f sales policy

politique du tourisme f tourism policy

pollution f pollution

pomme f apple

pomme de terre f potato

pomme de terre au four f baked potato

pomme de terre en robe de chambre f baked potato

pomme de terre en robe des champs f baked potato

pommes vapeur fpl boiled potatoes

pommes de terre frites fpl French fried potatoes, French fries

pompe à bière f beer pump

pont m bridge; [*de bateau*] deck

porc m pork

port m port, harbour

port fluvial m river port

port lacustre m lakeside port

port maritime m seaport

port d'arrivée m port of entry

port d'embarquement m port of embarkation

port d'escale m port of call

port de ferry m ferry port

port de plaisance m marina

porte f door; [*à aéroport*] gate

porte-bagage m luggage rack

porte-clef m key ring

porte coupe-feu f fire door

porte-fenêtre f French window

porte d'embarquement f boarding gate

porte de débarquement f (disembarkation) gate

porte de sortie f exit door

portes de chambres communiquantes fpl inter-connecting doors

porter plainte to lodge a complaint

porteur m porter

portier m doorman, porter, commissionaire

portier de nuit m night porter

porto m port

post-acheminement m transfer from main airport

poste restante f poste restante, general delivery *Am*

poste de pilotage m cockpit

poste de travail m work station

pot d'accueil m welcome drink

potage m soup

poulet m chicken

poulpe m octopus

pourboire m tip, gratuity

pour cent: 15 pour cent 15 percent

pourcentage de lits occupés m percentage sleeper occupancy

poursuivre en justice to sue

pré-acheminement m transfer to

main airport
précipitations *fpl* rainfall
pré-embarquement *m* pre-boarding
pré-embarquer to pre-board
pré-enregistrement *m* pre-registration
pré-inscription *f* pre-check-in
premier étage *m* first floor, second floor *Am*
première *f* first class; *voyager en première* to travel first class
première classe *f* first class
premiers soins *mpl* first aid
prénom *m* Christian name, first name
pré-paiement *m* pre-payment
préparation *f* preparation
préparer to prepare
pré-passerelle *f* pre-boarding bridge
préposé aux réservations *m* reservations clerk
présentation *f* presentation
Président-directeur général *m* Chairman and Managing Director, President *Am*
presse à pantalon *f* trouser-press
pressing *m* dry cleaning
pression *f* [*bière*] draught beer
pressographe *m* credit card machine, imprinter machine
prestataire de service *m* service provider
prestation *f* service
prestation de service: société de prestation de service *f* service provider
prévisions budgétaires *fpl* budget forecast
prévisions météorologiques *fpl* weather forecast
prévu au programme scheduled

prime *f* premium
printemps *m* spring
prise (femelle) *f* socket, outlet
prise (mâle) *f* plug
prise pour rasoir électrique *f* shaver socket
privatisation *f* privatization
privé private
prix *m* price, rate
prix fixe *m* fixed-rate
prix forfaitaire *m* all-inclusive price
prix minimum *m* minimum price
prix moyen des chambres *m* average room rate
prix net *m* net rate
prix standard *m* standard price
prix de vente *m* selling price
prix de vente moyen d'une chambre *m* average room rate
prix de la chambre *m* room rate
prix du couvert *m* cover charge
procédure de contrôle des coûts *f* cost control procedure
produit hôtelier *m* hotel product
Produit Intérieur Brut *m* Gross Domestic Product
Produit National Brut *m* Gross National Product
produit touristique *m* tourist product
profession touristique *f* tourist profession
profiterole *f* profiterole
programmateur de cartes-clés électroniques *f* electronic key encoding machine
programme de commercialisation *m* marketing programme
programme de fidélisation *m* frequent user programme
programme de voyage de

stimulation *m* incentive travel programme

programme du congrès *m* conference programme

projecteur *m* spotlight

projecteur de diapositives *m* slide projector

projecteur de films *m* film projector

projets de vacances *mpl* holiday plans

prolonger *m* [*séjour*] to extend

promotion *f* promotion

promotion des ventes *f* sales promotion

promouvoir to promote

propre clean

propreté *f* cleanliness

propriétaire *m* owner

propriété allégée *f* timeshare taken on a lease basis converting to ownership after 9 years

propriété-loisirs *f* = **propriété allégée**

propriété-vacances *f* = **propriété allégée**

prospectus *m* prospectus

pub *m* pub, public house

public *m* public; [*de conférence, cinéma*] audience

public public

publicité *f* advertising

publicité directe *f* below-the-line advertising

publicité interne *f* internal advertising

publicité pure *f* above-the-line advertising

publipostage *m* mailshot; *envoyer un publipostage à* to mailshot

pupitre *m* lectern

purée de pommes de terre *f* creamed potatoes, mashed potatoes

qualités touristiques *fpl* tourist qualities

quarantaine: mettre en quarantaine to put in quarantine

quatre étoiles four-star

quatre étoiles luxe five-star

questionnaire *m* questionnaire

questionnaire d'évaluation *m* [*remis aux clients*] customer satisfaction questionnaire

quinzaine *f* fortnight *Br*, two weeks

quitter to leave; [*chambre*] to vacate; *quitter l'hôtel* to check out, to check out of the hotel

quotidien daily

R

rabais *m* discount

radis *m* radish

rafraîchi cooled

rafraîchissements *mpl* refreshments

rafting *m* rafting

rage *f* rabies

raisin *m* grapes

rajustement des prix *m* backward pricing

randonnée *f* ramble, hike; [*sport*] rambling, trekking

randonnée sac au dos *f* backpacking (tour)

randonnée à dos de poney *f* pony-trekking

randonnée en montagne *f* hill walking, mountain trekking

randonnée en VTT *f* mountain biking

randonneur *m* rambler, hiker

rangement *m* storage

rappel *m* [*vaccin*] (vaccine) booster

rapport *m* statement, report

rapport financier *m* financial report

rapport journalier *m* daily report

rapport journalier de sécurité *m* daily security report

rapport d'exploitation *m* operating statement

rapport de caisse par service *m* department cash report

rapport de situation journalière *m* daily trading report

rapport de situation mensuelle *m* monthly trading report

rapport de la gouvernante *m* housekeeper's report

ratatouille *f* ratatouille

RATP = Régie Autonome des Transports Parisiens *f*

récapitulation des ventes journalières *f* traffic sheet

recensement d'hôtels *m* hotel registration

réceptif *m* incoming tour operator, ground operator

réception *f* reception; [*d'hôtel aussi*] front office, front of house; [*soirée*] reception, function

réception privée *f* private function

réception d'hôtel *f* hotel reception

réceptionnaire *mf* receptionist, desk clerk *Am*

réceptionniste *m* receptionist, reception clerk

réceptionniste d'hôtel hotel receptionist

réceptionniste de nuit *mf* night porter

récession *f* recession

recette moyenne par chambre *f* average return per room

recettes générées par le tourisme *fpl* tourism-generated revenue

réclamation *f* complaint
recommandation *f* referral
recommander to recommend
reconfirmation *f* reconfirmation
recouche *f* stay(-over); *liste des clients en recouche* stays list
recrutement *m* recruitment
reçu de change de devises *m* foreign exchange receipt
reçu de paiement anticipé *m* advance payment receipt
reçu pour paiement en espèces *m* cash receipt
récupérer [*bagages, TVA*] to reclaim
réduction *f* reduction, discount
réduction de tarif aérien *f* air fare discount
régate *f* regatta
Régie Autonome des Transports Parisiens *f* Paris public transport authority
régime *m* diet
régime spécial *m* special diet
Régime d'exportation pour la vente au détail *m* Foreign Exchange Tax Free Shopping
région *f* region
régional regional
registre *m* register
registre à feuillets rechargeables *m* loose-leaf register
registre de dépôt au coffre-fort *m* safe deposit receipt book
registre de sécurité *m* security register
registre des arrivées *m* arrivals register
registre des départs *m* departures book
registre du gardien de nuit *m* night porter's report book
règlement *m* payment

réglementation douanière *f* customs regulations
réglementation sur l'hygiène alimentaire *f* food hygiene regulations
réglementation sur l'hygiène et la sécurité *f* health and safety regulations
règlements et usages *mpl* code of practice
régler un compte to settle an account
régler une note to pay a bill
règles d'hygiène *fpl* hygiene regulations; *une règle d'hygiène* a rule of hygiene
regroupement *f* cluster
relais *m* post house
relais-château *m* country house hotel
relais de tourisme *m* country house hotel
relations publiques *fpl* public relations, PR
relevé *m* statement
relevé de communications téléphoniques *m* telephone call sheet
relevé de compte *m* statement of account
relevé des appels téléphoniques *m* telephone call sheet
remboursable refundable
remboursé reimbursed
remboursement *m* refund
rembourser to reimburse, to refund
remise *f* discount; [*activité*] discounting
remise compétitive *f* competitive discounting
remise pour les groupes *f* group discount

remonte-pente *m* ski lift, ski tow
remontées mécaniques *fpl* ski lifts
remparts *mpl* walls
rénovation *f* refurbishment
renseignements *mpl* information;
un renseignement a piece of
information
réparation *f* repair
repas *m* meal
repas chaud *m* hot meal
repas enfant *m* children's meal,
children's portion
repeindre to repaint
représentant *m* representative
représentant d'hôtel *m* hotel
representative
**Représentation française du
tourisme à l'étranger** *f*
organization which represents
French tourism abroad
responsable maintenance *m* head
of maintenance
résa (= réservation) *f* reservation,
booking, bkg
réseau *m* network
réseau aérien intérieur *m* internal
air network
réseau ferroviaire *m* rail network
réseau d'apport *m* feeder network
réservataire *m* party making a
reservation
réservation *f* booking, reservation,
advance booking
réservation ferme *f* firm
reservation
réservation informatisée *f*
computerized booking
réservation prioritaire *f* priority
booking
réservation télématique *f*
automated reservation
réservation téléphonique *f*
telephone reservation

réservation d'avion *f* flight
reservation
réservation de groupe *f* group
booking
réservation de place *f* seat
reservation
réservation en bloc *f* block-
booking
réservation par téléphone *f*
telephone reservation, telephone
booking
réservations centralisées *fpl*
central reservations
réserve *f* [*stock*] store; [*naturelle*]
(nature) reserve
réserve naturelle *f* conservation
area, nature reserve
réserve naturelle nationale *f*
National Nature Reserve
réserve d'animaux sauvages *f*
safari park
réserve de gibier *f* game reserve
réservé reserved
réserver to book, to make a
reservation, to reserve
résidence hôtelière *f* apartment
hotel
résidence secondaire *f* second
home, holiday home, vacation
home *Am*
résidence de tourisme *f* apartment
hotel
résident *m* resident
responsable: être responsable de
to be in charge of
responsable administratif *m*
executive manager
responsable maintenance *m*
maintenance engineer
responsable restauration *m*
restaurant manager
responsable de groupe *m* group
leader

responsable de l'approvisionnement *m* storekeeper, food and beverage manager

responsable de l'information *m* enquiry clerk

responsable de la formation *m* training officer

responsable de la sécurité *m* house security officer

responsable des achats *m* buyer

responsable des banquets *m* banqueting manager

responsable des congrès *m* conference coordinator

responsable des légumes *m* vegetable cook

responsable des réceptions *m* functions manager

responsable des réservations *m* reservations clerk

responsable des sauces *m* sauce cook

responsable des ventes *m* sales manager

responsable du courrier *m* mail clerk

responsable du hall *m* head hall porter

responsable du service à l'étage *m* room service manager

responsable du standard *m* head switchboard operator

responsable du vestiaire *m* cloakroom attendant

restaurant *m* restaurant

restaurant gastronomique *m* gourmet restaurant

restaurant libre-service *m* self-service restaurant

restaurant self-service *m* self-service restaurant

restaurant à thème *m* theme restaurant

restaurant d'altitude *m* mountain restaurant

restaurant de poissons *m* seafood restaurant

restaurant de spécialités *m* speciality restaurant

restaurateur *m* restaurant manager, restaurant owner, restaurateur

restauration *f* catering; [*industrie*] catering industry, catering business

restauration aérienne *f* in-flight catering, airline catering

restauration rapide *f* fast food

restoroute *m* motorway restaurant

restrictions gouvernementales *fpl* government restrictions

retapisser *vt* to redecorate

retard *m* delay; *être en retard* to be late; *le vol a du retard* the flight has been delayed

retenir [*chambre*] to block, to hold

retirer [*bagages*] to reclaim

retirer de l'argent to withdraw money

retour *m* [*voyage*] return journey

retrait des bagages *m* baggage claim

rétrocéder to release back

rétrocession *f* releasing back

rétroprojecteur *m* overhead projector

réunion *f* meeting; [*réception*] function

réveil automatique *m* automatic alarm

réveil(-matin) *m* alarm clock

réveil de voyage *m* travel alarm clock

réveil par la réception *m* wake-up call

réveiller to wake up; *souhaitez-vous être réveillé demain matin ?* would you like a wake-up call in the morning?

se **réveiller** to wake up

revenu *m* income

revenu disponible *m* disposable income

revenu passager-kilomètre *m* revenue passenger kilometre

Revue économique du tourisme mondial *f* Economic Review of World Tourism

rez-de-chaussée *m* ground floor, first floor *Am*

RFTE = Représentation Française du Tourisme à l'Étranger *f*

rhum *m* rum

rideau *m* curtain

rien à déclarer nothing to declare

RIHO (= Réseau Informatisé d'HOraires) *m* computerized SNCF timetable

rivière *f* river

riz *m* rice

rognon *m* kidney

rond de serviette *m* napkin ring

room-rack *m* room rack

room-service *m* room service

rôti *m* roast

rôti de bœuf *m* roast beef

rôtissage *m* roasting

rôtisseur roasting chef

rouge red

route des fromages *f* cheese route

route des vins *f* wine route

routier *m* transport café, truck stop *Am*

ruines *fpl* ruins

rumsteak *m* rumpsteak

rupture de contrat *f* breach of contract

rural rural

S

sable *m* sand

Sabre *m* Sabre

sac à dos *m* rucksack, backpack

sac de blanchisserie *m* laundry bag

sac de couchage *m* sleeping bag

sac de voyage *m* travel bag

sachet pour garniture périodique *m* sanitary disposal bag

safari *m* safari, safari holiday

saignant rare

saison *f* season; *de saison* seasonal

saison creuse *f* low season, off season

saison d'été *f* summer season
saison d'hiver *f* winter season
saisonnier seasonal
salade *f* salad
salade verte *f* green salad
salade de fruits *f* fruit salad
salle à manger *f* dining room
salle d'animation *f* entertainments room
salle d'arrivée *f* arrivals lounge
salle d'attente *f* waiting room
salle d'eau *f* shower room
salle d'embarquement *f* gate lounge
salle de bain *f* bathroom
salle de bain particulière *f* private bathroom, en-suite bathroom
salle de banquet *f* banqueting room
salle de billard *f* billiards room, pool room
salle de conférences *f* conference room, meeting room
salle de départ *f* departure lounge
salle de douches *f* shower room
salle de jeux *f* games room
salle de lecture *f* reading room
salle de musculation *f* fitness room, gym
salle de petit déjeuner *f* breakfast room
salle de projection *f* projection room
salle de réception *f* function room
salle de restaurant *f* dining room
salle de réunion *f* meeting room
salle de télévision *f* TV lounge, television room
salon *m* sitting room; [*dans hôtel, à l'aéroport*] lounge
Salon mondial du tourisme et des voyages *m* world travel and tourism fair

salon professionnel *m* trade fair
salon VIP *m* VIP lounge
salon de beauté *m* beauty salon
salon de bridge *m* card room
salon de coiffure *m* hair salon
salon de thé *m* tearoom, tea shop
sandwich *m* sandwich
sanglier *m* wild boar
sanitaires privatifs *mpl* en-suite facilities, private facilities
sauce *f* sauce
sauce salade *f* salad dressing
saucier *m* sauce chef
saucisse *f* sausage
saucisson (sec) *m* (salami-type) sausage
saumon *m* salmon
saumon fumé *m* smoked salmon
sauna *m* sauna
sauté sautéed
sauter to sauté
savon *m* soap
savonnette *f* soap
schweppes *m* tonic
SEAT = Service d'Études et d'Aménagement Touristique *m*
SEATER = Service d'Étude et d'Aménagement Touristique de l'Espace Rural *m*
SEATL = Service d'Étude et d'Aménagement Touristique du Littoral *m*
SEATM = Service d'Étude et d'Aménagement Touristique de la Montagne *m*
seau à glace *m* ice bucket
sec dry
sèche-cheveux *m* hair dryer
second (de cuisine) *m* senior sous chef; sous chef
seconde *f* second class; *voyager en seconde* to travel second class
seconde classe *f* second class

secrétaire *mf* secretary

secrétaire général *m* company secretary

secrétaire de direction *mf* executive secretary

secrétariat d'État au Tourisme *m* French Ministry for Tourism

secteur tertiaire *m* tertiary sector, service sector

secteur de l'hôtellerie et de la restauration *m* hotel and catering sector

secteur du tourisme *m* tourism sector

sécurité *f* safety; [*mesures contre délits*] security; *service de sécurité* security service

sécurité incendie *f* fire safety

segment de marché *m* market segment

segmentation du marché *f* market segmentation

séjour *m* stay

séjour discompté *m* bargain break

séjour éducatif *m* educational trip

séjour indépendant *m* self-catering holiday

séjour linguistique *m* language study trip

séjourner to stay

self(-service) *m* self-service restaurant

selle *f* [*de mouton, agneau*] saddle

selle à l'anglaise *f* [*de mouton, agneau*] saddle

semaine *f* week

séminaire *m* seminar

séminaire résidentiel *m* residential seminar

sentier *m* footpath, trail

sentier balisé *m* signposted footpath

sentier de grande randonnée *m* long-distance footpath

serrure électronique *f* electronic lock, computer-coded lock

serrure magnétique *f* magnetic lock

serrure à carte perforée *f* card-operated lock

serveur *m* waiter; [*de réseau informatique*] server

serveur minitel *m* minitel service provider

serveuse *f* waitress

service *m* service; *de service* duty; *être de service* to be on duty

service après-vente *m* after-sales service

service babyphone *m* baby-listening service

service compris *m* service included

service comptable *m* accounts (department)

service entretien *m* maintenance department

service ferroviaire *m* rail service

service hébergement *m* accommodation department, accommodation services department

service hôtelier *m* hotel service

service informations *m* enquiries

service international *m* international department

service médical *m* medical service

service réception *m* reception

service réception-accueil *m* front office department

service restauration *m* food and beverage service

service à bord *m* [*d'un avion*] in-flight service

service à table *m* table service, waiter service, waitress service

service à l'américaine *m*
American service

service à l'anglaise *m* English
service

service à l'assiette *m* plate service,
American service

service à la française *m* French
service

service à la russe *m* Russian
service

service au guéridon *m* gueridon
service, French service

service d'autobus *m* bus service

**Service d'étude et
d'aménagement touristique** *m*
body which implements tourism
policy

**Service d'étude et
d'aménagement touristique de
l'espace rural** *m* body which
deals with rural tourism

**Service d'étude et
d'aménagement touristique de
la montagne** *m* body which
researches tourism development
possibilities in mountain regions

**Service d'étude et
d'aménagement touristique du
littoral** *m* body which deals with
coastal tourism

service dans les chambres *m*
room service

service de blanchisserie *m*
laundry service

service de comptabilité *m*
accounts (department)

service de livraison à domicile *m*
home delivery service

service de navette *m* shuttle
service

service de réservation *m*
reservations department

service de restauration *m* [*dans
train*] buffet service

service de santé *m* health services

service de secrétariat *m*
secretarial service

service de voiturier *m* valet
parking

service de l'immigration *m*
immigration department

service des achats *m* purchasing
department

service des étages *m* housekeeping
department

service des réservations *m*
reservations department

service des ventes *m* sales
department

**service des ventes et du
marketing** *m* sales and
marketing department

service du marketing *m*
marketing department

service en chambre *m* room
service

services *mpl* services

services autoroutiers *mpl*
motorway services

Services Loisirs Accueil *mpl*
departmental association serving
as tourism information body and
ground handling agent

services à la clientèle *mpl*
customer care

**services de sûreté et de
surveillance** *mpl* security
services

serviette *f* [*de table*] napkin; [*de
toilette*] towel

servir to serve

SESAMTEL *m* computer
reservations system of
independent French hotels

session *f* session

set de table *m* table mat

sexe *m* sex
shaker *m* cocktail shaker
shampoing *m* shampoo
shopping *m* shopping
siège *m* seat
signalisation *f* sign-posting
signature *f* signature
signer to sign
signer le registre to sign the
  register
sirop *m* [*de fruit*] cordial
sirop d'érable *m* maple syrup
sirop d'orgeat *m* barley water
sirop de menthe *m* mint cordial,
  mint julep *Am*
site classé *m* conservation area
site historique *m* historical site
site touristique *m* tourist attraction
site d'intérêt touristique *m* site
  attraction
situation de caisse *f* cash position
Skal Club *m* club for members of
  tourism organizations and
  industries
ski *m* ski; [*sport*] skiing
ski nautique *m* water skiing
ski de fond *m* cross-country skiing
ski de piste *m* on-piste skiing
skier to ski
skieur *m* skier
SLA = Services Loisirs Accueil
  mpl
SME (= Système Monétaire
  Européen) *m* EMS
snack(-bar) *m* snack-bar
SNAV = Syndicat National des
  Agents de Voyages *m*
SNCF = Société Nationale des
  Chemins de Fer Français *f*
  French national railways
société d'assurance *f* insurance
  company
société de location *f* rental firm

société de location de voitures *f*
  car hire company
société de restauration *f* catering
  company
Socrate *m* SNCF computerized
  information system
soins esthétiques *mpl* beauty
  treatment
soins d'urgence *mpl* emergency
  treatment
soirée dansante *f* dance
soirée étape *f* stopover at an hotel
soirée à thème *f* theme evening
solarium *m* solarium
sole *f* sole
soleil *m* sun
solvabilité *f* credit rating
sommelier *m* cellarman,
  sommelier; [*serveur*] wine waiter
sommier *m* divan base
sortie *f* exit
sortie de secours *f* emergency exit
souffrance: en souffrance
  outstanding
soupe *f* soup
souper *m* supper
source *f* [*point d'eau*] spring
sous-bock *m* beermat
sous-directeur d'hôtel *m* deputy
  hotel manager, assistant hotel
  manager
sous-nappe *f* undercloth
soute *f* hold
soute à bagages *f* baggage hold
souvenir *m* souvenir
spaghettis *mpl* spaghetti
spécialité *f* speciality, specialty *Am*
spectacle *m* show
spectacle folklorique *m*
  performance of national or
  regional music or dancing
spectacle sons et lumières *m* son
  et lumière

spectacle de variétés *m* floor show

spiritueux *mpl* spirits

sport *m* sport

sports nautiques *mpl* water sports

sports d'hiver *mpl* winter sports

square *m* public gardens, square

squash *m* squash

stage *m* [*de tennis, peinture, etc.*] course

stand *m* stand, stall

standard informatisé *m* computerized switchboard

standard téléphonique *m* telephone switchboard

standardiste *mf* operator, switchboard operator, telephone operator

station *f* resort

station balnéaire *f* seaside resort, coastal resort

station climatique *f* health resort

station hydrominérale *f* spa resort

station thermale *f* spa

station verte *f* well-preserved and picturesque French rural town or village

station de métro *f* tube station, underground station, subway station *Am*

station de montagne *f* mountain resort

station de sports d'hiver *f* winter sports resort, ski resort

station de taxis *f* taxi rank

statistiques *fpl* statistics

statistiques du tourisme *fpl* tourism statistics

sterling *m* sterling

steward *m* steward, flight attendant, cabin attendant

stimulation *m* incentive

stockage *m* stocking

STOLPORT *m* STOLPORT

store *m* blind

structure tarifaire *f* fare structure

studio *m* flatlet, efficiency *Am*, studio

subvention *f* subsidy, grant

suite *f* [*dans hôtel*] suite

suite nuptiale *f* honeymoon suite, bridal suite

suite présidentielle *f* executive suite

suite royale *f* royal suite

suite de luxe *f* luxury suite; [*au dernier étage aussi*] penthouse suite

supérieur *m* supervisor

supplément *m* supplement, surcharge

supplément chambre individuelle *m* single room supplement

supplémentaire [*lit, etc.*] extra

surbook *m* overbooking; [*en double*] double booking

surbooké overbooked; [*en double*] double booked

surbooker to overbook; [*en double*] to double book

surbooking *m* overbooking; [*en double*] double booking

surclassement *m* upgrade

surclasser to upgrade

surlocation *f* overbooking, oversale *Am*; [*en double*] double booking

surlouer to overbook; [*en double*] to double book

surréservation *f* overbooking; [*en double*] double booking

surréserver to overbook; [*en double*] to double book

Syndicat national des agents de voyages *m* French national union of travel agents

syndicat d'initiative *m* tourist office, tourist information centre

System One *m* System One
système informatique de réservation *m* computer reservation system, automated reservation system
Système Monétaire Européen *m* European Monetary System
système d'aéroports central et d'apport extérieur *m* hub and spoke system
système de classement *m* grading system
système de détaxe à l'exportation *m* retail export scheme
système de facturation informatisé *m* computerized billing system

système de facturation au poids des bagages *m* weight system (for charging for baggage)
système de gestion des chambres *m* room management system
système de gestion et de facturation du téléphone *m* phone billing and management system
système de haut-parleurs *m* Tannoy system, public address system
système de réservation *m* reservations system
système de réservation manuel *m* manual reservation system

T

TAA (= Train Auto et moto Accompagnées) *m* Motorail
tabac *m* tobacco; [*débit de tabac*] tobacconist (which also sells stamps, phonecards, etc.)
table *f* table
table basse *f* coffee table
table roulante *f* trolley
table à découper *f* carving table
table d'hôte *f* table d'hôte
table de chevet *f* bedside table
table de deux *f* table for two

tableau noir *m* blackboard
tableau à clés *m* key board, key rack
tableau de service *m* rota
tableau de l'état des chambres *m* reception board, room rack
tableau de l'état des réservations *m* reservations rack
tableau des réservations *m* reservations chart
tablette *f* [*dans avion*] folding tray
tagliatelles *fpl* tagliatelle

taie d'oreiller *f* pillow-case

tampon *m* stamp

tampon dateur *m* date stamp

tapis rouge: dérouler le tapis rouge pour qn to give sb the red carpet treatment

tapis de livraison des bagages *m* baggage conveyor belt

tard late; **il arrivera tard** he will be a late arrival

tarif *m* [*liste des prix*] tariff; [*prix*] rate; [*transport*] fare

tarif adulte *m* adult fare

tarif aérien *m* air fare

tarif aérien aller-retour *m* return air fare, round-trip air fare *Am*

tarif aérien promotionnel *m* promotional air fare

tarif affaires *m* business rate; [*transport*] business fare

tarif aller simple *m* single fare, one-way fare *Am*

tarif APEX *m* APEX fare

tarif chambre + petit déjeuner anglais *m* Bermuda plan, bed and English breakfast

tarif chambre + petit déjeuner continental *m* continental plan *Am*, bed and continental breakfast

tarif chambre sans pension *f* room only, European plan *Am*

tarif commun *m* common rated fare, joint fare

tarif dégressif *m* sliding scale rate (for groups); [*transport*] group fare

tarif économique *m* economy rate; [*transport*] economy fare, budget fare

tarif équipage *m* crew rate; [*transport*] crew fare

tarif étudiant *m* student rate; [*transport*] student fare

tarif excursion *m* excursion fare, APEX fare

tarif famille *m* family rate; [*transport*] family fare

tarif fidélité *m* business house rate

tarif groupe chartérisé *m* travel group charter fare

tarif hebdomadaire *m* weekly rate

tarif hôtelier *m* hotel tariff

tarif IT *m* inclusive tour fare

tarif jeune *m* youth fare

tarif journalier *m* day rate

tarif libre *m* open rate

tarif plein aérien *m* normal air fare

tarif préférentiel *m* special rate, preferential rate

tarif promotionnel *m* promotional rate; [*transport*] promotional fare

tarif réduit *m* reduced rate, concession rate; [*transport*] concession fare

tarif saisonnier *m* seasonal tariff

tarif social *m* reduced train fare for the general public

tarif société *m* commercial rate, corporate rate

tarif spécial *m* preferential rate

tarif standby *m* standby fare

tarif vacances *m* holiday fare

tarif week-end *m* weekend rate; [*transport*] weekend fare

tarif (de) groupe *m* group rate; [*transport*] group fare

tarif de référence *m* basing fare

tarif des chambres *m* room rate

tarif en chambre double *m* double occupancy rate

tarif par personne supplémentaire *m* companion rate

tarifaire: politique tarifaire

pricing policy
tarification *f* setting of rates
tasse à café *f* coffee cup
tasse de café *f* cup of coffee
taux d'occupation *m* room occupancy, occupancy rate
taux d'occupation des hôtels *m* hotel occupancy
taux d'occupation des lits *m* guest occupancy
taux d'occupation des places *m* passenger seat occupancy
taux d'occupation des sièges *m* passenger load factor
taux de change *m* exchange rate
taux de change à l'achat *m* bank buying rate
taux de change à la vente *m* bank selling rate
taux de conversion *m* conversion rate
taux de fréquentation *m* [*des chambres*] sleeper occupancy
taux de marge *m* mark-up ratio
taux de marque *m* mark-up ratio
taxe touristique *f* tourist tax
taxe d'aéroport *f* airport tax
taxe d'atterrissage *f* airport landing tax
taxe d'entrée *f* [*taxe d'aéroport*] entry tax
taxe de départ *f* [*taxe d'aéroport*] departure tax
taxe de séjour *f* visitor tax
taxe sur l'hôtellerie *f* hotel tax
taxe sur la valeur ajoutée *f* value added tax
taxe sur les carburants *f* fuel tax
taxi *m* taxi
technique de marketing *f* marketing technique
télécarte *f* phonecard
télécopie *f* fax

télécopieur *m* fax (machine)
télégramme *m* telegram
télémarketing *m* telephone selling
téléphérique *m* cable-car
téléphone *m* telephone
téléphone direct *m* direct dial telephone
téléphone public *m* public telephone
téléphone à carte *m* card phone
téléphoner à qn to telephone sb
téléphones utiles *mpl* useful phone numbers
télésiège *m* chair lift
téléski *m* ski tow
télésurveillance *f* electronic surveillance
télévendeur *m* telesales person
télévente *f* telephone selling, telesales
télévision *f* television
télévision en circuit fermé *f* closed-circuit television
télévision par satellite *f* satellite television
télex *m* telex
température *f* temperature
tempéré temperate
temple *m* temple
temps *m* weather
temps libre *m* free time
temps universel *m* Greenwich Mean Time
tendance touristique *f* holiday propensity
teneur de livres *m* bookkeeper
tenir une conférence to hold a conference
tennis *m* tennis
tente *f* tent
tenue *f* uniform
tenue des livres *f* bookkeeping
TEP (= Terminal Électronique

de Paiement) *m* PDQ

terminal *m* [*aéroport*] terminal building; [*écran*] VDU, terminal

terminal électronique de paiement *m* credit card terminal, PDQ

terminal urbain *m* city terminal

terminal d'aérogare *m* air terminal

se **terminer** to terminate

terrain de camping *m* camping site, camp site

terrain de camping-caravaning *m* camping and caravan site

terrain de caravaning *m* caravan site

terrain de football *m* football pitch

terrasse *f* terrace

tétanos *m* tetanus

TGV = Train à Grande Vitesse *m*

thalassothérapie *f* seawater therapy, thalassotherapy

thé *m* tea

thé au citron *m* lemon tea, tea with lemon

thé au lait *m* tea with milk

théâtre *m* theatre

théière *f* teapot

thermalisme *m* water cures

thon *m* tuna

ticket-restaurant *m* luncheon voucher

ticket de bus *m* bus ticket

ticket de caisse *m* sales receipt

timbre *m* stamp

"time propriété" *f* timeshare

tir à l'arc *m* archery

tire-bouchon *m* corkscrew

titre de transport *m* ticket

toast *m* toast

toilettes *fpl* toilet, rest room *Am*

toilettes pour hommes *fpl* gents toilet, men's room *Am*

toilettes pour dames *fpl* ladies toilet, ladies' room *Am*

tomate *f* tomato

tonique *f* tonic

tonnage *m* tonnage

tonnage brut *m* gross tonnage

tonnage net *m* net tonnage

tonnage port en lourd *m* deadweight tonnage

tour *f* tower; [*d'habitation*] high-rise building

tour d'attente *f* stack

tour de contrôle *f* control tower

tour du monde *m* round the world journey; *faire le tour du monde* to go around the world

Touring Club de France *m* ≈ Automobile Association

tourismatique *f* computerized reservation systems

tourismatique aérienne *f* computerized airline reservation systems

tourisme *m* tourism; *faire du tourisme* to go sightseeing

tourisme agricole *m* agricultural tourism, agritourism

tourisme alpin *m* Alpine tourism

tourisme balnéaire *m* seaside tourism

tourisme blanc *m* winter sports tourism

tourisme culturel *m* cultural tourism, heritage tourism

tourisme écologique *m* eco-tourism

tourisme estival *m* summer tourism

tourisme hivernal *m* winter tourism

tourisme international *m* international tourism

tourisme ludique *m* leisure

tourism

tourisme national *m* national tourism, domestic tourism

tourisme organisé *m* package tourism

tourisme récepteur *m* inbound tourism

tourisme religieux *m* religious tourism

tourisme rural *m* rural tourism

tourisme scientifique et technique *m* scientific and technical tourism

tourisme social *m* social tourism

tourisme sportif *m* sports tourism

tourisme vert *m* green tourism

tourisme à la ferme *m* farm tourism

tourisme d'affaires *m* business tourism

tourisme d'exportation *m* export tourism

tourisme de loisirs *m* leisure tourism, holiday tourism

tourisme de masse *m* mass tourism, popular tourism

tourisme de santé *m* health tourism

tourisme de vacances *m* holiday tourism

touriste *mf* tourist

touriste international(e) *mf* international tourist

touriste d'affaires *mf* business tourist

touristique tourist, touristic

tour opérateur *m* tour operator

tournedos *m* tournedos

toutes taxes comprises inclusive of tax

trafic aérien *m* air traffic

trafic touristique *m* tourist traffic

train *m* train

train auto-couchettes *m* motorail, rail-drive

Train Auto et Moto Accompagnées *m* Motorail

Train Automobile Accompagnée *m* Motorail

train-couchettes *m* sleeper

train direct *m* through train

train interurbain *m* inter-city train

Train à Grande Vitesse *m* high speed train

train de croisière *m* luxury train

train de grandes lignes *m* inter-city train

traite bancaire *f* bank draft

traitement de faveur *m* preferential treatment, red carpet treatment

traitement de texte *m* word processor

traiteur *m* caterer

trajet *m* journey

tranche *f* slice

tranquille quiet

transat *m* recliner, sun lounger

transatlantique transatlantic

transbordeur *m* roll-on-roll-off ship

transférer to transfer

transfert *m* transfer

transfert de fonds électronique *m* electronic funds transfer

transit: en transit in transit

trans-Manche cross-Channel

transport *m* transport, transportation *Am*

transport aérien *m* air transport

transport civil aérien *m* civil air transport

transport ferroviaire *m* rail transport

transport individuel *m* private transport

transport maritime *m* sea transport

transport terrestre *m* surface transport

transport d'acheminement *m* transfer transport

transport de passagers *m* passenger transport

transport de voyageurs *m* passenger transport

transporteur *m* carrier

transporteur aérien *m* air carrier

transporteur international *m* international carrier

transporteur privé *m* private carrier

transports publics *mpl* public service transport

transports en commun *mpl* public transport

travail par roulement *m* shift work

travailler en équipe de roulement to work in shifts

travellers chèque *m* traveller's cheque, traveler's check *Am*

traversée *f* crossing

traversin *m* bolster

trekking *m* trekking

trésorerie *f* [*flux*] cashflow; [*service*] accounts (department)

triangle de présignalisation *m* hazard warning triangle

tripes *fpl* tripe

troisième âge Third Age; *personne du troisième âge* senior citizen; *réduction troisième âge* senior citizen's discount

tropiques *mpl* tropics

trousse de secours *f* first aid kit

trousse de secours de voyage *f* medical travel kit

truite *f* trout

TTC = Toutes Taxes Comprises

TU = Temps Universel *m*

tunnel sous la Manche *m* Channel tunnel, Chunnel

turbot *m* turbot

turista *f* holiday tummy

TVA (= Taxe sur la Valeur Ajoutée) *f* VAT

TVP *m* screen, display, VDU

U

UCCEGA = Union des Chambres de Commerce Gestionnaires d'Aéroports *f*

UNECTOUR = Union Nationale des Employés et Cadres du TOURisme *f*

uniforme *m* uniform

Union internationale routière *f* International Road Transport Union

Union nationale des associations de tourisme *f* national union of associated tourism

Union nationale des employés et cadres du tourisme *f* French national union for workers and managers in the tourist industry

Union nationale des organisateurs de séjours linguistiques *f* French union of language study trip organizers

Union des chambres de commerce gestionnaires d'aéroports *f* body which controls French airports other than those in Paris

Unité monétaire européenne *f* European Currency Unit

unité d'hébergement *f* accommodation unit

UNOSEL = Union Nationale des Organisateurs de Séjours Linguistiques *f*

urgence *f* emergency

vacances *fpl* holiday, holidays, vacation *Am*; *en vacances* on holiday

vacances actives *fpl* activity holiday

vacances studieuses *fpl* educational holiday, study holiday

vacances à la ferme *fpl* farm holiday

vacances à la montagne *fpl* mountain holiday

vacances aux sports d'hiver *fpl* winter sports holiday

vacances d'été *fpl* summer holidays

vacances d'hiver *fpl* winter holidays

vacances en bateau *fpl* boating holiday

vacances en camping *fpl* camping holiday

vacances en circuit *fpl* multi-centre holiday

Vacances pour Tous *f* association which organizes holidays for children from less well-off families

vacancier *m* holidaymaker, vacationer *Am*

vaccin *m* vaccine
vaccination *f* vaccination
vacciner to vaccinate
vaisselle *f* crockery
valable valid
validation *f* validation
validé validated
valise *f* suitcase
vanity case *m* vanity case
vapeur: à la vapeur steamed
varappe *f* rock-climbing
variable [*taux*] subject to variation
veau *m* veal
vedette *f* motor launch
végétalien vegan
végétarien vegetarian
véhicule de transport en commun *m* public service vehicle
veilleur de nuit *m* night watchman
vélo *m* bicycle, bike
vélo-tout-terrain *m* mountain bike
vente *f* sale; [*activité*] selling
vente directe *f* direct selling; [*une vente*] direct sale
vente à crédit *f* credit sale
vente (au) comptant *f* cash sale
vente au comptoir *f* over-the-counter sales
vente hors taxes *f* duty-free sales
vente par correspondance *f* mail order
vente sous douane *f* duty-free sales
ventilation *f* ventilation
vérification *f* [*de réservation*] confirmation
vérifier to confirm
verre *m* glass
verre à dents *m* tooth glass
verre à eau *m* water glass
verre à liqueur *m* liqueur glass
verre à vin *m* wine glass
verre à whisky *m* whisky glass
verres *mpl* glassware

verser to pour
vestiaire *m* cloakroom
via via
viande *f* meat
viande froide *f* cold meat
viande de cheval *f* horse meat
vidéo *f* video
vidéotex *m* videotex, viewdata
vider [*chambre*] to strip; [*cendrier*] to empty
vie nocturne *f* nightlife
villa *f* villa
villa de vacances *f* holiday home
village *m* village
village de loisirs *m* holiday village
village de pêcheurs *m* fishing village
village de vacances *m* holiday village
Villages-Vacances-Familles *m* association offering low-cost holiday centres for families
ville industrielle *f* industrial city
ville sainte *f* holy city, centre of pilgrimage
ville thermale *f* spa town
vin *m* wine
vin blanc *m* white wine
vin mousseux *m* sparkling wine
vin rosé *m* rosé
vin rouge *m* red wine
vin de table *m* table wine
vinaigre *m* vinegar
vinaigrette *f* vinaigrette
VIP *mf* VIP
visa d'entrée *m* entry visa
visa de sortie *m* exit visa
visite guidée *f* guided tour; [*de ville, etc. aussi*] sightseeing tour
visite pédagogique *f* educational visit
visite à pied *f* [*dans ville, etc.*] walking tour

visiter [*musée, etc.*] to visit
visiter une ville to go sightseeing
visiteur *m* visitor
visiteur en transit *m* transit visitor
visiteurs journaliers *mpl* daily visitors
vitrine d'exposition *f* display case
voie fluviale *f* inland waterway
voie navigable *f* waterway
voilage *m* net curtain
voile *f* sailing
voilier *m* yacht
voisin [*chambres*] adjoining
voiture *f* car; [*de train aussi*] coach
voiture-couchette *f* couchette car
voiture fumeurs *f* smoking carriage, smoker
voiture-lit *f* sleeping car, sleeper
voiture non fumeurs *f* no-smoking carriage, non-smoker
voiture-salon *f* saloon car, parlor car *Am*
voiture de location *f* rental car
voiturier *m* parking valet; *service de voiturier* valet parking
vol *m* flight; [*délit*] theft; *en vol* in-flight
vol aller-retour *m* return flight, round-trip flight *Am*
vol charter *m* charter flight
vol direct *m* direct flight
vol intérieur *m* domestic flight, internal flight
vol moyen-courrier *m* medium-haul flight
vol nolisé *m* charter flight
vol régulier *m* regular flight, scheduled flight
vol "sec" *m* flight only
vol d'apport *m* feeder flight
vol de correspondance *m* connecting flight
voler to fly; [*délit*] to steal

volets *mpl* shutters
volume *m* volume
voucher *m* voucher
voucher "crédit illimité" *m* unlimited value voucher, full credit coupon
voucher à valeur limitée *m* limited value voucher
voucher "sans valeur" *m* unlimited value voucher
voyage *m* journey, trip; *les voyages* travel
voyage accompagné *m* escorted trip; [*excursion*] escorted tour
voyage aller *m* outward journey
voyage aller-retour *m* round trip
voyage organisé *m* package holiday, package tour, inclusive tour
voyage professionnel *m* business trip; *les voyages professionnels* business travel
voyage retour *m* return journey
voyage scolaire *m* school trip
voyage à forfait *m* inclusive tour, package tour, all-expense tour, all-in tour
voyage à forfait personnalisé *m* independent inclusive tour
voyage à l'étranger *m* foreign trip; *les voyages à l'étranger* foreign travel
voyage d'affaires *m* business trip; *les voyages d'affaires* business travel
voyage d'études *m* study trip; [*d'encouragement*] familiarization tour
voyage de familiarisation *m* familiarization trip
voyage de noces *m* honeymoon
voyage de stimulation *m* incentive trip, incentive tour

voyage en autocar *m* coach trip; *les voyages en autocar* coach travel

voyager pour affaires to go on a business trip; *ceux qui voyagent beaucoup pour affaires* those who do a lot of business travel

voyages internationaux *mpl* world travel, international travel

voyages en avion *mpl* air travel

voyages en groupe *mpl* group travel

voyages en mer *mpl* sea travel

voyages en train *mpl* rail travel

voyageur *m* traveller

voyageur à haute contribution *m* full-fare paying passenger

voyageur d'affaires *m* business traveller

voyageur de commerce *m* travelling salesman

voyagiste *m* tour operator, operator; [*grossiste*] tour wholesaler

voyagiste réceptif *m* incoming tour operator, ground operator

VTT (= Vélo-Tout-Terrain) *m* mountain bike

vue sur mer *f* sea view

VVF = Villages-Vacances-Familles *m*

wagon-lit *m* sleeping car, sleeper

wagon-restaurant *m* restauran car, buffet car, dining car

W.-C. *mpl* WC

week-end à thème *m* theme weekend

week-end de Pâques *m* Easter weekend

whisky *m* whisky

xérès *m* sherry

yacht de croisière *m* cabin cruiser

yaourt *m* yoghurt

zone bleue *f* restricted parking zone

zone fumeurs *f* smoking area

zone hôtelière *f* hotel area

zone non fumeurs *f* no-smoking area

zone touristique *f* tourist area

zone d'apport *f* feeder zone

zone de trafic aérien *f* traffic conference area

zone sous douane *f* customs zone

zoo *m* zoo

A

AA = Automobile Association

AAA = American Automobile Association

Abacus [*computer reservation system*] Abacus *m*

abbey abbaye *f*

ABC = Advance Booking Charter

above-the-line advertising publicité pure *f*

abroad à l'étranger *m*

ABTA = Association of British Travel Agents

ABTA bonding scheme agrément ABTA *m*

Access carte Eurocard Mastercard *f*

accident accident *m*

accident book registre des accidents *m*

to **accommodate** héberger

accommodation hébergement *m*

accommodation capacity capacité d'accueil *f*

accommodation category catégorie d'hébergement *f*

accommodation department service hébergement *m*

accommodation industry industrie de l'hébergement *f*

accommodation management gestion de l'hébergement *f*

accommodation only logement sans restauration *m*

accommodation package forfait hébergement *m*

accommodation services department service hébergement *m*

accommodation survey enquête sur l'hébergement *f*

accommodation unit unité d'hébergement *f*

accommodation voucher bon d'hébergement *m*

accommodations *Am* hébergement *m*

accompanied baggage bagages accompagnés *mpl*

account compte *m*

account card fiche de compte *f*, fiche de facture *f*

account payable compte créditeur *m*

account receivable compte débiteur *m*

accountancy comptabilité *f*, compta *f*

accounts comptabilité *f*

accounts (department) service comptable *m*, service de comptabilité *m*

accreditation accréditation *f*

acculturation acculturation *f*

achieved room rate prix total des chambres *m*

acknowledgement of reservation confirmation de réservation *f*

activities animation *f*

activity break (courtes) vacances actives *fpl*

activity holiday vacances actives *fpl*

activity weekend week-end actif *m*

actual operating cost coût réel d'exploitation *m*

adaptor [*electric*] adaptateur *m*

additional holiday vacances supplémentaires *fpl*

add-on supplément *m*

add-on fare supplément *m*

adjoining voisin

adjoining rooms chambres attenantes *fpl*

A&D list = Arrival and Departure list

administration administration *f*

admission fee droit d'entrée *m*

adult fare tarif adulte *m*

advance: in advance à l'avance, d'avance

advance booking réservation (à l'avance) *f*

advance booking charter achat de bloc-sièges *m*

advance booking period délai de réservation *m*

advance payment receipt reçu de paiement anticipé *m*

Advance Purchase Excursion tarif (aérien) spécial sujet à des restrictions de délai d'achat *m*

advance reservation rack planning des réservations de type Whitney *m*

advance reservations office bureau des réservations *m*

advance reservations system système de réservation *m*

advance warning triangle triangle de présignalisation *m*

advanced check-in enregistrement anticipé *m*

advanced country pays riche *m*

advanced passenger train train à grande vitesse *m*, TGV *m*

advanced reservation card fiche de réservation *f*

adventure holiday circuit aventure *m*

advertising publicité *f*

advertising campaign campagne publicitaire *f*, campagne de publicité *f*

advertising director directeur de la publicité *m*

advertising manager directeur de la publicité *m*

AEA (= Association of European Airlines) AEA *f*

affinity group charter charter pour un groupe d'intérêt commun *m*

afternoon tea thé de cinq heures *m*, goûter *m*

after-sales service service après-vente *m*

age âge *m*

agency agence *f*

agency appointment [*authorization of travel agent by principal etc*] agrément *m*

agency fee frais d'agence *mpl*

agricultural museum musée de l'agriculture *m*

agricultural tourism tourisme agricole *m*

agritourism tourisme agricole *m*

AH&MA = American Hotel and Motel Association

AIEST (= International Association of Scientific Experts in Tourism) AIEST *f*

air broker courtier de l'air *m*

Airbus Airbus *m*
air carrier transporteur aérien *m*
air conditioning climatisation *f*,
air conditionné *m*
aircraft avion *m*
aircraft grounding interdiction de
vol *f*
aircraft identification code code
d'identification d'avion *m*
aircraft leasing location d'avions *f*
air fare tarif aérien *m*
air fare rebate réduction de tarif
aérien *f*
air hostess hôtesse de l'air *f*
air inclusive tour voyage à forfait
(par avion) *m*
airline compagnie d'aviation *f*,
compagnie aérienne *f*
airline club club de compagnie
aérienne *m*
airline code code compagnie
aérienne *m*
Airline Deregulation Act loi de
déréglementation des
compagnies aériennes *f*
airline identification code code
d'identification de compagnie
aérienne *m*
airline operator compagnie
aérienne *f*
airline passenger passager des
compagnies aériennes *m*
Airline Passengers Association
association des passagers des
compagnies aériennes *f*
airline ticket billet d'avion *m*
air link liaison aérienne *f*
air mile [*1.852 km*] mille
(aérien) *m*; *to collect air miles*
accumuler des Aéropoints
airpass carte d'abonnement de
transport aérien *f*
airplane avion *m*

airport aéroport *m*
airport apron aire de
stationnement (des avions) *f*
airport code code aéroport *m*
airport hotel hôtel d'aéroport *m*
airport landing tax taxe
d'atterrissage *f*
airport lounge hall d'aéroport *m*
airport service charge taxe
d'aéroport *f*
airport shop boutique d'aéroport *f*
airport tax taxe d'aéroport *f*
airport taxi taxi desservant
l'aéroport *m*
air/sea air/mer *m*
air service liaison aérienne *f*
air space espace aérien *m*
airstrip piste d'atterrissage *f*
air terminal terminal *m*,
aérogare *m*
air ticket billet d'avion *m*
air traffic trafic aérien *m*
air traffic controller contrôleur
de trafic aérien *m*
Air Transport Users Committee
comité des usagers des
transports aériens *m*
air travel voyages en avion *mpl*
air travel organizer organisateur
de voyages par avion *m*
air travel organizer's licence
licence d'organisateur de
voyages par avion *f*
Air Travel Reserve Fund Fonds
de réserve du transport aérien *m*
aisle seat place côté couloir *f*
AITO = Association of
Independent Tour Operators
alarm call appel de réveil *m*
alarm clock réveil *m*
alien étranger *m*
all-expense tour voyage à
forfait *m*

Alliance of Independent Travel Agents groupement national des agents de voyages indépendants *m*

all-inclusive price prix tout compris *m*, prix forfaitaire *m*

all-in tour voyage à forfait *m*

to **allocate** [*room*] attribuer

allotment [*of rooms*] allotement *m*, contingent *m*; [*of airplane seats*] bloc-siège *m*

allotment contract contrat d'allotement *m*, contrat de contingent *m*

all-you-can-eat nourriture à volonté *f*

Alpine tourism tourisme alpin *m*

Alpine Tourist Commission Commission de propagande touristique des pays alpins *f*

to **alter** [*ticket etc*] modifier

alternative airport [*for detour*] aéroport de déviation *m*; [*for overspill*] aéroport de remplacement *m*

alternative tourism tourisme vert *m*

altitude altitude *f*

Amadeus [*reservation system*] Amadeus *m*

amenities infrastructure *f*

American Automobile Association ≈ Touring Club de France *m*

American breakfast petit déjeuner américain *m*

American Express (card) carte American Express *f*

American Hotel and Motel Association association américaine des hôtels et motels *f*

American Plan *Am* pension complète *f*

American service service à l'américaine *m*, service à l'assiette *m*

American Society of Travel Agents association américaine des agents de voyages *f*

Amex carte Amex *f*

amount montant *m*

Amtrak société des chemins de fer interurbains des États-Unis *f*

Amtrak Rail Pass carte Amtrak *f*

anchovy anchois *m*

ancient monument monument historique *m*

angling pêche à la ligne *f*

animator animateur *m*

Antipodean day jour méridien *m*

ANTOR = Association of National Tourist Office Representatives

AONB = Area of Outstanding Natural Beauty

AP = American Plan

apartment appartement *m*

apartment hotel résidence hôtelière *f*, résidence de tourisme *f*

aperitif apéritif *m*

APEX (= Advance Purchase EXcursion) APEX *m*

APEX fare tarif APEX *m*

Apollo [*reservation system*] Apollo *m*

appetizer amuse-gueule *m*

apple pomme *f*

appointment [*of travel agent*] agrément *m*

après-ski après-ski *m*

apron [*airport*] aire de stationnement (des avions) *f*

APT (= Advanced Passenger Train) TGV *m*

Area of Outstanding Natural Beauty réserve classée pour sa beauté naturelle *f*

Area Tourist Board ≈ comité régional du tourisme *m*

armchair fauteuil *m*

arr. (= arrival) arr.

arrival arrivée *f*

arrival and departure list feuille des arrivées et des départs *f*, feuille des mouvements *f*

arrival form fichette d'arrivée *f*

arrival lounge salle d'arrivée *f*

arrival notification notification d'arrivée *f*

arrival time heure d'arrivée *f*

arrivals and departures arrivées et départs *mpl*

arrivals list liste des arrivées *f*

art gallery [*with items for sale*] galerie d'art *f*; [*museum*] musée *m*

artichoke artichaut *m*

arts festival festival culturel *m*

ashtray cendrier *m*

asparagus asperges *fpl*

assistant hotel manager sous-directeur d'hôtel *m*

assistant housekeeper aide-gouvernante *f*, assistante gouvernante *f*

assistant manager assistant de direction *m*

Association of British Travel Agents association des agents de voyage britanniques *f*

Association of European Airlines Association européenne des compagnies aériennes *f*

Association of Independent Tour Operators association des voyagistes indépendants *f*

Association of Independent Travel Agents groupement des agents de voyages indépendants *m*

Association of National Tourist Office Representatives association des représentants des offices du tourisme nationaux *f*

Assured Room Reservation Plan [*American Express*] système de réservation de chambres garantie *m*

ASTA = American Society of Travel Agents

ATB = Area Tourist Board

ATBP (= Automated Ticket and Boarding Pass) ATBP *m*

ATC = Alpine Tourist Commission

Athens Convention Convention d'Athènes *f*

ATOL = Air Travel Organizer's Licence

attractions attractions *fpl*

ATW (= Around The World) autour du monde

aubergine aubergine *f*

audience [*for product, advertisement*] public *m*

audio-visual equipment équipement audiovisuel *m*, matériel audiovisuel *m*

auditor auditeur *m*

auditorium auditorium *m*

automated reservation réservation télématique *f*

automated reservation system système informatique de réservation *m*

automated ticket billet informatisé *m*

Automated Ticket and Boarding Pass Automated Ticket and Boarding Pass *m*

automatic alarm réveil
automatique *m*
automatic key distributor
distributeur automatique de
clés *m*
automatic ticket distributor
distributeur automatique de
titres de transport *m*
automatic ticket machine
billetterie automatique *f*
automation automatisation *f*
Automobile Association ≈ Touring
Club de France *m*
autumn automne *m*
available disponible; [*room*] libre
available bed capacity capacité
d'accueil *f*
average length of stay durée
moyenne de séjour *f*
average room rate prix moyen des
chambres *m*
aviation aviation *f*
avocado avocat *m*

B

BABA = Book-A-Bed-Ahead
scheme
baby-changing area nurserie *f*,
point-bébé *m*
baby-listening microphone
babyphone *m*
baby-listening service service de
surveillance à distance des
bébés *m*, service babyphone *m*
baby sitting garde d'enfants *f*,
baby-sitting *m*
background music musique de
fond *f*
back of the house emplois
fonctionnels *mpl*
backpack sac à dos *m*
backpacker voyageur sac au dos *m*
backpacking tour randonnée sac
au dos *f*
back to back back to back, chaîne
de charters *f*
backward pricing rajustement des
prix *m*
bacon lard *m*
bacon and eggs œufs au bacon *mpl*
baggage bagages *mpl*
baggage allowance franchise de
bagages *f*
baggage check contrôle des
bagages *m*
baggage claim retrait des
bagages *m*
baggage claim area zone de
livraison des bagages *f*

baggage claim sticker étiquette autocollante d'identification de bagage *f*

baggage container conteneur à bagages *m*

baggage conveyor belt tapis de livraison de bagages *m*

baggage cover [*insurance*] assurance bagage(s) *f*

baggage handler bagagiste *m*

baggage lift ascenseur à bagages *m*

baggage room consigne *f*

baggage tag étiquette *f*

baked (cuit) au four

baked potato pomme de terre au four *f*, pomme de terre en robe des champs *f*

bakery boulangerie *f*

balcony balcon *m*

ballroom salle de réception *f*

BALPA = British AirLine Pilots Association

banana banane *f*

bank banque *f*

bank buying rate taux de change à l'achat *m*

bank cheque chèque bancaire *m*

bank draft traite bancaire *f*

bank holiday jour férié *m*

bank selling rate taux de change à la vente *m*

Bank Settlement Plan procédure de comptabilité normalisée de billetterie aérienne

banker's card carte bancaire *f*

banquet banquet *m*

banqueting manager responsable des banquets *m*

banqueting room or **suite** salle de réception *f*, salle de banquet *f*

bar bar *m*

barmaid barmaid *f*

barman barman *m*, garçon de comptoir *m*

bar meal repas au bar *m*

bar staff personnel de bar *m*

barbecue barbecue *m*

barbecued au barbecue

bareboat charter location de bateau(x) sans équipage *f*

bargain break séjour discompté *m*

barge péniche *f*

basing fare tarif de référence *m*

basing point [*location to/from which air fares are established*] point de référence *m*

basket of fruit corbeille de fruits *f*

bath bain *m*; [*tub*] baignoire *f*

bath rail barre de soutien dans la baignoire *f*

bathrobe peignoir de bain *m*

bathroom salle de bain *f*

baths bains *mpl*

BATO = British Association of Tourism Officers

B & B bed and breakfast *m*

BCC = Bus and Coach Council

beach plage *f*

beach hotel hôtel de plage *m*

beach tent tente de plage *f*

beauty salon institut de beauté *m*

beauty treatment soins esthétiques *mpl*

bed lit *m*

bed and board pension complète *f*

bed and breakfast bed and breakfast *m*, chambre d'hôte *f*

bed configuration configuration des lits *f*

bed linen draps et taies d'oreiller *mpl*

bed-night nuitée *f*

bed occupancy occupation des lits *f*

bed sheet drap *m*

bedside table table de chevet *f*
bedspace capacité d'accueil *f*
bedspread dessus de lit *m*
bedding matériel de couchage *m*,
　literie *f*
beef bœuf *m*
beer bière *f*
beer cellar brasserie *f*
beermat sous-bock *m*
beer pumpe pompe à bière *f*
beetroot betterave *f*
behaviour characteristics [*of
　tourists*] caractéristiques du
　comportement *fpl*
bellboy *Am* groom *m*, chasseur *m*;
　[*for lift*] garçon d'ascenseur *m*,
　liftier *m*
bell captain *Am* chef chasseur *m*
bellhop *Am* = **bellboy**
belly [*pork*] poitrine *f*
below-the-line advertising
　publicité directe *f*
Benelux Benelux *m*
Bermuda Agreement accord des
　Bermudes *m*
Bermuda Plan tarif chambre avec
　petit déjeuner anglais *m*
Berne Convention Convention de
　Berne *f*
berth [*on ship, train*] couchette *f*;
　[*small room*] cabine *f*; [*on train*]
　compartiment *m*
best available ce qu'il y a de
　mieux
best end of neck carré *m*
beverage boisson *m*,
　consommation *f*
BHA = **British Hospitality
　Association**
bible bible *f*
bicycle bicyclette *f*, vélo *m*
bidet bidet *m*
bike vélo *m*

bilateral agreement accord
　bilatéral *m*
bilingual bilingue
bill addition *f*; [*for hotel room*]
　note *f*
bill of exchange lettre de
　change *f*
billiards room salle de billards *f*
billing facturation *f*
billing machine caisse
　(enregistreuse) *f*
billing office bureau de
　facturation *m*
birth naissance *f*
birthday anniversaire *m*
biscuit biscuit *m*
bistro bistro(t) *m*
bitter bière (anglaise) *f*
bkg (= **booking**) résa *f*
blackberry mûre *f*
blackboard tableau noir *m*
black coffee café *m*, café noir *m*
blackcurrant cassis *m*
black list liste noire *f*
to **blanche** blanchir
bleeper bip *m*, alphapage *m*
blind [*on window*] store *m*
block [*of rooms*] contingent *m*
to **block** [*room*] retenir, bloquer
block booking réservation en
　bloc *f*; [*for hotel*] contrat de
　contingent *m*
block card fiche de blocage *f*
block of seats bloc-sièges *m*
blocked space espace réservé *m*
BNTS = **British National Travel
　Survey**
board: on board à bord
board and lodging hébergement
　en pension complète *m*
boarding bridge (pré-)passerelle *f*
boarding card carte
　d'embarquement *f*

boarding gate porte d'embarquement *f*

boarding house pension (de famille) *f*

boarding pass carte d'embarquement *f*

boat bateau *m*

boating holiday vacances en bateau *fpl*

to **boil** bouillir

boiled bouilli

boiled egg œuf à la coque *m*

boiled ham jambon blanc *m*

boiled potatoes pommes vapeur *fpl*

bolster traversin *m*

bomb scare alerte à la bombe *f*

bond obligation *f*

bonding scheme agrément *m*

bonus prime *m*

to **book** réserver

to **book sb out** trouver un autre hôtel pour qn

Book-A-Bed-Ahead scheme système de réservation de chambre d'hôtel par l'intermédiaire d'office du tourisme à partir d'une autre ville

book register registre de réservation *m*, cahier de réservation *m*

bookkeeper teneur de livres *m*

bookkeeping tenue des livres *f*

bookshop librairie *f*

booked up complet

booking réservation *f*

booking agency agence de réservation *f*

booking clerk responsable des réservations *m*

booking fee frais de réservation *mpl*

booking form feuille de réservations *f*, fiche de réservation *f*

booking office [*at railway etc*] bureau de réservations *m*

booking status état de la réservation *m*

bookings diary agenda de réservation *m*

Bord Fáilte comité du tourisme irlandais *m*

border frontière *f*

border controls contrôles aux frontières *mpl*

border crossing passage de frontière *m*

botanical gardens jardin botanique *m*

botel bateau-hôtel *m*; [*on barge*] péniche-hôtel *f*

bottle bouteille *f*

bottle-opener ouvre-bouteilles *m*

bottled water eau en bouteille *f*

bouquet bouquet *m*

bourbon bourbon *m*

BP = Bermuda Plan

braised braisé

braising braisage *m*

brandy cognac *m*

brandy glass verre à cognac *m*

brasserie brasserie *f*

breach of contract rupture de contrat *f*

bread pain *m*

bread roll petit pain *m*

break [*holiday*] courtes vacances *fpl*

to **break a journey** interrompre un voyage

breakfast buffet buffet du petit déjeuner *m*

breakfast chef chef de petit déjeuner *m*

breakfast cook cafetier *m*

breakfast order commande de petit déjeuner *f*

breakfast room salle de petit déjeuner *f*

breakfast tray plateau petit déjeuner *m*

breast of chicken blanc de poulet *m*

bridal suite suite nuptiale *f*

briefcase mallette *f*

brisket [*of beef*] poitrine *f*

British Airline Pilots Association association des pilotes des compagnies aériennes britanniques *f*

British Association of Tourism Officers association britannique de dirigeants de l'industrie touristique *f*

British Federation of Hotel, Guest House and Self catering Associations association d'hôteliers et de restaurateurs britanniques *f*

British Guild of Travel Writers association d'écrivains de tourisme britanniques *f*

British Hospitality Association association des hôteliers et restaurateurs britanniques *f*

British National Travel Survey étude sur le comportement touristique des britanniques *f*

British Rail Apex billet de train interurbain aller-retour réservé au moins 7 jours à l'avance à tarif préférentiel

British Rail Saver billet de train interurbain aller-retour *m*

British Rail Supersaver billet de train interurbain aller-retour valable certains jours à tarif réduit *m*

British Self-Catering Federation fédération britannique des professionnels de la para-hôtellerie *f*

British Summer Time heure d'été britannique *f*

British Tourist Authority ≈ conseil supérieur du tourisme britannique *m*

British Travel Education Trust association de promotion des études en tourisme *f*

British Travel Fair salon du tourisme britannique *m*

Britrail Pass [*for overseas visitors*] carte de train vendue hors GB, valable sur tout le réseau britannique

broccoli brocoli *m*

brochure brochure *f*, dépliant *m*

broker courtier *m*

broking courtage *m*

brown ale bière brune *f*

brunch brunch *m*

Brussels Convention Convention de Bruxelles *f*

BSCF = British Self-Catering Federation

BSP (= Bank Settlement Plan) BSP *m*

BST = British Summer Time

BTA = British Tourist Authority

bucket shop agence de voyages de discompte *f*

budget budget *m*

budget fare tarif économique *m*

budget forecast prévisions budgétaires *fpl*

budget hotel hôtel bon marché *m*

budget rate tarif économique *m*
buffet buffet *m*
buffet car wagon-restaurant *m*
buffet lunch déjeuner buffet *m*
buffet service [*on train*] service de restauration *m*
built attraction centre d'intérêt "non-naturel" *m*
bulb ampoule *f*
bulk fare tarif de groupe *m*
bulk reservation form formulaire de réservation de groupe *m*
bulk voucher bon de groupe *m*
bumping [*refusing transport in case of overbooking*] bumping *m*, refus d'embarquer suite à sur-réservation *m*
bunk beds lits superposés *mpl*
bureau de change bureau de change *m*
bus autobus *m*, bus *m*
Bus and Coach Council conseil des autobus et des autocars *m*
busboy *Am* aide-serveur *m*
bus depot gare routière *f*
bus service service d'autobus *m*
bus station gare routière *f*
bus ticket ticket de bus *m*
business card carte de visite *f*
business centre centre d'affaires *m*
business class classe affaires *f*
business fare tarif affaires *m*
business hotel hôtel d'affaires *m*

business house agency [*travel agency catering for business*] agence spécialisée dans le tourisme d'affaires *f*
business house rate tarif "fidélité" (accordé à certaines sociétés) *m*
business lounge centre d'affaires *m*
business lunch déjeuner d'affaires *m*
businessman homme d'affaires *m*
business tourism tourisme d'affaires *m*
business tourist touriste d'affaires *mf*
business travel voyages d'affaires *mpl*
business travel department implant *m*
business traveller voyageur d'affaires *m*
business trip voyage d'affaires *m*; *to go on a business trip* voyager pour affaires
businesswoman femme d'affaires *f*
busy [*period*] chargé; [*roads*] encombré; [*line*] occupé
butter beurre *m*
buttery restaurant *m*
buyer acheteur *m*, responsable des achats *m*

C

CAA (=Civil Aviation Authority) ≈ DGAC *f*
CAB (=Civil Aeronautics Board) ≈ DGAC *f*
cabana [*room by beach/swimming pool*] cabine de bain *f*
cabaret cabaret *m*
cabbage chou *m*
cabin [*on ship, aircraft*] cabine *f*; [*log cabin etc*] case *f*, bungalow *m*
cabin attendant [*male*] steward *m*; [*female*] hôtesse de l'air *f*
cabin baggage bagages à main *mpl*
cabin crew équipage *m*
cabin cruiser yacht de croisière *m*
cabin staff personnel de cabine *m*, membres de l'équipage *mpl*
cabin steward steward *m*
cable car funiculaire *m*
cabotage cabotage *m*
cabotage fare tarif de cabotage *m*
cabotage rights droits de cabotage *mpl*
cabotage route itinéraire de cabotage *m*
café café *m*
café complet [*mid-morning/afternoon snack*] café complet *m*
café-owner cafetier-limonadier *m*
cafeteria cafétéria *f*
cafeteria manager directeur de cafétéria *m*

cake gâteau *m*
cake shop pâtisserie *f*
cakes pâtisserie *f*
call [*wake-up call*] appel de réveil *m*
call sheet feuille des réveils *f*
camp camp *m*
to **camp** camper
camp bed lit de camp *m*
camp site terrain de camping *m*, camping *m*
campaign campagne *f*
camper [*person*] campeur *m*
camper (van) camping-car *m*
camping camping *m*
Camping and Caravanning Club of Great Britain and Ireland Ltd fédération de camping-caravaning de Grande-Bretagne et d'Irlande *f*
camping-caravanning campage-caravanage *m*, camping-caravaning *m*
camping ground terrain de camping *m*
camping holiday vacances (en) camping *fpl*
camping site camping *m*, terrain de camping *m*
canal canal *m*
to **cancel** [*booking etc*] annuler
cancellation annulation *f*
cancellation charge *or* **fee** frais d'annulation *mpl*

cancellation form bon d'annulation *m*, bulletin d'annulation *m*

cancellation holiday vacances annulées et soldées *fpl*

canoeing canoë-kayac *m*

capacity [*of plane*] capacité *f*

capacity occupancy occupation maximale *f*

capacity utilization utilisation maximale *f*

capital capitale *f*

capital goods biens d'équipement *mpl*

captain [*of plane*] commandant *m*; [*Am, in restaurant*] chef de rang *m*

captive [*market*] captif

car voiture *f*

car ferry car-ferry *m*, ferry(-boat) *m*

car hire location de voitures *f*

car hire company société de location de voitures *f*

car park parking *m*, parc de stationnement *m*

car recovery insurance assurance dépannage *f*

car rental location de voitures *f*

carafe carafe *f*

caravan caravane *f*

caravan park terrain de caravaning *m*

caravan site terrain de caravaning *m*

caravanning caravaning *m*, caravanage *m*

card: visiting card carte de visite *f*

card index fichier *m*

card key carte-clé *f*

card-operated lock serrure à carte perforée *f*

card room salon de bridge *m*

carnet [*customs pass*] carnet de passage en douanes *m*

carnival carnaval *m*

carousel carrousel *m*

carpet moquette *f*

carrier transporteur *m*

carrot carotte *f*

carrying capacity [*of tourist attraction*] capacité d'accueil *f*

carry-on baggage bagages à main *mpl*

carte: à la carte à la carte

to **carve** [*meat*] découper

carvery grill *m*

carving table table à découper *f*

cash espèces *fpl*, argent comptant *m*; [*actual coins and notes*] monnaie *f*, liquide *m*; *to pay cash* payer comptant

to **cash** encaisser

to **cash up** faire les comptes

cash report (form) situation de caisse *f*

cash book livre de caisse *m*

cashflow trésorerie *f*

cash position situation de caisse *f*

cash receipt reçu pour paiement en espèces *m*

cash sale vente (au) comptant *f*

cashier caissier *m*

cashier's desk comptoir-caisse *m*

cashier's office bureau du caissier *m*

cashier's record form feuille des recettes *f*

casino casino *m*

castle château *m*

catalogue catalogue *m*

category catégorie *f*

caterer traiteur *m*

catering restauration *f*

catering company société de restauration *f*

catering industry industrie de la restauration *f*

catering manager directeur de la restauration *m*

catering staff personnel de restauration *m*

cathedral cathédrale *f*

cauliflower chou-fleur *m*

caviar caviar *m*

CDW = Collision Damage Waiver

celery céleri *m*

cellar cave *f*; [*for wine, provisions also*] cellier *m*

cellarman sommelier *m*

central buying group centrale d'achat(s) *f*

central heating chauffage central *m*

central office bureau central *m*

central purchasing group centrale d'achat(s) *f*

central reservation office centrale de réservation *f*

central reservation system système de réservation central *m*

central reservations réservations centralisées *fpl*

central reservations office centrale de réservation *f*

central reservations unit centrale de réservation *f*

Central Standard Time *Am* heure normale du Centre (États-Unis, Canada) *f*

cereals céréales *fpl*

certificate of airworthiness certificat de navigabilité aérienne *m*

Certificate of Tour Operating Practice diplôme de voyagiste *m*

Certificate of Tourist Information Centres Competence diplôme d'agent d'Office du tourisme *m*

Certificate of Travel Agency Competence diplôme d'agent de voyages *m*

Certificate of Travel Agency Management diplôme de gestion d'agence de voyages *m*

certified cheque chèque certifié *m*

ch = central heating

chain chaîne *f*

chain hotel hôtel de chaîne *m*

chair chaise *f*

chair lift télésiège *m*

Chairman and Chief Executive Officer Président-directeur général *m*

Chairman and Managing Director président-directeur général *m*

chalet chalet *m*

chalet park parc résidentiel de loisirs *m*

chamber maid femme de chambre *f*

Chamber of Commerce chambre de Commerce *f*

champagne champagne *m*

champagne flute flûte à champagne *f*

champagne glass coupe à champagne *f*

champagne reception réception avec champagne *f*

chance customer client imprévu *m*

chance guest client sans réservation *m*

to **change money** changer de l'argent

changeover day [*when weekly tariffs start and finish*] jour de changement de tarif *m*

Channel tunnel tunnel sous la Manche *m*, Eurotunnel *m*

charge prix *m*; ***our charges*** notre tarif; ***to be in charge of*** être responsable de

charge account compte de crédit *m*

to **charge to an account** mettre sur un compte

charge card carte accréditive *f*

to **charter** [*plane*] affréter

charter flight vol charter *m*, vol nolisé *m*

charter plane avion charter *m*

charterer affréteur *m*

chartering chartérisation *f*, nolisation *f*

chauffeur-driven avec chauffeur

cheap day return aller-retour à tarif réduit valable une journée *m*

check *Am* chèque *m*; [*in restaurant etc*] addition *f*

check-in enregistrement *m*

to **check in** *vi* [*at airport*] enregistrer; [*at hotel*] arriver; [*fill in forms etc*] remplir la fiche du voyageur

to **check in** *vt* [*person*] inscrire; [*luggage*] enregistrer

check-in clerk [*at airport*] employé à l'enregistrement des bagages *m*

check-in desk comptoir d'enregistrement *m*

check-in time heure limite d'enregistrement *f*

to **check out** *vi* quitter (l'hôtel); [*pay bill*] régler la note au départ

to **check sb out** encaisser la note de qn

check-out time heure de départ *f*; [*when room has to be vacated*] heure limite d'occupation des chambres *f*

checked baggage bagages enregistrés *mpl*

cheese fromage *m*

cheese board plateau de fromages *m*

chemist's pharmacie *f*

cheque chèque *m*

cheque card carte bancaire *f*

cherry cerise *f*

chest of drawers commode *f*

Chicago Convention Convention de Chicago *f*

chicken poulet *m*

chicken breast blanc de poulet *m*

chicory endive *f*

child enfant *m*

child-minding garde d'enfants *f*

children's area coin enfants *m*

children's meal repas enfant *m*

children's menu menu enfant *m*

children's portion repas enfant *m*

chilled frais

chips frites *fpl*

chuck *Am* paleron *m*

Chunnel tunnel sous la Manche *m*, Eurotunnel *m*

church église *f*

cider cidre *m*

cigar cigare *m*

cigarette cigarette *f*

cigarette machine distributeur de cigarettes *m*

cigarillo cigarillo *m*

cinema cinéma *m*

citizenship citoyenneté *f*

city break court séjour en ville *m*

city centre centre ville *m*

city centre agent [*travel agent*] agent en ville *m*

city centre hotel hôtel situé dans le centre ville *m*

city code code ville *m*

city hall hôtel de ville *m*

city ledger débiteurs divers *mpl*

city terminal terminal urbain *m*

Civil Aeronautics Board *Am* ≈ Direction générale de l'Aviation civile *f*

civil airline compagnie d'aviation civile *f*

civil air transport transport aérien civil *m*

Civil Aviation Act loi sur l'aviation civile *f*

Civil Aviation Authority [*UK*] ≈ Direction générale de l'Aviation civile *f*

to **classify** classer

clean propre

to **clean** nettoyer

cleaning nettoyage *m*

cleaning staff personnel de nettoyage *m*

cleanliness propreté *f*

client file dossier client *m*, fichier client *m*

clientele clientèle *f*

climate climat *m*

climbing alpinisme *m*; [*rock climbing*] escalade *f*

clipper class classe affaires *f*

cloakroom [*for coats*] vestiaire *m*

cloakroom attendant employé du vestiaire *m*

clocking-in card fiche de pointage *f*

closed-circuit TV télévision en circuit fermé *f*

closet *Am* placard *m*

clothes closet *Am* penderie *f*

club club *m*; [*disco*] boîte *f*

club class classe affaires *f*

cluster [*of tourist attractions etc*] regroupement *f*

coach car *m*, autocar *m*; [*on train*] voiture *f*

coach party groupe voyageant en autocar *m*; *we have three coach parties coming tomorrow* il y a trois cars qui arrivent demain

coach shuttle autocar navette *m*

coach station gare routière *f*

coach tour voyage en autocar *m*, circuit en car *m*

coach tour operator autocariste *m*

coach trip excursion en car *f*

coast côte *f*, littoral *m*

coastal resort station balnéaire *f*

coaster dessous-de-verre *m*

cocktail bar bar (*plus chic*) *m*

cocktail party cocktail *m*, réception avec cocktail *f*

cocktail shaker shaker *m*

cod morue *f*

code of conduct code de conduite *m*

code of practice règlements et usages *mpl*

code sharing usage d'un code commun *m*

coffee café *m*

coffee cup tasse à café *f*

coffee pot cafetière *f*

coffee shop café *m*, coffee shop *m*

coffee table table basse *f*

cognac cognac *m*

cold buffet buffet froid *m*

cold drink boisson fraîche *f*

cold meat viande froide *f*

collision damage waiver suppression de franchise pour les dommages causés aux véhicules *f*

colour coding code couleurs *m*

combination [*for lock*] combinaison *f*

comfort confort *m*

comfortable confortable

comment card fiche d'observations *f*

commercial airline compagnie aérienne commerciale *f*
commercial freedoms libertés commerciales *fpl*
commercial hospitality [*hospitality industry*] hospitalité commerciale *f*
commercial hotel hôtel de tourisme *m*
commercial rate tarif société *m*
commis chef commis *m*, commis cuisinier *m*, commis de cuisine *m*
commis waiter commis *m*
commission commission *f*
commissionaire commissionnaire *m*, portier *m*, chasseur *m*
common carrier entreprise de transport public *f*
common fund fonds commun *m*
common interest group groupe d'intérêt commun *m*
common interest tourism tourisme pour groupes d'intérêt commun *m*
common rated fare tarif commun *m*
common rated points destinations pour lesquelles les tarifs sont identiques à partir d'un même point de départ
communal collectif
communications communications *fpl*
commuter airline compagnie d'aviation "court-courrier" *f*
commuter line [*train*] ligne de banlieue *f*
commuter plane commuter *m*
companion fare [*for additional person*] tarif par personne supplémentaire *m*
compartment compartiment *m*

compensation dédommagement *m*
competitive discounting remise compétitive *f*
complaint plainte *f*, réclamation *f*
complaints book cahier de réclamations *m*
complimentary gracieux
complimentary room chambre offerte *f*
computer ordinateur *m*
computer-controlled lock serrure électronique *f*
computer terminal terminal (informatique) *m*
computerized informatisé
computerized airline reservations tourismatique aérienne *f*
computerized billing system système de facturation informatisé *m*
computerized booking réservation informatisée *f*
computerized key clé magnétique *f*
computerized reservation system tourismatique *f*, système informatique de réservation *m*
computerized switchboard standard informatisé *m*
concert concert *m*
concessionary rate tarif réduit *m*
concierge concierge *mf*
concierge's desk comptoir du concierge *m*
concierge's slip débours concierge *m*
concourse hall *m*
condiments condiments *mpl*
conditions of entry and movement conditions d'entrée et de circulation *fpl*
conditions of reservation conditions de réservation *fpl*

conditions of sale conditions de vente *fpl*

conducted tour visite guidée *f*

Confederation of Tourism, Hotel and Catering Management confédération de la gestion du tourisme, des hôtels et des restaurants *f*

conference congrès *m*

conference centre centre de conférences *m*

conference coordinator responsable des congrès *m*

conference delegate congressiste *m*

conference organizer organisateur de conférences *m*, organisateur de congrès *m*

conference pack dossier offert aux conférenciers avec informations générales sur la conférence, petits cadeaux, etc.

conference room salle de conférence *f*

configuration [*of seats*] configuration *f*

to **confirm** vérifier; [*booking*] confirmer

confirmation vérification *f*; [*of booking*] confirmation *f*

confirmation form formulaire de confirmation *m*

confirmation invoice facture de confirmation *f*

confirmed seat place confirmée *f*

conglomerate conglomérat *m*

congress congrès *m*

conjunction tickets billets complémentaires *mpl*

connecting flight vol de correspondance *m*, correspondance *f*

connecting rooms chambres communicantes *fpl*

connecting time temps de correspondance *m*

connection correspondance *f*

consecutive consécutif

conservation area site classé *m*, réserve naturelle *f*

consolidation [*combining bookings*] groupage *m*

consolidator groupeur *m*

consommé consommé *m*

consumer behaviour comportement du consommateur *m*

contact staff personnel en contact avec la clientèle *m*

contagious disease maladie contagieuse *f*

Continent: the Continent l'Europe continentale *f*

continental breakfast petit déjeuner continental *m*

Continental Plan *Am* tarif chambre avec petit déjeuner continental *m*

contract of carriage contrat de transport *m*

contract of employment contrat de travail *m*

control office bureau de contrôle *m*

control tower tour de contrôle *f*

controller contrôleur *m*

convention convention *f*; [*conference*] congrès *m*

conversion rate taux de conversion *m*

convertible currency devise convertible *f*

cook cuisinier *m*, chef *m*

cooked breakfast petit déjeuner à l'anglaise *m*

cool frais

cooled rafraîchi

co-ownership copropriété *f*
cordial sirop *m*
cork bouchon *m*
cork charge droit de bouchon *m*
corkscrew tire-bouchon *m*
corkage droit de bouchon *m*
corked bouchonné
corn on the cob épi de maïs *m*
corporate tarif préférentiel pour sociétés ou agences *m*
corporate hospitality accueil d'invités d'entreprises *m*
corporate-operated group chaîne intégrée *f*
corporate rate tarif préférentiel de fidélité *m*, tarif société *m*
to **cost sth** [*work out cost of*] évaluer les coûts de qch
cost analysis évaluation des coûts *f*
cost centre centre d'analyse *m*
cot lit de bébé *m*, lit d'enfant *m*; *Am* lit de camp *m*
COTAC = Certificate Of Travel Agency Competence
COTAM = Certificate Of Travel Agency Management
cotel *Am* auberge de jeunesse *f*
COTICC = Certificate Of Tourist Information Centres Competence
COTOP = Certificate Of Tour Operating Practice
couchette couchette *f*
couchette car voiture-couchette *f*
to **countersign** contresigner
country pays *m*
country code code pays *m*
country house hotel relais-château *m*, auberge *f*
country inn auberge rurale *f*, auberge de campagne *f*
country of origin pays d'origine *m*
country park base de loisirs *f*

countryside campagne *f*, paysage *m*
countryside conservation designation scheme plan de classification et de protection du paysage *m*
country-town agency [*travel agent*] agence de ville de campagne *f*
couple couple *m*
coupon bon *m*
courgette courgette *f*
courier accompagnateur *m*; accompagnatrice *f*
course [*of meal*] plat *m*; [*educational*] stage *m*
courtesy bus navette gratuite *f*
courtesy car voiture gratuite *f*
cover couvert *m*
cover charge prix du couvert *m*
CP = Continental Plan
crab crabe *m*
craft centre centre d'artisanat *m*
craftwork artisanat *m*
crazy-golf mini-golf *m*
cream crème *f*
cream tea thé de cinq heures avec gâteaux à la crème *m*
creamed potatoes purée de pommes de terre *f*
creaming écrémage *m*
creche garderie *f*
credit crédit *m*; *to give credit* faire crédit
credit account compte à crédit *m*
credit card carte de crédit *f*
credit card machine pressographe *m*
credit card reader lecteur de cartes *m*
credit card terminal terminal électronique de paiement *m*, TEP *m*

credit card voucher note de débit *f*
credit file dossier crédit *m*
credit manager directeur du
   crédit *m*
credit policy politique de crédit *f*
credit rating solvabilité *f*
credit sale vente à crédit *f*
crew équipage *m*
crew rate tarif équipage *m*
crewed charter location de bateau
   avec équipage *m*
CRO = Central Reservations
   Office
crockery vaisselle *f*
cross-Channel [*ferry*] trans-
   Manche
cross-Channel car ferry ferry
   trans-Manche *m*
crossing traversée *f*, passage *m*
Crown rating system système de
   classement (des hôtels
   britanniques) *m*
CRS = Computerized
   Reservation System
cruise croisière *f*
cruise director animateur de
   croisière *m*
cruise ship bateau de croisière *m*
crushed ice glace pilée *f*
CST = Central Standard Time
cucumber concombre *m*
culinary culinaire
cultural culturel
cultural event manifestation
   culturelle *f*
cultural exchange échange
   culturel *m*
cultural heritage patrimoine
   culturel *m*
cultural tourism tourisme
   culturel *m*
culture culture *f*
cupboard placard *m*

currency devise *f*
currency code code devise *m*
currency surcharge supplément
   en cas de variation des parités
   monétaires *m*
current assets actif circulant *m*
current expenditure dépenses
   courantes *fpl*
current liabilities dettes à court
   terme *fpl*
curried au curry *m*
curtain rideau *m*
customer client *m*
customer care services à la
   clientèle *mpl*
customer satisfaction
   questionnaire formulaire
   d'appréciation *m*, fiche
   d'appréciation *f*
customs douane *f*
customs allowance franchise
   douanière *f*
customs clearance
   dédouanement *m*
customs control contrôle
   douanier *m*
customs duties droits de
   douane *mpl*
customs formalities formalités
   douanières *fpl*
customs regulations
   réglementation douanière *f*
cut-price bradé
to **cut prices** baisser les prix
cutlery couverts *mpl*
to **cycle** aller à bicyclette
cycle path piste cyclable *f*
cycling by train carte Train
   Évasion Randonnée (billet
   SNCF train + vélo) *f*
cycling holiday(s)
   cyclotourisme *m*
cyclist cycliste *m*

D

daily [*sailing etc*] quotidien
daily occupancy forecast planning d'occupation journalière *m*
daily report rapport journalier *m*
daily security report rapport journalier de sécurité *m*
daily trading report rapport de situation journalière *m*
daily visitors visiteurs journaliers *mpl*
damage dommages *mpl*
dance danse *f*
dance band orchestre de danse *m*
database base de données *f*
DATAS II [*reservation system*] DATAS II *m*
date of birth date de naissance *f*
date of departure date de départ *f*
date of return date de retour *f*
date stamp tampon dateur *m*
to **date-stamp** composter
date-stamping compostage *m*
day jour *m*; *per day* par jour
day book livre de main-courante *m*
day let day used
daylight saving time heure d'été *f*
day rate tarif journalier *m*
day return aller-retour dans la journée *m*
day tour excursion d'une journée *f*
day trip excursion d'une journée *f*
day tripper excursionniste *mf*
day visitor excursionniste *mf*

day visits survey étude sur les déplacements d'une journée pour loisir ou affaires *f*
deadhead flight parcours à vide *m*
deadweight tonnage [*of ship*] tonnage port en lourd *m*
debit note note de débit *f*
decaf déca *m*
decaffeinated coffee café décaféiné *m*
deck pont *m*
deckchair chaise longue *f*
to **declare** déclarer
decor décoration *f*
deep-fat frying cuisson en bain de friture *f*
deep-sea passenger ship paquebot de haute mer *m*
degree in hotel and catering diplôme en hôtellerie-restauration *m*
delay retard *m*
delayed: the flight has been delayed le vol a été retardé, le vol a du retard
delinquent account compte en souffrance *m*
deluxe luxueux
deluxe cabin cabine de luxe *f*
deluxe room chambre catégorie "luxe" *f*
demand for tourism demande touristique *f*
demi-pension demi-pension *f*

demographic factors facteurs démographiques *mpl*

denied boarding compensation dédommagement de non accès à bord *m*

density chart feuille d'occupation journalière *f*

density reservation chart feuille des réservations journalières *f*

dentist dentiste *m*

dep. (= departure) dép. *m*

department service *m*

department head chef de service *m*

departmental cash report rapport de caisse par service *m*

departure départ *m*

departure date date de départ *f*

departure gate porte (départ) *f*

departure list liste des départs *f*

departure lounge salle de départ *f*

departure notification notification de départ *f*

departure tax taxe de départ *f*

departures book registre des départs *m*

to **deplane** débarquer

deposit arrhes *fpl*

deputy manager directeur adjoint *m*

designated carrier compagnie aérienne désignée dans un accord bilatéral pour assurer les liaisons entre deux pays *f*

desk clerk *Am* réceptionnaire *mf*

dessert dessert *m*, entremets *m*

dessert spoon cuillère à dessert *f*

dessert trolley chariot de desserts *m*

destination destination *f*

destination management company [*organizes services eg transfers*] agence de réceptif *f*

destination survey étude sur les destinations *f*

developed country pays industrialisé *m*

developing country pays en voie de développement *m*

Development of Tourism Act loi sur le développement du tourisme *f*

diabetic diabétique

diary agenda *m*

die plate [*for tickets*] plaque d'imprimante de billets *f*

diet régime *m*

differential fare structure structure tarifaire différentielle *f*

differential pricing établissement des prix différentiels *m*

Digest of Tourism Statistics rapport statistique sur le tourisme *m*

to **dine out** dîner dehors

diner client *m*; [*restaurant*] restaurant *m*

Diner's Club (card) carte Diner's Club *f*

dining car wagon-restaurant *m*

dining room salle à manger *f*, salle de restaurant *f*

dinner dîner *m*

dinner dance dîner dansant *m*

direct direct

direct air link liaison aérienne directe *f*

direct dial telephone ligne téléphonique directe *f*, téléphone direct *m*

direct flight vol direct *m*

direct mail advertising publicité directe par courrier *f*

direct sale vente directe *f*

direct selling vente directe *f*

director directeur *m*
disabled handicapé
disabled access facilité d'accès
pour personnes handicapées *f*
disabled person personne
handicapée *f*
Disabled Persons' Railcard carte
de train pour personnes
handicapées *f*
disbursement voucher bon de
décaissement *m*
disco(theque) discothèque *f*
discount rabais *m*, réduction *f*,
remise *f*
discount coach card carte de
réduction sur les lignes
d'autocars *f*
discount tariff tarif réduit *m*
discount ticket agency agence
spécialisée dans la vente de
billets bradés *f*
discount travel card carte de
réduction pour les transports *f*
discount voucher bon de
réduction *m*
discounted air ticket billet
d'avion à tarif réduit *m*
discounted ticket billet bradé *m*
discounting remise *f*
dish plat *m*
dishwasher [*person*] plongeur *m*
display [*on screen*] affichage *m*
display case vitrine d'exposition *f*
to **display prices** afficher les prix
disposable [*cups etc*] jetable
distribution channel circuit de
distribution *m*
district manager directeur
régional *m*
disturb: do not disturb ne pas
déranger
divan base sommier *m*
to **dive** plonger

diverting airport aéroport de
déroutement *m*
dividend dividende *m*
diving plongée (sous-marine) *f*
divisional director directeur de
division *m*
doctor médecin *m*
documents papiers *mpl*
dog chien *m*; *dogs welcome* chiens
acceptés
domestic airline ligne intérieure *f*
domestic excursionist
excursionniste (dans son propre
pays) *mf*
domestic flight vol intérieur *m*
domestic route ligne intérieure *f*
domestic same-day visitor
excursionniste (dans son propre
pays) *mf*
domestic tourism tourisme
national *m*
domestic tourist touriste (dans son
propre pays) *mf*
domestic travel voyages
domestiques *mpl*
domestic visitor touriste (dans son
propre pays) *mf*
door attendant portier *m*
doorman portier *m*
dormitory dortoir *m*
double bed grand lit *m*
to **double book** sur-réserver
double glazing double vitrage *m*
double occupancy occupation
double *f*
double occupancy rate tarif par
personne en chambre double *m*
double room chambre double *f*
to **downgrade** déclasser
draught beer bière pression *f*
dressing table coiffeuse *f*
drink boisson *f*
drinking water eau potable *f*

drinks dispenser *or* **machine**
distributeur de boissons *m*
drive-in restaurant *Am* restaurant
drive-in *m*
drive-through restaurant *Am*
restaurant drive-in où l'on peut
aussi manger à l'intérieur
drumstick [*of chicken*] pilon *m*
dry sec
dry cleaning nettoyage à sec *m*,
pressing *m*
dry lease location d'avion ou de
bateau sans carburant ni
équipage *f*
Dublin Bay prawn langoustine *f*
duck canard *m*
dumb waiter [*food stand*]
guéridon *m*; [*lift*] monte-plats *m*

dumping dumping *m*
duplex duplex *m*
duty: to be on duty être de
service
duty-free hors-taxe, exempt de
droits de douane
duty-free goods marchandise hors
taxe *f*
duty-free sales vente hors taxes
duty-free shop boutique hors
taxes *f*
duty housekeeper gouvernante
(qui est) de service *f*
duty manager directeur (qui est)
de service *m*
duty paid droits acquittés *mpl*
duvet couette *f*
DVS = Day Visits Survey

E

E111 E111 *m*
early arrival arrivée anticipée *f*
early departure départ anticipé *m*
early morning arrival arrivée
matinale *f*
early morning call appel
matinal *m*
early morning departure départ
matinal *m*
early morning tea thé du
matin *m*

easel chevalet *m*
Easter holidays vacances de
Pâques *fpl*
Easter weekend week-end de
Pâques *m*
Eastern Standard Time *Am* heure
de l'Est
to **eat in** consommer sur place
to **eat out** déjeuner/dîner à
l'extérieur
eatery *Am* restaurant *m*

EC (= European Community)
CE *f*

ECAC (= European Civil Aviation Conference) CEAC *f*

Economic Review of World Tourism Revue économique du tourisme mondial *f*

economy class classe économique *f*

economy fare tarif économique *m*

eco-tourism tourisme écologique *m*

ecu (= European Currency Unit) écu *m*

educational éducatif; [*trip*] d'études

educational holiday vacances studieuses *fpl*

educational tour Éductour *m*, voyage d'études *m*

educational trip séjour éducatif *m*

educational visit visite pédagogique *f*

eel anguille *f*

EFCT (= European Federation of Conference Towns) FEVC *f*

EFTPOS = Electronic Fund Transfer From The Point-Of-Sale

egg œuf *m*

eggplant *Am* aubergine *f*

eiderdown édredon *m*

electricity électricité *f*

electronic billing machine caisse électronique *f*

electronic card lock serrure à carte perforée *f*

electronic funds transfer transfert de fonds électronique *m*

electronic funds transfer from the point-of-sale système de transfert de fonds électronique à partir du point de vente *m*

electronic key card carte-clé *f*

electronic key encoding machine programmateur de cartes-clés électroniques *m*

electronic lock serrure électronique *f*

elevator *Am* ascenseur *m*

elevator attendant *Am* liftier *m*

embargo embargo *m*

embarkation embarquement *m*

embarkation card carte d'embarquement *f*

emergency urgence *f*

emergency exit issue de secours *f*, sortie de secours *f*

emergency lighting éclairage de sécurité *f*

emergency medical kit trousse de secours *f*

emergency telephone téléphone d'urgence *m*

emergency treatment soins d'urgence *mpl*

EMS (= European Monetary System) SME *m*

encashment *Br* encaissement *m*

engineer [*on plane*] ingénieur *m*

English breakfast petit déjeuner à l'anglaise *m*

English service service à l'anglaise *m*

English Tourist Board ≈ comité du tourisme anglais *m*

to **enplane** embarquer

enquiries service informations *m*

enquiry card fiche de demande de renseignements *f*

enquiry clerk responsable de l'information *m*

enquiry desk bureau de renseignements *m*

en-suite [*bathroom*] particulier, privatif

en-suite facilities sanitaires privatifs *mpl*

entertainment divertissement *m*, distractions *fpl*

entertainments director directeur de l'animation *m*

entertainments officer animateur *m*

entertainments team équipe d'animation *f*

entrance entrée *f*

entrance hall hall d'entrée *m*

entrecôte steak entrecôte *f*

entry card fiche de police (au débarquement) *f*

entry requirements formalités d'entrée *fpl*

entry tax taxe d'entrée *f*

entry visa visa d'entrée *m*

environment environnement *m*

environmental impact impact sur l'environnement *m*

Environmentally Sensitive Area zone de protection de la nature désignée par la CE où les agriculteurs doivent utiliser des méthodes traditionnelles

EP = European Plan

ERM = Exchange Rate Mechanism

escape route plan d'évacuation *m*

escorted tour voyage accompagné *m*

EST = Eastern Standard Time

establishment établissement *m*

Estimated Time of Arrival heure d'arrivée prévue *f*

Estimated Time of Departure heure de départ prévue *f*

ETA = Estimated Time of Arrival

ETAG = European Tourism Action Group

ETB = English Tourist Board

ETC (= European Travel Commission) CET *f*

ETD = Estimated Time of Departure

ethnic tourism [*travel to ancestral country*] tourisme ethnique *m*

EU = European Union

Eurailpass eurailpass *m*

Eurobudget eurobudget *m*

Eurobudget fare tarif eurobudget *m*

Eurocheque eurochèque *m*

Eurodollar eurodollar *m*

European Association of Hotel and Tourism Schools AEHT *f*, Association européenne des écoles d'hôtellerie et du tourisme *f*

European Civil Aviation Conference Commission européenne de l'aviation civile *f*

European Community Communauté européenne *f*

European Currency Unit Unité monétaire européenne *f*

European Federation of Camping Site Organisations Fédération européenne de l'hôtellerie de plein air *f*

European Federation of Conference Towns Fédération européenne des villes de congrès *f*

European Monetary System Système monétaire européen *m*

European Passenger Train Timetable Conference CEH *f*, Conférence européenne des horaires des trains de voyageurs *f*

European plan *Am* tarif chambre sans pension *m*

European Tourism Action Group Groupe d'action du tourisme européen *m*

European Travel Commission Commission européenne du tourisme *f*

European Union Union européenne *f*

Eurotourism eurotourisme *m*

evening meal dîner *m*

event événement *m*; [*cultural, at festival etc*] manifestation *f*

event attraction attrait touristique lié à une manifestation *m*

event management organisation de manifestations *f*

excess baggage excédent de bagages *m*

excess fare supplément *m*

excess mileage excédent de kilométrage *m*

excess value excédent de valeur *m*

excess weight excédent de poids *m*

exchange controls contrôle des changes *m*

exchange rate cours des changes *m*, taux de change *m*

Exchange Rate Mechanism mécanisme des taux de change *m*

excursion excursion *f*

excursion fare tarif excursion *m*

excursionist excursionniste *mf*

executive cadre *m*

executive chef cuisinier en chef *m*, maître-coq *m*

executive class classe affaires *f*

executive director directeur administratif *m*, directeur-gérant *m*

executive housekeeper gouvernante générale *f*

executive secretary secrétaire de direction *mf*

executive suite suite présidentielle *f*

executive travel voyages d'affaires *mpl*

exhibition exposition *f*

exhibition centre parc des expositions *m*

exit sortie *f*

exit door porte de sortie *f*

exit visa visa de sortie *m*

expenditure dépenses *fpl*

expenses claim form note de frais *f*

export exportation *f*

export tourism tourisme d'exportation *m*

express [*train*] express *m*

express train train direct *m*

to **extend** prolonger

extra extra *m*

extra [*bed etc*] supplémentaire

extra charge supplément *m*

extras bill facture des extras *f*

F

to **face** donner sur
facecloth gant de toilette *m*
facilities installations *fpl*
fair foire *f*
fall *Am* automne *m*
fam trip Famtour *m*
familiarization trip [*for sales agents*] voyage d'études *m*, voyage de familiarisation *m*
family famille *f*
family fare tarif famille *m*
Family Railcard carte de train "famille" *f*, ≈ carte Kiwi *f*
family rate tarif famille *m*
family room chambre "famille" *f*
family-run [*hotel, restaurant*] géré en famille, familial
family-run boarding house pension de famille *f*
family-run hotel hôtel familial *m*
Fantasia [*reservation system*] Fantasia *m*
fare tarif *m*
Fare Construction Unit ancienne base de calcul des tarifs aériens établie par l'IATA *f*
fare level niveau tarifaire *m*
fare list [*of carrier*] liste des tarifs *f*
fare payment règlement du tarif *m*
fare structure structure tarifaire *f*
farm camping camping à la ferme *m*

farm holiday vacances à la ferme *fpl*
farmhouse accommodation logis à la ferme *m*
farm tourism tourisme "fermier" *m*, tourisme agricole *m*
fast food restauration rapide *f*
fast food restaurant fast-food *m*
fax télécopie *f*, fax *m*
to **fax** [*document*] faxer
fax (machine) télécopieur *m*
FB = Full Board
FCU = Fare Construction Unit
feasibility study étude de faisabilité *f*
federation fédération *f*
feeder airline compagnie aérienne d'apport *f*
feeder flight vol d'apport *m*
feeder network réseau d'apport *m*
ferry ferry *m*
ferry port port de ferry *m*
festival festival *m*, fête *f*
FFP = Frequent Flyer Programme
FGTO (= Foreign Government Tourist Offices) ONET *m*
fictitious fare construction points escales fictives d'établissement de tarif *fpl*
file fichier *m*
fillet filet *m*
film projector projecteur de films *m*

finance finances *fpl*
financial controller contrôleur
  financier *m*
financial report rapport
  financier *m*
financing financement *m*
fire alarm alarme incendie *f*
fire blanket couverture pare-
  flamme *f*
fire door porte coupe-feu *f*
fire drill exercices d'évacuation en
  cas d'incendie *mpl*
fire escape escalier de secours *m*
fire extinguisher extincteur *m*
fire hydrant bouche d'incendie *f*
fire notice consignes en cas
  d'incendie *fpl*
fireplace cheminée *f*
fire regulations consignes en cas
  d'incendie *fpl*
fire safety sécurité incendie *f*
firm reservation réservation
  ferme *f*
first aid premiers soins *mpl*
first aid kit trousse de secours *f*
first class première classe *f*,
  première *f*; *to travel first class*
  voyager en première
first class ticket billet de
  première *m*
first floor premier étage *m*; *Am*
  deuxième étage *m*
fish poisson *m*
fishing pêche *f*
fishing village village de
  pêcheurs *m*
fishmonger poissonnier *m*
FIT = Fully Independent Travel
fitness centre club de
  gymnastique *m*
fitness room salle de
  musculation *f*
fittings installations *fpl*

five-star hotel hôtel cinq étoiles
  m, hôtel quatre étoiles-luxe *m*
fixed assets immobilisations *fpl*
fixed-centre holiday vacances
  avec hébergement fixe *fpl*
fixed-price menu menu à prix
  fixe *m*
fixed rate prix fixe *m*
fixed-term contract contrat à
  durée déterminée *m*, CDD *m*
flag airline compagnie aérienne
  nationale *f*
flag carrier compagnie de
  transports nationale *f*
flagship [*best hotel, restaurant
  etc*] fleuron *m*
flambé flambé
flat swapping échange
  d'appartement *m*
flatlet studio *m*
flea market marché aux puces *m*
fleet flotte *f*
flexibility flexibilité *f*
flexible ticket billet sans
  condition *m*
flight vol *m*
flight attendant hôtesse de l'air *f*;
  steward *m*
flight coupon coupon de vol *m*
flight crew équipage (d'avion) *m*,
  personnel navigant *m*, membres
  de l'équipage
flight engineer ingénieur de vol *m*
flight number numéro de vol *m*
flight only vol "sec" *m*
flight personnel personnel de
  cabine *m*
flight reservation réservation
  d'avion *f*
flight time durée de vol *f*; [*take-off
  time*] heure du vol *f*
float [*in cash register*] fonds de
  caisse *m*

floor [*storey*] étage *m*
floor clerk responsable d'étage *m*
floor housekeeper gouvernante d'étage *f*
floor plan plan d'étage *m*
floor show spectacle de variétés *m*
floor waiter garçon d'étage *m*
floral arrangement décoration florale *f*
florist fleuriste *m*
florist's boutique de fleurs *f*
flower fleur *f*
to **fly** voler
fly cruise forfait avion et croisière *m*
fly drive forfait avion + location de voiture *m*
fly-drive holiday forfait vacances avion + voiture de location *m*
fly fishing pêche à la mouche *f*
fly rail forfait avion + train *m*
flying vol *m*
foldaway bed lit pliant *m*
folder classeur *m*
folding bed lit pliant *m*
folding tray tablette *f*
folk *adj* folklorique
folk museum musée des arts et traditions populaires *m*, musée du folklore *m*
food nourriture *f*
food and beverage manager directeur des approvisionnements *m*, contrôleur restauration *m*
food and beverage service service de restauration *m*
food chain chaîne de restauration *f*
food checker contrôleur de la restauration *m*
food court [*in airport*] zone de restauration *f*

food critic critique gastronomique *m*
food hygiene regulations réglementation sur l'hygiène alimentaire *f*
foot passenger passager à pied *m*, passager piéton *m*
footpath sentier *m*; [*for hikers*] chemin de randonnée *m*
Forces Railcard carte de train délivrée par les autorités militaires *f*
forecast chart [*in hotel*] feuille d'occupation journalière *f*
foreign capital investment investissement de capitaux étrangers *m*
foreign country pays étranger *m*
foreign currency devise étrangère *f*
foreign currency earnings apport de devises étrangères *m*
foreign exchange receipt reçu de change de devises *m*
Foreign Exchange Tax Free Shopping régime d'exportation pour la vente au détail *m*
Foreign Government Tourist Offices Offices nationaux étrangers du tourisme *mpl*
foreign language langue étrangère *f*
foreign travel voyages à l'étranger *mpl*
foreign travel currency allowance franchise de devises étrangères *f*
foreign travel expenditure dépenses de devises à l'étranger *fpl*
foreigner étranger *m*; étrangère *f*
fork fourchette *f*
fortnight quinzaine *f*

fourposter bed lit à baldaquin *m*

four-star hotel hôtel quatre étoiles *m*

foyer hall de réception *m*

franchise franchise *f*

franchise agreement accord de franchise *m*

franchised chain chaîne franchisée *f*

franchisee franchisé *m*

franchising franchisage *m*, franchising *m*

franchisor franchiseur *m*

free [*room*] libre

free house *Br* pub qui vend différentes marques de bière *m*

free movement of people libre circulation de personnes *f*

free place [*additional*] place gratuite *f*

free time temps libre *m*

freebie cadeau *m*

freedom to land for technical reasons droit d'escales techniques *m*

freedom to overfly a country without landing droit de survol d'un État *m*

freedoms of the air libertés de l'air *fpl*

French civil aviation authority Direction générale de l'aviation civile

French dressing vinaigrette *f*

French fried potatoes pommes de terre frites *fpl*

French fries frites *fpl*

French Ministry for Tourism Secrétariat d'État au tourisme *m*

French national railway Société Nationale des Chemins de Fer Français *f*, SNCF *f*

French service service à la française *m*, service au guéridon *m*

French window porte-fenêtre *f*

frequent-flyer club club de fidélité de compagnie aérienne *m*

frequent flyer programme programme de fidélisation des passagers de compagnies aériennes *m*

frequent user card carte de fidélité *f*

frequent user programme programme de fidélisation *m*

fresh frais

fresh orange orange pressée *f*

freshwater fish poisson d'eau douce *m*

freshly squeezed fruit juice jus de fruit pressé *m*

freshly squeezed lemon juice citron pressé *m*

freshly squeezed orange juice orange pressée *f*

fried frit

fried egg œuf au plat *m*

to **frisk** fouiller (manuellement)

from de

fromage frais fromage blanc *m*, fromage frais *m*

front desk réception *f*

front of house accueil *m*

front of house manager directeur de l'hébergement *m*

front office réception *f*, accueil *m*

front office cashier caissier de la réception *m*

front office (department) service réception-accueil *m*

front office manager chef de la réception *m*

fruit fruit *m*

fruit juice jus de fruit *m*

fruit salad salade de fruits *f*
frying friture *f*
fuel surcharge surcharge due à l'augmentation du prix du carburant *f*
fuel tax taxe sur les carburants *f*
full board pension complète *f*
full credit voucher bon plein crédit *m*
full-fare paying passenger voyageur à haute contribution *m*
full pension pension complète *f*
full-price plein tarif *m*
full-time à plein temps
fully booked complet
fully inclusive tour voyage à forfait tout compris *m*

fully licensed [*hotel, restaurant etc*] qui a obtenu une licence pour la vente d'alcool
function réunion *f*, réception *f*
function bar bar (de salle de réception) *m*
function room salle de réception *f*, salle de réunion *f*
functions manager responsable des réceptions *m*
furnished meublé
furnished house maison meublée *f*
furnishings mobilier *m*, ameublement *m*
furniture meubles *mpl*, ameublement *m*

G

gala dinner dîner de gala *m*
Galileo [*reservation system*] Galileo *m*
galley [*kitchen*] cuisine *f*
game jeu *m*; [*venison etc*] gibier *m*
game reserve réserve de gibier *f*
games room salle de jeux *f*
garage garage *m*
garage attendant gardien de parking *m*
garden jardin *m*
gardener jardinier *m*

garlic ail *m*
garnished garni
gastronomy gastronomie *f*
gate [*at airport*] porte *f*
gate lounge salle d'embarquement *f*
gateway [*city as main point of access*] porte *f*
GB plate plaque GB *f*
GB sticker autocollant GB *m*
GDP (= Gross Domestic Product) PIB *m*

Gemini [*reservation system*] Gemini *m*

general cash book livre de trésorerie générale *m*

general sales agent agent général *m*

generator [*electricity*] groupe électrogène *m*

gents toilet toilettes pour hommes *fpl*

geographical mile [*1.852 km*] mille *m*

gherkin cornichon *m*

giblets abats *mpl*

gift cadeau *m*

gift shop boutique de cadeaux *f*

gin gin *m*

gin and tonic gin tonic *m*

giveaway cadeau publicitaire *m*

glass verre *m*

glassware verres *mpl*

GMT (= Greenwich Mean Time) TU *m*

GNP (= Gross National Product) PNB *m*

goat's cheese fromage de chèvre *m*

goat's milk lait de chèvre *m*

golf golf *m*

golf course parcours de golf *m*

good food guide guide gastronomique *m*

gourmet restaurant restaurant gastronomique *m*

government restrictions restrictions gouvernementales *fpl*

to **grade** [*hotels, accommodation*] classer

grant subvention *f*

grapes raisin *m*

grapefruit pamplemousse *m*

gratuity pourboire *m*

Green Belt zone "verte" de protection du paysage rural contre l'urbanisation

green card [*insurance*] carte verte *f*

green channel file "rien à déclarer" *f*

green salad salade verte *f*

green tourism tourisme vert *m*

Greenwich Mean Time Temps Universel *m*, TU *m*

to **greet** accueillir

greeting accueil *m*

Greyhound Pass abonnement de car valable aux États-Unis mais vendu à l'extérieur

grill grill *m*

grilled grillé

grilling cuisson au grill *f*

gross domestic product produit intérieur brut *m*

gross holiday propensity tendance touristique générale *f*

gross national product produit national brut *m*

gross tonnage tonnage brut *m*

gross vacation propensity *Am* tendance touristique générale *f*

ground arrangements [*at airport*] services au sol *mpl*

ground costs frais au sol *mpl*

ground floor rez-de-chaussée *m*

ground handling agency agence de réceptif *f*, agence réceptive *f*

ground handling agent agent de réceptif *m*

ground operator [*organizes services, eg transfers*] voyagiste de réceptif *m*, agence de réceptif *f*, réceptif *m*

ground staff personnel au sol *m*

grounds parc *m*

group groupe *m*

group booking réservation de
   groupe *f*
group discount remise pour les
   groupes *f*
group fare tarif de groupe *m*
group leader responsable de
   groupe *m*
group organizer organisateur de
   groupe *m*
group rate tarif groupe *m*
group travel voyages en
   groupe *mpl*
grouse lagopède d'Écosse *f*,
   grouse *f*, coq de bruyère *m*
guarantee garantie *f*
to **guarantee** garantir
guaranteed [*reservation etc*]
   garanti
gueridon guéridon *m*
guest client *m*
guest bill facture client *f*

guest comments commentaires
   clients *mpl*
guest folio fiche client *f*
guest history card fiche Kardex *f*
guest history file fichier clients *m*
guest house pension *f*
guest laundry blanchisserie (à la
   disposition des clients) *f*
guest list liste des clients *f*
guest occupancy taux
   d'occupation des lits *m*
guest speaker conférencier *m*
guide guide *mf*,
   accompagnateur *m*,
   accompagnatrice *f*
guide book guide (touristique) *m*
guide dog chien d'aveugle *m*
guidelines directives *fpl*
guided tour visite guidée *f*
Gulliver Gulliver *m*
gym salle de musculation *f*

H

haddock aiglefin *m*
hair dryer sèche-cheveux *m*
hair salon salon de coiffure *m*
half-board demi-pension *f*
half-bottle demi-bouteille *f*
half-fare ticket billet
   demi-tarif *m*
halibut flétan *m*

hall foyer *m*
hall porter concierge *m*
ham jambon *m*
hand baggage bagage(s) à
   main *m(pl)*
hand baggage check contrôle des
   bagages à main *m*
handbook guide *m*

hand luggage bagage(s) à
main *m(pl)*
handicapped handicapé
handyman homme à tout faire *m*
hanger cintre *m*
happy hour l'heure où les
boissons sont moins chères *f*
harbour port *m*
harbour terminal gare
maritime *f*
hard-boiled egg œuf dur *m*
hard currency devise forte *f*
hare lièvre *m*
HB = Half Board
H&C = Hot and Cold
HCIMA = Hotel, Catering and
Institutional Management
Association
HCITB = Hotel and Catering
Industry Training Board
HCTC = Hotel and Catering
Training Company
head accountant chef
comptable *m*
head barman chef barman *m*
head cashier chef caissier *m*
head chef chef de cuisine *m*
head concierge chef concierge *m*
head hall porter chef
concierge *m*, responsable du
hall *m*
head housekeeper gouvernante
générale *f*
head of department chef de
service *m*, directeur de
service *m*
head of maintenance responsable
maintenance *m*
head of section chef de service *m*
headphones écouteurs *mpl*
head porter chef concierge *m*
head receptionist chef de
réception *m*

head switchboard operator chef
standardiste *m*, responsable du
standard *m*
head waiter maître d'hôtel *m*
health and fitness centre centre
de sport et de remise en forme *m*
health and safety regulations
réglementation sur l'hygiène et
la sécurité *f*
health resort station climatique *f*;
[*by sea*] station balnéaire *f*
health services services de
santé *mpl*
health tourism tourisme de
santé *m*
heart [*offal*] cœur *m*
heated [*swimming pool etc*]
chauffé
heating chauffage *f*
helicopter hélicoptère *m*
heliport héliport *m*
Helsinki Accord accords
d'Helsinki *mpl*
hepatitis hépatite *f*
herbal tea infusion *f*
heritage patrimoine *m*
heritage attraction attraction
touristique patrimoniale *f*
Heritage Coast côtes anglaises et
galloises, sites classés pour leur
beauté naturelle *fpl*
heritage site site patrimoine *m*
heritage tourism tourisme
culturel *m*
high-rise building tour *f*
high season haute saison *f*, pleine
saison *f*
high speed train TGV *m*, train à
grande vitesse *m*
**Highlands and Islands
Enterprise** conseil du
développement des Highlands et
des îles écossaises *m*

to **hike** marcher

hiker randonneur *m*

hiking marche *f*

hill walking randonnée en montagne *f*

HIMG = Hotel Industry Marketing Group

Hindu Hindou *m*

to **hire** louer

hiring location *f*

historic monument monument historique *m*

historic town cité historique *f*

historical monument monument historique *m*

historical site site historique *m*

to **hitch-hike** faire de l'autostop

HM Customs and excise service des douanes et des taxes britannique *m*

HM Immigration service de l'immigration en Grande-Bretagne *m*

hold [*on ship, plane*] cale *f*; [*for luggage on plane*] soute *f*

to **hold** [*airline seat*] bloquer

to **hold a conference** tenir une conférence

hold baggage bagages de soute *mpl*

holiday vacances *fpl*, congé *m*; *on holiday* en vacances

to **holiday** passer les vacances

holiday accommodation hébergement de vacances *m*

holiday bond [*form of timeshare*] obligation "vacances" *f*

holiday brochure catalogue de vacances *m*

holiday camp camp de loisirs *m*, camp de tourisme *m*, colonie de vacances *f*

Holiday Care Service association britannique qui aide les personnes dont l'âge ou un handicap pose des problèmes en vacances

holiday centre centre de vacances *m*

holiday club club de vacances *m*

holiday complex complexe touristique *m*

holiday cottage gîte *m*

holiday entitlement droit aux vacances *m*

holiday fare tarif vacances *m*

holiday frequency fréquence de prise de vacances *f*

holiday home résidence secondaire *f*

holiday insurance assurance vacances *f*

holidaymaker vacancier *m*

holiday market marché du tourisme *m*

holiday period période de fêtes *f*

holiday plans projets de vacances *mpl*

holiday propensity tendance touristique *f*

holiday property immobilier de loisir *m*

holiday property bond obligation de résidence de tourisme *f*

holiday resort lieu de vacances *m*, villégiature *f*

holiday spot endroit de vacances *m*, villégiature *f*

holiday survey étude sur le tourisme de loisir *f*

holiday tourism tourisme de loisir *m*

holiday tourist touriste *m*

holiday tummy turista *f*, diarrhée du voyageur *f*

holiday village village de vacances *m*, village de loisirs *m*

holidays vacances *fpl*, congés *mpl*

home delivery service service de livraison à domicile *m*

home-made fait maison

honesty system système faisant appel à l'honnêteté du client *m*

honeymoon voyage de noces *m*, lune de miel *f*

honeymoon suite suite nuptiale *f*

horizontal integration intégration horizontale *f*

hors d'œuvre hors-d'œuvre *m*

horse meat viande de cheval *f*

horseradish raifort *m*

horse riding équitation *f*

hospitality hospitalité *f*

hospitality business hôtellerie *f*

hospitality industry industrie hôtelière *f*

hospitality management gestion hôtelière *f*

hospitality tray plateau de courtoisie *m*

hostel auberge *f*

hostess hôtesse *f*

hot and cold running water eau courante chaude et froide *f*

hot and cold water eau chaude et froide *f*

hot chocolate chocolat chaud *m*

hot drink boisson chaude *f*

hot-line number numéro de téléphone accessible 24 heures sur 24 *m*

hot meal repas chaud *m*

hot meal tray plateau repas (chaud) *m*

hotel hôtel *m*

hotel *adj* hôtelier

hotel accommodation hébergement à l'hôtel *m*

hotel accountant comptable d'hôtel *m*

hotel administration gestion hôtelière *f*

Hotel and Catering Benevolent Association association d'assistance aux retraités de l'industrie hôtelière et de la restauration, ainsi qu'aux jeunes employés

hotel and catering industry industrie de l'hôtellerie et de la restauration *f*

Hotel and Catering Industry Training Board centre de formation de l'industrie hôtelière et de la restauration *m*

hotel and catering management gestion d'hôtel et de restaurant *f*

hotel and catering sector secteur de l'hôtellerie et de la restauration *m*

Hotel and Catering Training Company centre de formation de l'industrie hôtelière et de la restauration *m*

hotel area zone hôtelière *f*

hotel bed lit d'hôtel *m*

hotel business hôtellerie *f*

Hotel, Catering and Institutional Management Association association de l'hôtellerie, de la restauration et de la gestion d'institutions *f*

hotel chain chaîne hôtelière *f*

hotel classification classement hôtelier *m*

hotel clerk employé d'hôtel *m*

hotel complex complexe hôtelier *m*

hotel coupon coupon hôtel *m*

hotel director directeur d'hôtel *m*, directeur hôtelier *m*

hotel division division hôtellerie *f*

hotel grading notation hôtelière *f*
hotel group groupe hôtelier *m*
hotel industry industrie hôtelière *f*, hôtellerie *f*
Hotel Industry Marketing Group société spécialisée dans le marketing de l'industrie hôtelière
hotelkeeping hôtellerie *f*
hotel law droit hôtelier *m*
hotel lobby hall (d'entrée) d'hôtel *m*
hotel management gestion hôtelière *f*
hotel manager gérant d'hôtel *m*, directeur hôtelier *m*, directeur d'hôtel *m*
hotel occupancy taux d'occupation des hôtels *m*
hotel operator hôtelier *m*
hotel product produit hôtelier *m*
Hotel Proprietors Act loi sur la responsabilité des propriétaires d'hôtels *f*
hotel reception réception d'hôtel *f*
hotel receptionist réceptionniste d'hôtel *mf*
hotel register agenda de réservation *m*, livre de réservation *m*
hotel registration [*of guests*] enregistrement des clients *m*; [*registering of hotels*] recensement d'hôtels *m*
hotel representative représentant d'hôtel *m*
hotel school école hôtelière *f*
hotel tariff tarif hôtelier *m*
hotel tax taxe sur l'hôtellerie *f*
hotel taxi taxi desservant les hôtels *m*
hotel transfer transfert (de la gare ou l'aéroport à l'hôtel) *m*

hotel voucher bon d'hôtel *m*
hotelier hôtelier *m*
HOTREC (= Confederation of National Hotel and Restaurant Associations of the European Community) HOTREC *f*
houseboat house-boat *m*
house-detective détective d'hôtel *m*
housekeeper gouvernante *f*
housekeeper's report rapport de la gouvernante *m*
housekeeping entretien *m*
housekeeping department service des étages *m*
houseman homme de ménage *m*
house manager gérant *m*
house wine cuvée de la maison, cuvée du patron *f*
hovercraft hydroglisseur *m*, aéroglisseur *m*
hub [*main airport*] "hub" *m*
hub airport aéroport "hub" *m*, aéroport central *m*
hub and spoke system système d'aéroports central et d'apport extérieur *m*
human resources management gestion des ressources humaines *f*
humid humide
to **hunt** chasser
hunting chasse *f*
hydrant bouche d'incendie *f*
hydrofoil hydrofoil *m*, hydroptère *m*
hygiene hygiène *f*
hygiene regulations règles d'hygiène *fpl*
hypothetical fare construction points étapes hypothétiques pour l'établissement des tarifs *fpl*

I

IACVB = International Association of Convention and Visitor Bureaux

IATA (= International Air Transport Association) IATA *f*

IATA bonding scheme agrément IATA *m*

IATA licence agrément IATA *m*

IATM = International Association of Tour Managers

ICAO (= International Civil Aviation Organization) OACI *f*

ice glace *f*

ice bucket seau à glace *m*

ice-cream glace *f*

ice cube glaçon *m*

iced frappé

icon icône *f*

ID = IDentification

identification pièce d'identité *f*

identity card carte d'identité *f*

IFAPA = International Foundation of Airline Passengers Associations

IFCA = International Flight Catering Association

IHA (=International Hotel Association) AIH *f*

immigration immigration *f*

immigration control contrôle de l'immigration *m*

immigration department service de l'immigration *m*

immunization immunisation *f*

import importation *f*

imprinter machine [*for credit cards*] pressographe *m*

inbound tourism tourisme récepteur *m*, tourisme réceptif *m*

inbound travel tourisme récepteur *m*

incentive stimulation *m*

incentive company agence spécialisée dans le voyage de stimulation *f*

incentive fare tarif de stimulation *m*

incentive tour voyage de stimulation *m*

incentive tourism tourisme de stimulation *m*

incentive travel voyages de stimulation *mpl*

incentive travel programme programme de voyage de stimulation *m*

incentive trip voyage de stimulation *m*

incidentals faux frais *mpl*

included inclus, compris

inclusive of tax TTC, toutes taxes comprises

inclusive tour voyage à forfait *m*, voyage organisé *m*, inclusive tour *m*

inclusive tour by charter voyage à forfait en charter *m*

inclusive tour by excursion forfait excursion *m*

inclusive tour fare tarif de voyage à forfait *m*

Inclusive Tours on Scheduled Services voyages à forfait sur des lignes régulières *mpl*

income revenu *m*

incoming tour operator voyagiste de réceptif *m*

independent inclusive tour voyage à forfait personnalisé *m*

independent operator voyagiste indépendant *m*

independent travel voyages indépendants *mpl*

indirect route principle principe de l'itinéraire indirect *m*

indoor (swimming pool) piscine intérieure *f*, piscine couverte *f*

indoor visitor attraction centre d'intérêt couvert *m*

industrial city ville industrielle *f*

industrialized country pays industrialisé *m*

infant bébé *m*

in-flight en vol, à bord

in-flight catering restauration aérienne *f*

in-flight entertainment distractions en vol *fpl*

in-flight magazine magazine distribué dans les avions *m*

in-flight service service à bord (d'un avion) *m*

information renseignements *mpl*

information centre centre d'information *m*

information desk bureau de renseignements *m*

information office bureau d'information *m*

information sheet fiche explicative *f*

in-house interne

in-house laundry buanderie *f*

in-house travel agency implant *m*

inland waterway voie fluviale *f*

inn auberge *f*

Innkeepers Liability Act loi autorisant les hôteliers à garder certaines affaires du client pour lutter contre les impayés

innkeeper's lien droit qu'ont les hôteliers de garder certaines affaires du client pour lutter contre les impayés

inoculation inoculation *f*

in-plant agency *Am* implant *m*

in-room video [*promotional tool*] cassette vidéo publicitaire *f*

Institute of Travel and Tourism institut de voyages et du tourisme *m*

instruction directive *f*, instruction *f*

instructor moniteur *m*

insurance assurance *f*

insurance company société d'assurance *f*

insurance contract contrat d'assurance *m*

insurance cover couverture d'assurance *f*

insurance form formulaire d'assurance *m*

insurance policy police d'assurance *f*

InterCity train interurbain *m*

inter-city line grande ligne *f*

inter-city rail service lignes de chemin de fer interurbaines *fpl*

inter-city train train interurbain *m*, train de grandes lignes *m*

inter-connecting doors portes de chambres communiquantes *fpl*

intercontinental intercontinental

interest intérêt *m*

interior decorator décorateur d'intérieur *m*

interline [*involving 2 or more carriers*] inter-compagnie

interline sale vente inter-compagnie *f*

interlining accord inter-compagnie *m*

intermodal travel voyages par différents moyens de transport *mpl*

internal advertising publicité interne *f*

internal air network réseau aérien intérieur *m*

internal flight vol intérieur *m*

internal mail courrier interne *m*

internal travel voyages à l'intérieur d'un même pays *mpl*

International Academy of Tourism Académie internationale du tourisme *f*

International Air Transport Association Association internationale des transporteurs aériens *f*

International Association of Convention and Visitor Bureaux association internationale des bureaux de congrès et de tourisme *f*

International Association of Scientific Experts in Tourism association internationale d'experts scientifiques du tourisme *f*

International Association of Tour Managers association internationale de tour managers *f*

International Bureau for Youth Tourism and Exchanges Bureau international pour le tourisme et les échanges de la jeunesse *m*

International Bureau of Social Tourism Bureau international du tourisme social *m*

international carrier transporteur international *m*

International Civil Aviation Organization Organisation aéronautique civile internationale *f*

international currency devise internationale *f*

International Date Line ligne de de changement de date *f*, ligne de changement de jour *f*

international department service international *m*

international excursionist [*visitor who does not stay overnight*] excursionniste international *m*

International Federation of Camping and Caravanning Fédération internationale de camping et de caravaning *f*

International Flight Catering Association Association internationale de restauration aérienne *f*

International Foundation of Airline Passengers Associations Fondation internationale des associations de passagers aériens *f*

International Hotel Association Association internationale de l'hôtellerie *f*

international nautical mile [*1.852 km*] mille nautique international *m*

International Passenger Survey
étude internationale auprès des
passagers *f*

international same-day visitor
[*stays less than 24 hours/not
overnight*] excursionniste
international *m*

**International Student Identity
Card** carte internationale
d'étudiant *f*

international tourism tourisme
international *m*

international tourism destination
destination touristique
internationale *f*

**international tourism
expenditure** dépenses
touristiques internationales *fpl*

international tourist touriste
international *m*

international travel voyages
internationaux *mpl*

international visitor visiteur
international *m*

**International Youth Hostel
Federation** Fédération
internationale des auberges de
jeunesse *f*

**Interparliamentary Association
for Tourism** Association
interparlementaire du tourisme *f*

interpretation interprétation *f*

interpreter interprète *mf*

Inter-Rail Card carte inter-rail *f*

interstate carrier transporteur
inter-État *m*

intrastate carrier transporteur
intra-État *m*

investment investissement *m*

invisible exports exportations
invisibles *fpl*

invisible imports importations
invisibles *fpl*

invoice facture *f*

to **invoice for** facturer

invoicing facturation *f*

**IPS = International Passenger
Survey**

Irish Tourist Board ≈ comité du
tourisme irlandais *m*

iron fer à repasser *m*

ironing board planche à
repasser *f*, table de repassage *f*

**ISIC = International Student
Identity Card**

island île *f*

**island hopping: to go island
hopping** aller d'une île à l'autre

issuing office [*for ticket etc*]
bureau d'émission *m*

IT (=Inclusive Tour) IT *m*

ITB = Irish Tourist Board

ITC = Inclusive Tour by Charter

itinerary itinéraire *m*

IT (= Inclusive Tour) number
numéro d'IT *m*

**ITT = Institute of Travel and
Tourism**

ITX = Inclusive Tour fare

**ITX = Inclusive Tours on
Scheduled Services**

**ITX = Inclusive Tour by
eXcursion**

**IYHF (= International Youth
Hostel Federation)** FIAJ *f*

J

jab injection *f*
jack plug fiche *f*
jack socket prise (femelle) à fiche *f*
jacuzzi jacuzzi *m*
jam confiture *f*
jardiniere jardinière *f*
jet avion à réaction *m*
jetfoil hydroglisseur *m*
jet-lag: to have jet lag souffrir du décalage horaire

jet-skiing jet-ski *m*
jetty jetée *f*, embarcadère *f*
joint fare tarif commun *m*
joint venture contrat d'association *m*
journey voyage *m*, trajet *m*
journey time durée du voyage *f*
jug cruche *f*, pichet *m*
juice jus *m*
jumbo jet jumbo-jet *m*
junior suite petite suite *f*

K

kennel chenil *m*
key clé *f*, clef *f*
key and mail rack casier à clés et à courrier *m*
key board tableau des clés *m*
key card carte-clé *f*
key clerk responsable des clés *m*
key depository dépôt des clés *m*
key rack tableau des clés *m*

key ring porte-clé *m*
kidney rognon *m*
king-size bed lit king size *m*
kipper kipper *m*
kitchen cuisine *f*
kitchen assistant aide-cuisinier *m*
kitchen hand aide de cuisine *mf*
kitchen porter aide-cuisine *m*
kitchen steward aide-cuisine *m*

kitchenette cuisinette *f*, coin-cuisine *m*
knife couteau *m*
knot [*measure of speed*] nœud (marin) *m*

knuckle [*of veal, beef*] jarret *m*
knuckle end [*of pork*] jambonneau *m*
kosher cacher

L

ladies toilet toilettes pour dames *fpl*
lager bière blonde *f*
lake lac *m*
lake cruise croisière lacustre *f*
lamb agneau *m*
lamb chop côte d'agneau *f*
lamp lampe *f*
to **land** atterir
landing atterrissage *m*
landing card carte de débarquement *f*
landscape gardener architecte paysagiste *m*
language exchange holiday échange linguistique *m*
language group groupe linguistique *m*
language study trip séjour linguistique *m*
larder cellier *m*
larder chef chef de partie boucher *m*
lasagne lasagnes *fpl*

late arrival arrivée tardive *f*; *he will be a late arrival* il arrivera tard
late availability disponibilité de dernière minute *f*
late cancellation annulation de dernière minute *f*
lateral integration intégration horizontale *f*
latitude latitude *f*
launch vedette *f*
laundry blanchisserie *f*, buanderie *f*
laundry bag sac de blanchisserie *m*
laundry room buanderie *f*
laundry service service de blanchissage *m*
to **lay the table** dresser la table, mettre la table
layover escale *f*
leader [*of group*] accompagnateur *m*; accompagnatrice *f*
leaflet dépliant *m*, brochure *f*

leakage fuite *f*
least-cost route itinéraire le moins cher *m*
to **leave the key** déposer la clé
lectern pupitre *m*
lecture hall amphithéâtre *m*
ledger grand livre *m*
leek poireau *m*
left luggage (office) consigne *f*, consigne bagages *f*
leg [*as food*] cuisse *f*; [*of veal*] cuisseau *m*; [*of lamb*] gigot *m*; [*of pork*] jambon *m*; [*in air transport*] parcours *m*; **empty leg** parcours à vide
legal aid assistance juridique *f*
leisure loisir *m*
leisure activities loisirs *mpl*
leisure break court séjour de détente *m*
leisure centre centre de loisirs *m*
leisure club club de loisirs *m*
leisure industry industrie des loisirs *f*
leisure market marché des loisirs *m*
leisure park parc de loisirs *m*
leisure sailing navigation de plaisance *f*
leisure tourism tourisme de loisir *m*, tourisme ludique *m*
lemon citron *m*
lemon sole sole limande *f*
lemon tea thé au citron *m*
lemonade limonade *f*
length of stay durée du séjour *f*
lentils lentilles *fpl*
to **let** louer
letter lettre *f*
letter of confirmation lettre de confirmation *f*
letter of credit lettre de crédit *f*, accréditif *m*

lettuce laitue *f*
LF = Load Factor
licence licence *f*
licensed [*agent*] licencié; [*for alcohol*] habilité à vendre de l'alcool
life jacket gilet de sauvetage *m*
lift ascenseur *m*
lift attendant garçon d'ascenseur *m*
lift pass forfait de remontées mécaniques *m*
light meal collation *f*
light plane avion petit porteur *m*
lighting éclairage *m*
lime citron vert *m*
limited value voucher voucher à valeur limitée *m*
linen linge *m*
linen-keeper lingère *f*
linen room lingerie *f*
linen store lingerie *f*
liner paquebot de ligne *m*, paquebot *m*
links [*for golf*] parcours de golf *m*
liqueur liqueur *f*
liqueur glass verre à liqueur *m*
listed building monument classé *m*
listed monument monument classé *m*
live-in accommodation [*for staff*] logement à demeure *m*
liver foie *m*
liveried [*uniformed*] en livrée, en uniforme
load factor [*number on plane*] coefficient de remplissage *m*
lobby hall *m*
lobster homard *m*
local hotel association association d'hôtels locaux *f*
location emplacement *m*
loch [*in Scotland*] lac *m*

121

lodge chalet *m*

to **lodge a complaint** porter plainte

lodging industry *Am* industrie hôtelière *f*

logbook [*of plane, ship*] cahier de bord *m*; [*for vehicle*] carte grise *f*, [*de réceptionniste*] cahier de consignes *m*

logo logo *m*

loin [*of veal, pork*] longe *f*

long-distance call communication interurbaine *f*

long-distance footpath sentier de grande randonnée *m*

long haul [*flight, route*] long-courrier

long holidays grandes vacances *fpl*

long-stay car park parking longue durée *m*

long vacation *Am* grandes vacances *fpl*

longitude longitude *f*

loose-leaf register registre à feuillets rechargeables *m*

loss [*of luggage etc*] perte *f*

lost and found *Am* objets trouvés *mpl*

lost property objets trouvés *mpl*

lough [*in Ireland*] lac *m*

lounge [*at airport etc*] salon *m*

lounge bar partie plus chic d'un pub où les boissons sont plus chères *f*

lounge car voiture salon *f*

low season basse saison *f*, saison creuse *f*

luggage bagages *mpl*

luggage lockers consigne automatique *f*

luggage porter bagagiste *m*, chasseur-bagagiste *m*

luggage rack porte-bagage *m*

luggage trolley chariot (à bagages) *m*

lunch déjeuner *m*

to **lunch** déjeuner

lunch menu menu déjeuner *m*

luncheon déjeuner *m*

luncheon voucher chèque-restaurant *m*, ticket-restaurant *m*

luxury luxe *m*

luxury hotel hôtel de luxe *m*

M

MA (= **routing Mid-Atlantic**) itinéraire qui passe par le milieu de l'Atlantique *m*

mackerel maquereau *m*

magnetic boarding pass carte magnétique d'accès à bord *f*

magnetic lock serrure
magnétique *f*
maid femme de chambre *f*
maid service [*at self-catering
apartment*] service de femme de
ménage *m*
mail box *Am* boîte aux lettres *f*
mail clerk *Am* responsable du
courrier *m*
mail-it-home scheme service de
livraison à domicile *m*
mail order vente par
correspondance *f*
mail pay *Am* paiement du port du
courrier *m*
mail rack casier à courrier *m*
mailshot publipostage *m*,
mailing *m*
to **mailshot** envoyer un
publipostage à
main course plat principal *m*
main holiday grandes vacances *fpl*
mainland continent *m*; ***mainland
Scotland*** le continent écossais
(par rapport aux îles)
maintenance maintenance *f*,
entretien *m*
maintenance department
maintenance *f*, service
entretien *m*
maintenance engineer
responsable maintenance *m*,
responsable d'entretien *m*
maintenance man ouvrier
d'entretien *m*
maintenance staff personnel
d'entretien *m*
maintenance team équipe
d'entretien *f*
maintenance work request
demande d'intervention de
réparation *f*
maître d' *Am* maître d'hôtel *m*

maize maïs *m*
major carrier très importante
compagnie de transport *f*
to **make a bed** faire un lit
management direction *f*, gestion *f*
management contract contrat de
gestion *m*
manager directeur *m*, gérant *m*
manageress directrice *f*
managing director directeur
général *m*
manifest [*list of passengers*]
manifeste *m*
man-made attraction centre
d'intérêt "non-naturel" *m*
manor (house) manoir *m*
manual reservation system
système de réservation manuel *m*
MAP = Modified American Plan
map carte *f*; [*of city*] plan *m*
marginal cost coût marginal *m*
marginal cost pricing fixation du
prix au coût marginal *f*
marina marina *f*, port de
plaisance *m*
marinated mariné
market marché *m*
market research étude de
marché *f*
market segment segment de
marché *m*
market segmentation
segmentation du marché *f*
market share part de marché *m*
marketing [*discipline*]
marketing *m*, mercatique *f*; [*of
product, city etc*]
commercialisation *f*
marketing and sales department
service du marketing et des
ventes *m*
marketing audit audit
marketing *m*

marketing campaign campagne de marketing *f*

marketing department service du marketing *m*

marketing director directeur du marketing *m*

marketing manager directeur du marketing *m*

marketing planning planification du marketing *f*

marketing programme programme de commercialisation *m*

marketing strategy stratégie marketing *f*

marketing technique technique de marketing *f*, mercatique *f*

mark-up ratio taux de marge *m*, taux de marque *m*

marmalade marmelade *f*

mashed potatoes purée de pommes de terre *f*

mass tourism tourisme de masse *m*

Masta = Medical Advisory Services for Travellers Abroad

Mastercard carte Eurocard Mastercard *f*

master key passe *m*, clef passe-partout *f*

matches allumettes *fpl*

mattress matelas *m*

maximum permitted mileage kilométrage maximal autorisé *m*

mayonnaise mayonnaise *f*

MCO (= Miscellaneous Charges Order) MCO *m*

MCT = Minimum Connecting Time

meal tray plateau repas *m*

means of payment moyen de paiement *m*

meat viande *f*

mechanic mécanicien *m*

medallion, médaillon médaillon *m*

Medical Advisory Services for Travellers Abroad service britannique de conseil médical pour les personnes qui partent à l'étranger *m*

medical card carte de santé *f*

medical care assistance sanitaire *f*

medical expenses frais médicaux *mpl*

medical insurance assurance médicale *f*

medical travel survival kit trousse de secours de voyage *f*

medium-haul [*flight, route*] moyen-courrier

medium-haul flight vol moyen-courrier *m*

medium-rare à point

meeting point lieu de rendez-vous *m*

meeting room salle de conférence *f*, salle de réunion *f*

mega-resort mégastation *f*, station très importante *f*

melon melon *m*

membership card carte d'adhérent *f*

memo note (de service) *f*

memo pad bloc-notes *m*

memorandum carnet de bord *m*, cahier de bord *m*

menu menu *m*

menu design conception des menus *f*

menu planning établissement des menus *m*

meridian méridien *m*

Meridian Day jour méridien *m*

meringue meringue *f*

message message *m*

message form fiche-message *f*

meter compteur (de taxes) *m*

method of payment mode de paiement *m*

microphone micro *m*

mid-category hotel hôtel milieu-de-gamme *m*

middle neck [*of beef*] côtes découvertes *fpl*

midweek en milieu de semaine

migration migration *f*

mile mille *m*

mileage-based fare system système de tarification basé sur la distance *m*

mileage system [*in air travel*] système de kilométrage *m*

milk lait *m*

milk run parcours de routine *m*

milk-shake milk-shake *m*

mineral water eau minérale *f*

mini bar mini-bar *m*

mini-break mini-séjour *m*

minibus minibus *m*

mini-cruise mini-croisière *f*

minimum charge prix minimum *m*

minimum connecting time temps minimal de correspondance *m*

minimum land package *Am* voyage à forfait proposant une formule d'hébergement minimum *m*

minimum-rated package tour voyage à forfait proposant une formule d'hébergement minimum *m*

minimum stay package forfait hébergement de courte durée *m*

Minister for Tourism ministre du Tourisme *m*

Ministry of Tourism ministère du Tourisme *m*

mini-weekend package forfait week-end *m*

minor operated departments départements de services secondaires *mpl*

mirror miroir *m*

miscellaneous divers

miscellaneous charges order bon de paiement émis par une ligne aérienne *m*

misunderstanding malentendu *m*

mobile home camping-car *m*, mobil-home *m*; [*non-motorized*] caravane *f*

MOD = Minor Operated Departments

modified American Plan *Am* tarif demi-pension *m*

monastery monastère *m*

money argent *m*

money belt pochette *f*

money order mandat postal *m*

money transfer transfert de fonds *m*

month mois *m*

monthly trading report rapport de situation mensuelle *m*

monument monument *m*

more distant point principle principe des points les plus éloignés *m*

morning coffee café (servi le matin) *m*

mosque mosquée *f*

mosquito moustique *m*

motel motel *m*

motivation motivation *f*

motorail train auto-couchettes *m*, TAA *m*, Train Auto et Moto accompagnées *m*

motorbike moto *f*

motorcycle motocyclette *f*

motor-home *Am* auto-caravane *f*, camping-car *m*

motor hotel motel *m*

motor inn motel *m*

motor launch vedette *f*
motor lodge *Am* motel *m*
motorway autoroute *f*
motorway restaurant restoroute *m*
motorway services services autoroutiers *mpl*
motoring organization association d'automobilistes *f*
mountain montagne *f*
mountain biking randonnée en VTT *f*
mountain holiday vacances à la montagne *fpl*
mountain resort station de montagne *f*, station montagnarde *f*
Mountain Standard Time *Am* heure normale des Montagnes Rocheuses *f*
mountain trekking randonnée en montagne *f*
mountain village village de montagne *m*, village montagnard *m*
mountaineering alpinisme *m*
movie screen *Am* écran de cinéma *m*

MPM = Maximum Permitted Mileage
MST = Mountain Standard Time
muesli müesli *m*, musli *m*
multi-carrier journey voyage effectué sur plusieurs compagnies aériennes *m*
multi-centre holiday vacances en circuit *fpl*
multinational multinationale *f*
multi-ownership multipropriété *f*
multiple société à succursales multiples *f*
multiplier concept concept multiplicateur *m*
multi-sector journey voyage multi-secteur *m*
multi-sector ticketing délivrance de billets multi-secteurs *f*
Murphy bed lit escamotable *m*
museum musée *m*
mushroom champignon *m*
music festival festival de musique *m*
Muslim musulman
mussels moules *fpl*
mutton mouton *m*

N

NA (= routing via North Atlantic) itinéraire qui passe par l'Atlantique-Nord *m*

NAITA = National Association of Independent Travel Agents

napkin serviette *f*

napkin ring rond de serviette *m*

narrow bodied aircraft avion petit porteur *m*

National Association of Independent Travel Agents association nationale des agents de voyages indépendants britanniques *f*

national holiday survey étude nationale sur le tourisme de loisirs *f*

national nature reserve réserve naturelle nationale *f*

national park parc national *m*, parc naturel national *m*

national scenic area zone protégée pour la beauté de son paysage *f*

national tourism tourisme national *m*

National Tourism Office Office national du tourisme *m*

National Tourism Organization Office national du tourisme *m*

national tourism survey étude nationale sur le tourisme *f*

National Tourist Office Office national du tourisme *m*

national travel survey étude nationale sur les voyages *f*

National Trust organisme britannique qui gère les sites et les monuments historiques *m*

national vacation survey *Am* étude nationale sur les vacances *f*

nationality nationalité *f*

natural attraction attraction naturelle *f*

natural heritage patrimoine naturel *m*

nature reserve parc naturel *m*, réserve *f*, réserve naturelle *f*

nature trail sentier aménagé dans la nature *m*

naturism naturisme *m*, nudisme *m*

nautical mile [*1.852 km*] mille nautique *m*

net curtain voilage *m*, rideaux *mpl*

net holiday propensity tendance touristique nette *f*

net rate prix net *m*

net tonnage [*of ship*] tonnage net *m*

net vacation propensity *Am* tendance touristique nette *f*

network réseau *m*

network access costs coûts d'accès au réseau *mpl*

Network Railcard carte de réduction de train valable uniquement sur le réseau Sud-Est de l'Angleterre

Neutral Unit of Construction
[*used to calculate air fare*] base
de calcul des tarifs aériens
établie par l'IATA *f*
New World Nouveau Monde *m*
newspaper journal *m*
newspaper stand kiosque à
journaux *m*
newsstand kiosque à journaux *m*
niche marketing marketing
ciblé *m*
night nuit *f*
night auditor caissier de nuit *m*
night auditor's report balance du
caissier de nuit *f*
night clerk réceptionniste de
nuit *mf*
nightclub boîte *f*, night-club *m*
nightlife vie nocturne *f*
night manager directeur de nuit *m*
night porter concierge de nuit *m*
night porter's report book
registre du concierge de nuit *m*
night report rapport de l'activité
du jour (établi par le directeur de
nuit) *m*
night shift équipe de nuit *f*
night watchman veilleur de
nuit *m*
**NIHCA = Northern Ireland
Hotels and Caterers'
Association**
**NITB = Northern Ireland Tourist
Board**
no-cancellation policy police de
non-annulation *f*
non-alcoholic non alcoolisé
non-alien non-étranger *m*,
autochtone *m*
non-refundable non-remboursable
non-scheduled stop étape non-
prévue *f*

non-stop flight vol direct *m*
Nordic countries pays
nordiques *mpl*
no-reservations system système
de non-réservation *m*
normal air fare tarif plein
aérien *m*
**Northern Ireland Hotels and
Caterers' Association**
association des hôteliers et des
restaurateurs de l'Irlande du
Nord *f*
Northern Ireland Tourist Board
≈ comité régional du tourisme
d'Irlande du Nord *m*
no-show no-show *m*,
désistement *m*, défection *f*
no-smoking non-fumeurs
no-smoking area zone non-
fumeurs *f*
no-smoking carriage voiture non-
fumeurs *f*
no-smoking compartment
compartiment non-fumeurs *m*
no-smoking seat place non-
fumeur *f*
note pad bloc-notes *m*
nothing to declare rien à déclarer
nouvelle cuisine nouvelle cuisine *f*
no vacancies [*sign*] complet
**NP (= routing via North/Central
Pacific)** itinéraire qui passe par
le nord/centre du Pacifique *m*
NTO = National Tourist Office
**NTO = National Tourism
Organization**
**NUC = Neutral Unit of
Construction**
number numéro *m*; *0800
telephone number* numéro
vert *m*

O

OAG = Official Airline Guide
occupancy occupation *m*
occupancy forecast prévision du taux d'occupation *f*
occupancy levels niveaux d'occupation *mpl*
occupancy rate taux d'occupation *m*
occupation profession *f*
occupied occupé
ocean liner paquebot de haute mer *m*
octopus poulpe *m*
OECD (= Organization for Economic Cooperation and Development) OCDE *f*
off [*room*] hors d'usage; *the chicken is off today* il n'y a pas de poulet aujourd'hui
offal abats *mpl*
office bureau *m*
office automation bureautique *f*
official officiel
Official Airline Guide guide officiel des compagnies aériennes *m*
Official Hotel and Resort Guide guide officiel des stations touristiques et des hôtels *m*
off-licence [*shop*] magasin de vins et spiritueux *m*
off-line area [*where carrier has no right to operate*] zone interdite *f*
off-line connection [*changing*

plane with different airline] correspondance avec changement de compagnie aérienne *f*
off-peak creuse, en dehors des heures de pointe
off season saison creuse *f*
off-season *adj* hors-saison
OHRG = Official Hotel and Resort Guide
oil huile *f*
OK OK
Old World Ancien Monde *m*
olive olive *f*
omnibus survey étude de marché standard *f*
one-star hotel hôtel une étoile *m*
one-way ticket aller simple *m*, billet aller (simple) *m*
onion oignon *m*
on-line area [*area where carrier has right to operate*] zone autorisée *f*
on-line connection [*changing plane with same airline*] correspondance avec un avion d'une même compagnie *f*
onward connection correspondance *f*
onward flight continuation en vol *f*
onward journey: we wish you a pleasant onward journey bonne continuation de voyage
open-air à ciel ouvert, de plein air

open air pool piscine de plein air *f*

open-date ticket billet open *m*, billet ouvert *m*

open-jaw trip voyage à retour ouvert *m*

open rate [*for routes for which fares have not been agreed*] tarif libre *m*

open ticket billet open *m*

opening ceremony cérémonie d'ouverture *f*

opening hours heures d'ouverture *fpl*

opera opéra *m*

operating profit bénéfice d'exploitation *f*

operating statement rapport d'exploitation *m*

operational costs coûts d'exploitation *mpl*, frais d'exploitation *mpl*

operational lease [*of aircraft*] location d'avion de courte durée *f*

operations manager directeur des exploitations *m*, directeur d'exploitation *m*

operator [*tour operator*] tour opérateur *m*, voyagiste *m*; [*telephone*] opérateur *m*, opératrice *f*; [*hotel etc*] standardiste *mf*

optimal route itinéraire optimal *m*

option option *f*; *to take an option* prendre une option

optional en option, optionnel

orange orange *f*

orange juice jus d'orange *m*

order: in order [*room*] à blanc; *out of order* hors service

to **order** commander

ordinary normal

organization organisation *f*

Organization for Economic Cooperation and Development Organisation de coopération et de développement économiques *f*

origin origine *f*

originating airline [*airline with whom journey has started*] compagnie aérienne de départ *f*

outbound tourism tourisme émetteur *m*

outdoor activity activité de plein air *f*

outside line ligne extérieure *f*

outstanding en souffrance

outward bound for/from en partance pour/de

outward journey voyage aller *m*

to **overbook** surbooker, faire de la sur-réservation

overbooked surbooké

overbooking surbook *m*, surbooking *m*, surlocation *f*

to **overcharge** faire payer trop cher

overcooked trop cuit

overhead projector rétroprojecteur *m*

overheads frais généraux *mpl*

overland par voie de terre

to **overlook** [*window*] donner sur

overnight [*travel*] de nuit

overnight stay séjour d'une nuit *m*, nuitée *f*

override commission extra *f*

overriding commission commission extra *f*

oversale *Am* surlocation *f*

overseas d'outre-mer

overtime heures supplémentaires *fpl*

OW (= One Way) AS *m*

owner propriétaire *m*

owner-managed [*hotel*] familial

oyster huître *f*

P

PA (= **routing via PAcific**)
itinéraire qui passe par le
Pacifique *m*
PA assistant *m*; assistante *f*
Pacific Standard Time heure
normale du Pacifique *f*
to **pack** faire ses bagages
package forfait *m*
package deal forfait *m*
package holiday séjour à forfait
m; [*tour*] voyage organisé *m*
package tour voyage à forfait *m*,
voyage organisé *m*
package tourism tourisme
organisé *m*
packed lunch panier-repas *m*
packed meal panier-repas *m*
page groom *m*
to **page** [*call out name of*] appeler;
to have sb paged faire appeler qn
page boy groom *m*
paging system système d'appel
d'un client (qui se trouve dans
l'hôtel mais pas dans sa
chambre)
PAI = **Personal Accident
Insurance**
paid holidays congés payés *mpl*
paidout form bon de
décaissement *m*
paidout voucher bon de débours *m*
palace palais *m*
pancake house crêperie *f*
parallel of latitude parallèle de

latitude *m*
parcel paquet *m*
park jardin public *m*, parc *m*
parking attendant gardien de
parking *m*
parking lot *Am* parking *m*
parlor car *Am* voiture-salon *f*
PARS PARS *m*
part charter charter partiel *m*
part-time à temps partiel
part-time contract contrat à
temps partiel *m*
partnership association *f*
party [*of guests*] groupe *m*
passage passage *m*
passenger passager *m*
passenger aircraft avion de
ligne *m*
passenger kilometre kilomètre-
passager *m*
passenger load factor taux
d'occupation des places *m*
passenger seat occupancy taux
d'occupation des places (d'un
moyen de transport) *m*
Passenger Shipping Association
association de compagnies
maritimes de tourisme *f*
passenger transport transport de
passagers *m*
Passenger Transport Authority
régie de transports en commun
(municipale) *f*
passkey clé passe-partout *f*

passport passeport *m*

passport control contrôle des passeports *m*

passport number numéro de passeport *m*

passport-sized photograph photo d'identité *f*

pasta pâtes *fpl*

pastry chef chef pâtissier *m*

pastry cook pâtissier *m*, cuisinier-pâtissier *m*

PA system système de haut-parleurs *m*

pâté pâté *m*

to **pay** payer; *to pay a bill* régler une note

paying guest [*in boarding house*] pensionnaire *m*

paying-in encaissement *m*

payment card carte de paiement *f*

PDQ (= Processes Data Quickly) machine terminal électronique de paiement *m*, TEP *m*

peak period période de pointe *f*

peak summer period haute saison estivale *f*

peak time heure de pointe *f*

peas petits pois *mpl*

pedal boat pédalo *m*

pedalo pédalo *m*

peg board panneau alvéolé *m*

pension pension *f*; *en pension* en pension

penthouse suite suite de luxe au dernier étage *f*

pepper poivre *m*; [*capsicum*] poivron *m*

per par

percent: 15 percent 15 pour cent

percentage sleeper occupancy pourcentage de lits occupés *m*

perfume parfum *m*

permanent contract contrat à durée indéterminée *m*, CDI *m*

permanent site [*caravan site*] terrain de caravaning permanent *m*

personal accident insurance assurance pour les personnes transportées *f*

personal assistant assistant *m*; assistante *f*

personal cheque chèque *m*

personal property insurance assurance sur les objets personnels *f*

personnel personnel *m*

personnel director directeur du personnel *m*

personnel manager directeur du personnel *m*

pest control désinsectisation *f*; dératisation *f*

pet animal domestique *m*; *no pets* les animaux domestiques ne sont pas admis

petits fours petits fours *mpl*

petty cash petite caisse *f*

petty cash voucher bon de (petite) caisse *m*

PEX = Public Excursion Fare

pheasant faisan *m*

phone billing and management system système de gestion et de facturation du téléphone *m*

phonecard télécarte *f*, carte de téléphone *f*

photocopier photocopieuse *f*

to **photocopy** photocopier

phrase book guide de conversation *m*

physical planning aménagement du territoire *m*

physically handicapped handicapé physique

picnic area *or* **site** aire de

pique-nique *f*
pictogram pictogramme *m*
piece system [*to charge for excess baggage*] tarification d'excédent de bagages *f*
pied-à-terre pied-à-terre *m*
pigeon pigeon *m*
pigeonhole case *f*
pilgrim pèlerin *m*
pilgrimage pèlerinage *m*
pillow oreiller *m*
pillowcase, pillowslip taie d'oreiller *f*
pineapple ananas *m*
PIR = Property Irregularity Report
pitch [*between seats*] espacement *m*
to **pitch a tent** planter une tente
pizza parlor pizzeria *f*
pizzeria pizzeria *f*
place-name [*card*] carte marque-place *f*
place setting couvert *m*
plaice carrelet *m*
plan [*map*] plan *m*
plane avion *m*
plane ticket billet d'avion *m*
planned preventative maintenance entretien de prévention prévu *m*
planning planification *f*
plant plante *f*
plastic key clé en plastique *f*
plate assiette *f*
plate service service à l'assiette *m*
play area aire de jeux *f*
pleasure boat bateau d'excursion *m*, bateau de plaisance *m*
pleasure cruising navigation de plaisance *f*
PO (= routing via POlar route)

itinéraire qui passe par le pôle *m*
to **poach** pocher
poached egg œuf poché *m*
podium podium *m*
POE = Port Of Embarkation
POE = Port Of Entry
point of arrival point d'arrivée *m*
point of departure point de départ *m*
point of sale point de vente *m*
point-to-point traffic trafic d'un point à un autre *m*
police police *f*
pollution pollution *f*
pony-trekking randonnée à dos de poney *f*
pool room salle de billard *f*
pooling [*sharing revenue of particular route*] partage du revenu entre compagnies aériennes sur certains trajets *m*
popular tourism tourisme de masse *m*
pork porc *m*
pork butchery/delicatessen charcuterie *f*
port port *m*; [*drink*] porto *m*
port of call port d'escale *m*
port of embarkation port d'embarquement *m*
port of entry port d'arrivée *m*
portable computer ordinateur portable *m*
porter [*carries bags*] [*at airport, station*] porteur *m*; [*at hotel*] chasseur-bagagiste *m*; [*doorman*] portier *m*
porter's desk comptoir du concierge *m*
POS (= Point Of Sale) PDV *m*
post courrier *m*
postbox boîte aux lettres *f*
postcard carte postale *f*

post house relais *m*

post office bureau de poste *m*

post office cheque chèque postal *m*

poste restante poste restante *f*

potato pomme de terre *f*

to **pour** verser

powder room toilettes (pour dames) *fpl*

PPM = Planned Preventative Maintenance

PR = Public Relations

prawn crevette *f*

prawn cocktail cocktail de crevettes *m*

to **pre-board** pré-embarquer

pre-boarding pré-embarquement *m*

pre-check-in pré-inscription *f*

preferential rate tarif spécial *m*

preferential treatment traitement de faveur *m*

premium [*insurance*] prime *f*

premium cabin [*aircraft*] première classe *f*

pre-paid payé à l'avance, payé d'avance

pre-paid ticket advice avis de billet payé d'avance *m*

preparation préparation *f*

to **prepare** préparer

pre-payment pré-paiement *m*

pre-registration pré-enregistrement *m*

presentation présentation *f*

preserves conserves *fpl*

president [*Am, of company*] Président-directeur général *m*

price prix *m*

price competition concurrence des prix *f*

price discrimination discrimination par les prix *f*

price elasticity élasticité des prix *f*

price fixing [*of air fares*] établissement des prix *m*

pricing établissement des prix *m*, prisée *f*

primary departments [*rooms, food etc*] services principaux *mpl*

primary tourist enterprise entreprise touristique primaire *f*

printer imprimante *f*

printout impression *f*

principal [*in transaction*] comettant *m*

priority booking réservation prioritaire *f*

private privé, privatif; [*bathroom*] particulier

private airline compagnie aérienne privée *f*

private bathroom salle de bain particulière *f*

private beach plage privée *f*

private carrier transporteur privé *m*

private facilities sanitaires privatifs *mpl*

private function réception privée *f*

private parking parking privé (réservé à la clientèle) *m*

private transport transport individuel *m*

privately-owned [*hotel etc*] familial *m*

privatization privatisation *f*

PR manager directeur des relations publiques *m*

professional hospitality industrie de l'hôtellerie *f*

professional qualification in hotelkeeping brevet de technicien hôtelier *m*

professional qualification in

tourism and leisure brevet de technicien supérieur de tourisme-loisirs *m*
profile characteristics [*of tourists*] caractéristiques *fpl*
profit bénéfice *m*
profit margin marge bénéficiaire *f*
profiterole profiterole *f*
projection room salle de projection *f*
projection screen écran de projection *m*
to **promote** promouvoir
promotion [*advertising*] promotion *f*
promotional air fare tarif aérien promotionnel *m*
promotional fare tarif promotionnel *m*
promotional offer offre promotionnelle *f*
proof of identity pièce d'identité *f*
prop jet avion à hélices *m*
property irregularity report formulaire rempli à l'aéroport en cas de perte de bagages *m*
prospectus prospectus *m*
provisioned charter [*fuel and provisions*] location de bateau avec carburant et provisions *f*
PSA = Passenger Shipping Association
PSA Bonding Scheme accréditation de l'association de compagnies maritimes de tourisme *f*
PST = Pacific Standard Time
PTA = Prepaid Ticket Advice
pub pub *m*
pub food *or* **grub** plats servis dans les pubs *mpl*
public address system système de haut-parleurs *m*

public areas locaux communs *mpl*
public bar partie moins chic d'un pub où les boissons sont moins chères *f*
public beach plage publique *f*
public entrance entrée principale *f*
public excursion fare tarif excursion *m*
public gardens jardin public *m*, square *m*
public holiday jour férié *m*
public house pub *m*
public liability insurance assurance responsabilité civile *f*
public relations relations publiques *fpl*
public relations director directeur des relations publiques *m*
public relations manager directeur des relations publiques *m*
public room salle de réception *f*
public sales office [*of an airline etc*] agence commerciale *f*
public service transport transports publics *mpl*
public service vehicle véhicule de transport en commun *m*
public telephone téléphone public *m*
public transport transports en commun *mpl*
pudding dessert *m*
Pullman Pullman *m*
purchase achat *m*
to **purchase** acheter
purchase order bon de commande *m*
purchaser acheteur *m*
purchasing department service des achats *m*
purser [*on ship*] commissaire de bord *m*

Q

quail caille *f*
qualification diplôme *m*
qualified staff personnel
  qualifié *m*
quarantine quarantaine *f*
queen-size bed grand lit double *m*

query demande *f*
questionnaire questionnaire *m*
quiet tranquille
quilt couette *f*
to **quote a price** faire un devis

R

rabbit lapin *m*
rabies rage *f*
RAC = Royal Automobile Club
rack casier *m*
rack rate plein tarif *m*
rack slip fiche de réservation *f*
radio radio *f*
radish radis *m*
rafting rafting *m*
RAGB = Restaurateurs'
  Association of Great Britain
rail: by rail en train
railcard carte de train *f*
rail-drive train + auto *m*

rail network réseau ferroviaire *m*
rail pass carte de train *f*
rail service service ferroviaire *m*
rail transport transport
  ferroviaire *m*
rail travel voyages en train *mpl*
rainbow trout truite arc-en-ciel *f*
rainfall précipitations *fpl*
ramble randonnée *f*
rambler randonneur *m*
rambling randonnée *f*
range [*of prices etc*] gamme *f*
rank [*for taxis*] station de taxis *f*
rapid transit link [*for connecting*

flights] liaison de transit rapide *f*

rare [*meat*] saignant; **very rare** bleu

raspberry framboise *f*

rate prix *m*

rate-of-return pricing fixation de prix rentables *f*

rate spread gamme de prix *f*

raw cru

R&B =Room and Board

reading light [*on train,plane*] liseuse *f*

reading room salle de lecture *f*

receiving agent agent de réceptif *m*

reception réception *f*, accueil *m*

reception area réception *f*

reception board tableau (de l'état) des chambres *m*

reception clerk receptionniste *mf*

reception desk comptoir de réception *m*

reception manager chef de réception *m*

receptionist réceptionniste *mf*

recession récession *f*

to **reclaim** [*baggage*] retirer

to **reclaim VAT** récupérer la TVA

to **recommend** recommander

reconfirmation reconfirmation *f*

record [*in database*] enregistrement *m*

recreation détente *f*

recreation centre centre de loisirs *m*

recreation facilities installations de loisirs *fpl*

recreational vehicle *Am* camping-car *m*

recruitment recrutement *m*

red rouge

red carpet treatment: to give sb the red carpet treatment dérouler le tapis rouge pour qn

red channel file pour les passagers qui ont des objets à déclarer à la douane *f*

to **redecorate** retapisser et repeindre

to **reduce** [*sauce etc*] faire réduire

reduced rate tarif réduit *m*

reduction [*in fare etc*] réduction *f*

referral recommandation *f*

referral system système de réservations recommandées inter-hôteliers *m*

refreshments rafraîchissements *mpl*

refrigerated self-service cabinet armoire réfrigérée de self-service *f*

refund remboursement *m*

to **refund** rembourser

refundable remboursable

refurbishment rénovation *f*

regatta régate *f*

region région *f*

regional régional

regional airport aéroport régional *m*

regional development développement régional *m*

regional manager directeur régional *m*

regional planning planification du développement économique et social d'une région *f*

Regional Tourism Council conseil régional du tourisme *m*

Regional Tourist Association association de promotion du tourisme régional *f*

Regional Tourist Board ≈ comité régional du Tourisme *m*

register registre *m*

to **register** s'inscrire

registered but not assigned client

137

inscrit mais chambre non affectée *m*

registering enregistrement *m*

registration card [*for foreign guests*] fiche voyageur *f*; [*for non-EC guests*] fiche de police *f*

registration desk bureau d'inscriptions *m*

registration form bulletin d'inscription *m*; [*in hotel*] fiche d'accueil *f*, fiche d'arrivée *f*, fiche d'inscription *f*

regular habitué *m*

regular bodied aircraft avion moyen porteur *m*

regular client client régulier *m*

to **reimburse** rembourser

to **release back** [*rooms*] rétrocéder

releasing back rétrocession *f*

relief staff [*cover staff*] personnel extra *m*

religious service service religieux *m*, office religieux *m*

religious tourism tourisme religieux *m*

to **rent** louer

rental car voiture de location *f*

rental firm société de location *f*

rented accommodation logement en location *m*, location *f*

renting location *f*

repair réparation *f*

repair order ordre de réparation *m*

reply-paid reservation postcard carte postale de réservation avec port payé *f*

report rapport *m*

representative représentant *m*

request: on request sur demande

to **re-register** se réinscrire

re-routing déroutement *m*

reservation réservation *f*, résa *f*; *to* ***make a reservation*** réserver,

effectuer une réservation; *the* ***party making a reservation*** le réservataire

reservation agent agent de réservation *m*

reservation card kardex *f*, fiche de réservation *f*

reservation centre [*for car hire*] centre de réservation *m*

reservation chart tableau des réservations *m*

reservation department service réservation *m*

reservation file fichier des réservations *m*

reservation form fiche de réservation *f*, formulaire de réservation *m*

reservation list liste des réservations *f*

reservation rack tableau (de l'état) des réservations *m*

reservation rack card fiche pour le tableau des réservations *f*, fiche de blocage *f*

reservation record enregistrement des réservations *m*

reservation sheet feuille de réservation *f*, bordereau de réservations *m*

reservation ticket coupon de réservation *m*

reservations book agenda de réservation *m*, livre de réservation *m*

reservations bureau bureau des réservations *m*

reservations chart liste des réservations *f*

reservations clerk employé aux réservations *m*

reservations console console de réservation *f*

reservations department service des réservations *m*

reservations manager directeur des réservations *m*

reservations system système de réservation *m*

reserve réserve *f*

to **reserve** réserver

reserved réservé

residence tax *Am* taxe de séjour *f*

resident résident *m*

resident manager directeur qui habite sur place *m*

residential seminar séminaire résidentiel *m*

residents' average daily spend dépense moyenne journalière par client *f*

resort station *f*

resort hotel hôtel saisonnier *m*, hôtel touristique *m*

resort representative correspondant local *m*

resort tax [*hotel tax*] taxe sur l'hôtellerie *f*

resource-based [*attraction*] faisant usage de ressources naturelles ou monument déjà sur place

response rate taux de réponse *m*

responsible tourism [*green tourism*] tourisme vert *m*

rest room salle de repos *f*; *Am* toilettes *fpl*

restaurant restaurant *m*

restaurant car wagon-restaurant *m*

restaurant chain chaîne de restaurants *f*

restaurant manager responsable de la restauration *m*, directeur de restaurant *m*

restaurant owner restaurateur *m*

restaurateur restaurateur *m*

Restaurateurs' Association of Great Britain association des restaurateurs de Grande-Bretagne *f*

restrictions restrictions *fpl*

Retail Export Scheme système de détaxe à l'exportation *m*

retail trade commerce de détail *m*

retail travel agency agence de voyages distributrice *f*

retail travel agent agent de voyages détaillant *m*

return air fare tarif aérien aller-retour *m*

return journey retour *m*, voyage retour *m*

return ticket aller-retour *m*, billet aller-retour *m*

revalidation sticker [*if ticket is changed*] autocollant de revalidation *m*

revenue load factor revenu de coefficient de remplissage *m*

revenue passenger mile revenu passager-kilomètre *m*

rib steak entrecôte *f*

rice riz *m*

river rivière *f*

river-cruise croisière fluviale *f*

RNA = Registered but Not Assigned

road service licence autorisation de service routier *f*

roadside assistance assistance technique aux véhicules *f*

roast rôti *m*

roast beef rôti de bœuf *m*

roasting rôtissage *m*

roasting chef rôtisseur *m*

rock-climbing varappe *f*, escalade *f*

rock lobster langouste *f*

roll petit pain *m*

roll-on roll-off ferry ferry roulier *m*

room chambre *f*, unité chambre *f*; [*not bedroom*] pièce *f*

room and board pension complète *f*

room attendant femme de chambre *f*

room audit [*for phonecalls*] facture de téléphone détaillée par chambre *f*

room availability chart planning de disponibilité des chambres *m*

room availability report rapport de disponibilité des chambres *m*

room card fiche de la chambre *f*

room change délogement *m*

room clerk réceptionniste *mf*

room index card fiche de la chambre *f*

room information sheet note d'informations générales (que l'on trouve dans les chambres)

room key clé de la chambre *f*; *your room key* la clé de votre chambre

room letting sheet planning d'occupation des chambres *m*

room linen inventory inventaire du linge des chambres *m*

room management system système de gestion des chambres *m*

room night nuitée *f*

room number numéro de chambre *m*

room occupancy occupation des chambres *f*, taux d'occupation *m*

room occupancy chart liste d'occupation des chambres *f*

room rack room-rack *m*, tableau (de l'état) des chambres *m*

room rack card fiche client *f*, fiche d'occupation *f*

room rack slip fiche client *f*

room rate [*for one room*] prix de la chambre *m*; [*for all rooms*] tarif des chambres *m*

room record card fiche de chambre *f*

room sale vente de chambre *f*

room service room-service *m*, service aux chambres *m*, service en chambre *m*, restauration d'étages *f*

room service manager responsable du service à l'étage *m*

room servicing entretien des chambres *m*

room status [*of one room*] état et disponibilité d'une chambre *m*; [*of all rooms*] état des chambres *m*

room status indicator indicateur de l'état des chambres *m*

room tax [*hotel tax*] impôt sur l'hôtellerie *m*

room temperature: at room temperature chambré

rooms division manager directeur de l'hébergement *m*

rosé vin rosé *m*

to **roster** planifier

rota tableau de service *m*

round-the-world ticket billet de tour du monde *m*

round trip voyage aller-retour *m*

round-trip flight vol aller-retour *m*

round-trip passenger passager aller-retour *m*

round-trip ticket aller-retour *m*

route parcours *m*, itinéraire *m*

routing parcours *m*, itinéraire *m*

Royal Automobile Club ≈ Touring Club de France *m*

royal suite suite royale *f*

RPM = Revenue Passenger Mile

RT (= Return Ticket) AR *m*
RTA = Regional Tourist Association
RTB (= Regional Tourist Board) ≈ CRT *m*
RTC = Regional Tourism Council
rte = route
RTW = Round The World

rucksack sac à dos *m*
ruins ruines *fpl*
rum rhum *m*
rump steak [*of beef*] culotte *f*, rumsteak *m*
rural tourism tourisme rural *m*
Russian service [*from silver salver onto plate*] service à la russe *m*
RV = Recreational Vehicle

S

SA (routing via South Atlantic) itinéraire qui passe par l'Atlantique Sud *m*
Sabre [*US airline reservation system*] Sabre *m*
saddle [*of lamb, mutton*] selle à l'anglaise *f*
saddle of lamb selle d'agneau *f*
safari safari *m*
safari holiday safari *m*
safari park réserve d'animaux sauvages *f*
safe coffre *m*, coffre-fort *m*
safe deposit receipt bulletin de dépôt au coffre *m*
safe deposit receipt book registre de dépôt au coffre-fort *m*
safety sécurité *f*
safety deposit box coffre(-fort) *m*
safety drill exercice

d'évacuation *m*
to **sail** [*leave*] partir
sailing [*departure*] départ *m*; [*sport*] voile *f*
sailing schedule horaires de départ *mpl*
salad salade *f*
salad bar buffet de salades *m*
salad dressing sauce salade *f*
sale vente *f*
sales [*turnover*] chiffre d'affaires *m*
sales and marketing director directeur des ventes et du marketing *m*
sales consultant conseiller commercial *m*
sales department service des ventes *m*
sales director directeur commercial *m*

sales incentive holiday voyage d'encouragement pour les bons vendeurs *m*

sales manager chef des ventes *m*, directeur commercial *m*

sales outlet point de vente *m*

sales policy politique de vente *f*

sales promotion promotion des ventes *f*

salmon saumon *m*

sample survey enquête par sondage *f*

sampling échantillonnage *m*

sand sable *m*

sandwich sandwich *m*

sanitary disposal bag sachet pour garniture périodique *m*

sanitized label [*on toilet*] bandelette de propreté pour WC *f*

satellite television télévision par satellite *f*

sauce sauce *f*

sauce chef *or* **cook** saucier *m*, responsable des sauces *m*

sauerkraut choucroute *f*

sauna sauna *m*

sausage [*cooked*] saucisse *f*; [*cured*] saucisson (sec) *m*

to **sauté** sauter

sautéed sauté

scenery paysage *m*

scenic panoramique

scenic route itinéraire panoramique *m*

schedule [*for trains etc*] horaires *mpl*, indicateur horaire *m*

scheduled [*activities, excursions*] prévu au programme

scheduled ancient monument monument historique classé *m*

scheduled flight vol régulier *m*

school party groupe scolaire *m*

school trip voyage scolaire *m*

Scottish Tourist Board ≈ comité du tourisme écossais *m*

Scottish Tourist Guides Association association des guides touristiques écossais *f*

scrag [*of veal*] collet *m*

scrambled egg(s) œufs brouillés *mpl*

screen écran *m*

scuba diving plongée sous-marine *f*

sea mer *f*

sea crossing traversée *f*

sea cruising area zone de croisière *f*

seafish poisson de mer *m*

seafood fruits de mer *mpl*

seafood restaurant restaurant de poissons *m*

seaplane hydravion *m*

seaport port maritime *m*

seaside bord de mer *m*; *at the seaside* au bord de la mer

seaside resort station balnéaire *f*

seaside tourism tourisme balnéaire *m*

sea travel voyages en mer *mpl*

sea view vue sur mer *f*

seawater therapy thalassothérapie *f*

to **search** [*baggage*] fouiller; [*computer*] *to do a search for sth* rechercher qch

season saison *f*

to **season** assaisonner

season ticket abonnement saisonnier *m*

seasonal saisonnier, de saison

seasonal adjustment ajustement saisonnier *m*

seasonal employment emploi saisonnier *m*

seasonal fluctuation fluctuation saisonnière *f*

seasonal tariff tarif saisonnier *m*

seat siège *m*; [*in plane, train etc*] place (assise) *f*

to **seat** [*customers in restaurant*] installer; *the hall seats 230* la salle peut contenir 230 personnes

seat belt ceinture de sécurité *f*

seat number numéro de place (assise) *m*

seat pitch espacement des sièges *m*

seat reservation réservation des places *f*; *to make a seat reservation* réserver une place

seating capacity capacité d'accueil *f*

seating plan affectation des places *f*

second class seconde classe *f*, seconde *f*; *to travel second class* voyager en seconde

second class ticket billet de seconde *m*

second holiday: to take a second holiday reprendre des vacances

second home résidence secondaire *f*

secondary departments [*laundry, casino etc in hotel*] départements de services secondaires *mpl*

secondary tourist enterprise entreprise touristique secondaire *f*

secretarial service service de secrétariat *m*

secretarial staff personnel de secrétariat *m*

secretary secrétaire *mf*

security sécurité *f*

security alert alerte au danger *f*

security officer agent de sécurité *m*

security register registre de sécurité *m*

security risk risque pour la sécurité *m*

self-catering location de vacances *f*; *to go self-catering* partir en location; *to prefer self-catering* préférer les vacances en location

self-catering accommodation meublé de tourisme *m*

self-catering apartment appartement en location *m*

self-catering holiday *m* vacances en location *fpl*; *to be on a self-catering holiday* être en location

self-drive sans chauffeur

self-service restaurant self(-service) *m*, restaurant libre-service *m*

selling price prix de vente *m*

seminar séminaire *m*, colloque *m*

senior citizen personne âgée *f*, personne du troisième âge *f*

Senior (Citizen's) Railcard carte de réduction dans les trains pour le troisième âge *f*, ≈ carte Vermeil *f*

senior management direction générale *f*

senior sous chef second de cuisine *m*

to **serve** servir; [*airport*] desservir

server serveur *m*; serveuse *f*

service service *m*; *service included* service compris

to **service a room** faire une chambre

service accommodation hébergement avec restauration *m*

service areas locaux de service *mpl*

service bell sonnette (pour appeler un employé de l'hôtel) *f*

service (charge) service *m*

service department département du service *m*

service industry industrie des services *f*

service lift monte-charge *m*, ascenseur de service *m*

service provider prestataire de services *m*

service sector secteur tertiaire *m*

serviced [*apartment etc*] avec service d'entretien

serviced accommodation [*apartment*] résidence hôtelière *f*

serviced accommodation business para-hôtellerie *f*

serviced apartment appartement dans une résidence hôtelière *m*

services prestations *fpl*, services *mpl*

serving dish plat *m*, assiette de service *f*

serving hatch passe-plat *m*

session session *f*

set menu menu à prix fixe *m*

to **set the table** dresser la table, mettre le couvert, mettre la table

setting of rates tarification *f*

to **settle an account** régler un compte

sewing kit nécessaire de couture *m*

sex sexe *m*

shampoo shampo(o)ing *m*

shandy panaché *m*

to **share** [*room etc*] partager

shareholder actionnaire *mf*

shaver socket prise pour rasoir électrique *f*

sheet drap *m*

shellfish crustacés *mpl*

sherry xérès *m*

shift work travail par roulement *m*

shin [*of beef*] gîte de devant *m*

ship bateau *m*

shipowner armateur *m*

shipping conference conférence maritime *f*

shipping line compagnie maritime *f*

shirt laundering service service de blanchisserie (pour les chemises) *m*

shoe-polishing machine machine à cirer les chaussures *f*

shooting chasse *f*

shop magasin *m*, boutique *f*

shopping shopping *m*

shopping arcade galerie marchande *f*

shopping centre centre commercial *m*

shopping mall *Am* centre commercial *m*

shore excursion excursion (lors d'une escale) *f*

short break mini-séjour *m*

short-haul [*flight, route*] court-courrier

short-staffed à court de personnel

short-stay accommodation hébergement de courte durée *m*

short-stay car park parking courte durée *m*

Short Take-off and Landing Airport STOLPORT *m*

shoulder épaule *f*

shoulder fare tarif moyenne saison *m*

shoulder period [*between high and low season*] moyenne saison *f*

shoulder rate tarif moyenne saison *m*

shoulder season moyenne

saison *f*
show spectacle *m*
to **show** [*person to table, room etc*]
  conduire
shower douche *f*
shower cap bonnet de douche *m*
shower gel gel douche *m*
shower room salle de douches *f*,
  salle d'eau *f*
shrimp crevette *f*
shutters volets *mpl*
shuttle navette *f*
to **shuttle between** faire la navette
  entre
shuttle service service de
  navette *m*
sights attractions (touristiques) *fpl*
sightseeing: to do some
  sightseeing faire du tourisme; *to*
  go sightseeing faire du tourisme
sightseeing tour visite guidée *f*
sign enseigne *f*; [*small, in hotel*
  etc] panonceau *m*; [*road sign*]
  panneau *m*
to **sign** signer; *to sign the register*
  signer le registre
sign-posted footpath sentier
  balisé *m*
sign-posting signalisation *f*
signature signature *f*
silver salver plateau en argent *m*
silver service waiter serveur pour
  service au guéridon *m*
silver service waitress serveuse
  pour service au guéridon *f*
silverside [*of beef*] gîte à la noix *m*
silverware argenterie *f*
to **simmer** laisser frémir, faire
  cuire à feu doux
single bed lit une place *m*
single fare tarif aller (simple) *m*
single occupancy occupation par
  une seule personne *f*

single room chambre
  individuelle *f*, chambre simple *f*
single room supplement
  supplément chambre
  individuelle *m*
single supplement supplément
  chambre individuelle *m*
single ticket aller simple *m*, billet
  aller *m*
sink évier *m*
sirloin aloyau *m*
site [*of building etc*]
  emplacement *m*
site attraction site d'intérêt
  touristique *m*
Sites of Special Scientific Interest
  sites d'un intérêt scientifique
  particulier *mpl*
sitting room salon *m*
sixth freedom liberté de
  cabotage *f*
skewer brochette *f*
to **ski** skier
ski club club de ski *m*
ski instructor moniteur de ski *m*
ski lift remonte-pente *m*, téléski *m*
ski pass forfait de ski *m*
ski resort station de sports
  d'hiver *f*
ski slope piste de ski *f*
ski tow remonte-pente *m*
skier skieur *m*; skieuse *f*
skiing ski *m*
skiing area domaine skiable *m*
skiing centre station de sports
  d'hiver *f*
to **skip** [*leave without paying*] filer
  à l'anglaise
skipper [*leaves without paying*
  bill] client qui part sans payer *m*
sleeper couchette *f*, voiture-lit *f*;
  [*train*] train couchette *m*
sleeper night nuitée *f*

sleeper occupancy taux de fréquentation *m*

sleeping car voiture-lit *f*, wagon-lit *m*

slice tranche *f*

slide projector projecteur de diapositives *m*

slip [*paper*] bon *m*

slot [*for take-off etc*] créneau *m*

to **slow cook** mijoter

smoke detector détecteur de fumée *m*

smoked fumé

smoked haddock haddock *m*

smoked salmon saumon fumé *m*

smoking [*seats etc*] fumeurs

smoking area zone fumeurs *f*

smoking carriage voiture fumeurs *f*

smoking compartment compartiment fumeurs *m*

smoking seat place fumeur *f*

snack collation *f*

snack-bar snack(-bar) *m*

snail escargot *m*

snow neige *f*

to **snow** neiger

soap savon *m*; [*guest size*] savonnette *f*

social director directeur de l'animation *m*

social officer [*on ship*] animateur *m*

social tourism tourisme social *m*

socio-economic factors facteurs socio-économiques *mpl*

socio-economic group groupe socio-économique *m*

sofa sofa *m*, canapé *m*

sofa bed canapé-lit *m*

soft currency devise faible *f*

soft drink boisson non-alcoolisée *f*, boisson sans alcool *f*

soft tourism [*green tourism*] tourisme vert *m*

solarium solarium *m*

sole [*fish*] sole *f*

sole agent agent exclusif *m*

sole proprietor propriétaire exclusif *m*

sommelier sommelier *m*

son et lumière spectacle son et lumière *m*, son et lumière *m*

soundproofing insonorisation *f*, isolation phonique *f*

soup potage *m*, soupe *f*

soup spoon cuillère à soupe *f*

soured cream crème fraîche *f*

sous chef second *m*, assistant du chef de cuisine *m*

souvenir souvenir *m*

souvenir shop boutique de souvenirs *f*

spa station thermale *f*

spa bath bain bouillonnant *m*

spa hotel hôtel médicalisé *m*

spa resort station hydrominérale *f*

spa town ville thermale *f*

spaghetti spaghettis *mpl*

spare rib [*pork*] côtelette *f*

sparkling [*wine*] mousseux

sparkling water eau gazeuse *f*

special diet régime spécial *m*

special indications [*on ticket*] indications spéciales *fpl*

special offer offre spéciale *f*

special rate tarif préférentiel *m*

speciality specialité *f*

speciality restaurant restaurant de spécialités *m*

to **spend the night** passer la nuit

spinach épinards *mpl*

spirits spiritueux *mpl*

spit [*for cooking*] broche *f*

split charter charter partagé entre plusieurs voyagistes *m*

spoke [*airport*] aéroport
d'apport *m*

spoon cuillère *f*

sporting event manifestation
sportive *f*

sports centre centre sportif *m*

sports club club de sport *m*

sports facilities installations
sportives *fpl*

sports instruction monitorat
sportif *m*

sports tourism tourisme sportif

spotlight projecteur *m*

spring [*water*] source *f*; [*season*]
printemps *m*

square pin socket prise mâle à
fiche carrée *f*

squash [*sport*] squash *m*

squid calamar *m*

**SSSI = Sites of Special Scientific
Interest**

Stabilizer accord d'exclusivité
entre l'ABTA et les voyagistes
(GB) *m*

stack [*of aircraft*] tour
d'attente *m*

stag party réunion entre hommes
organisée par le marié la veille
de son mariage *f*

stairs escalier *m*

stairwell cage d'escalier *f*

stall stand *m*

stamp timbre *m*; [*date stamp etc*]
tampon *m*, cachet *m*

stand stand *m*

standard class deuxième classe *f*

standby fare tarif standby *m*, tarif
de réservation sans garantie *m*

standby passenger passager avec
billet standby *m*

star rating classement par
étoiles *m*

starter hors-d'œuvre *m*

state code code État *m*

state-owned national(isé)

stateroom [*on ship*] cabine de
luxe *f*

stately home château *m*, grande
demeure *f*

statement relevé *m*, rapport *m*

statement of account relevé de
compte *m*, extrait de compte *m*

static site [*caravan site*] terrain de
caravaning permanent *m*

station waiter chef de rang *m*

stationery papier à lettres *m*

statistics statistiques *fpl*

statute mile mille *m*

stay séjour *m*

to **stay** séjourner

stay-over chambre en recouche *f*,
recouche *f*

stay requirement durée de séjour
nécessaire pour bénéficier de
certains tarifs *f*

staying visitor voyageur qui passe
au moins une nuit *m*

stays list liste des clients en
recouche *f*

STB = Scottish Tourist Board

steak bifteck *m*; [*of fish*] darne *f*;
thick slice of beef steak
pavé *m*

steakhouse grill *m*

steam bath bain de vapeur *m*

steam room chambre de
vapeur *f*

steamed à la vapeur, cuit à
l'étouffée

steaming cuisson à la vapeur *f*

sterling sterling *m*

steward steward *m*

stewardess hôtesse *f*

**STGA = Scottish Tourist Guides
Association**

still [*wine*] non mousseux

still mineral water eau plate *f*

stock book livre d'inventaire *m*

stock control contrôle des stocks *m*

stocking [*of supplies*] stockage *m*

STOLPORT (= Short Take-Off and Landing airPORT) STOLPORT *m*

stop-list [*for lost cheques*] liste de chèques volés ou perdus *f*

stopover escale *f*

storage rangement *m*

store réserve *f*

storekeeper responsable de l'approvisionnement *m*, manutentionnaire *m*

storeman manutentionnaire *m*

storey étage *m*

strawberry fraise *f*

to **strip** [*rooms*] vider; [*beds*] défaire

student étudiant *m*; étudiante *f*

student rate tarif étudiant *m*

studio studio *m*

studio bed canapé-lit *m*

study day journée d'étude *f*

study trip voyage d'études *m*

stuffed farci

stuffing farce *f*

subject to variation variable

subsidiary filiale *f*

subsidy subvention *f*

suburban agency [*travel agent*] agence de banlieue *f*

subway *Am* métro *m*

to **sue** poursuivre en justice

suitcase valise *f*

suite suite *f*

summer été *m*

summer break petites vacances d'été *fpl*

summer holidays vacances d'été *fpl*

summer hotel hôtel ouvert seulement l'été *m*

summer season saison d'été *f*, période estivale *f*

summer timetable horaires d'été *mpl*

summer tourism tourisme estival *m*

sun soleil *m*

sunshine ensoleillement *m*

sun terrace terrasse *f*

sundries articles divers *mpl*

supersonic transport aircraft avion supersonique *m*

supervisor supérieur *m*

supper souper *m*

supplement supplément *m*

supplementary tourist accommodation [*youth hostels, holiday centres etc*] hébergement touristique qui n'entre pas dans la catégorie "hôtellerie"

supplier fournisseur *m*

supplies approvisionnement *m*

surcharge supplément *m*

surety caution *f*

surface transport transport terrestre ou maritime *m*

survey enquête *f*

sustainable tourism tourisme vert *m*

sweet [*dessert*] entremets *m*

sweet doux

sweet corn maïs *m*

to **swim** nager

swimming natation *f*

swimming pool piscine *f*

switchboard operator standardiste *mf*

swordfish espadon *m*

synagogue synagogue *f*

System One System One *m*

T

tab [*Am, bill*] note *f*
table table *f*
table centre décor de table *m*
tablecloth nappe *f*
table d'hôte table d'hôte *f*
table d'hôte menu menu table
 d'hôte *m*
table linen linge de table *m*
table mat set de table *m*
table service service à table *m*
table tent [*cards on tables in
 restaurants*] carte de menu
 suggéré *f*
table wine vin de table *m*
tabular ledger grand livre *m*
tagliatelle tagliatelles *fpl*
tailor-made sur mesure
tailor-made itinerary itinéraire
 sur mesure *m*
to take away emporter
take-away restaurant restaurant
 de plats à emporter
take-off décollage *m*
to take off [*plane*] décoller
take-off slot créneau horaire de
 décollage *m*
take-off weight poids au
 décollage *m*
Tannoy haut-parleur *m*
Tannoy system système de haut-
 parleurs *m*
tap water eau du robinet *f*
tape recorder magnétophone *m*
target market marché-cible *m*

target marketing marketing
 ciblé *m*
tariff tarif *m*
tariff change notification form
 bulletin de changement de
 tarif *m*
tariff manual cahier des tarifs *m*
task sheet fiche de poste *f*
tax-free shop boutique hors taxes *f*
tax-free shopping shopping hors
 taxes *m*
Tax-Free Shopping Form
 formulaire de détaxe *m*
taxi taxi *m*
taxiplane avion-taxi *m*
taxi rank station de taxis *f*
tea thé *m*; [*meal*] goûter *m*; *tea
 with milk* thé au lait; *tea with
 lemon* thé citron
tea and coffee making facilities
 nécessaire pour préparer le thé et
 le café *m*
teapot théière *f*
tearoom salon de thé *m*
tea shop salon de thé *m*
teaspoon cuillère à thé *f*
technician technicien *m*
telegram télégramme *m*
telephone téléphone *m*
to telephone sb téléphoner à qn
telephone booking réservation par
 téléphone *f*
telephone booth *Am* cabine
 téléphonique *f*

telephone box cabine téléphonique *f*

telephone call appel (téléphonique) *m*

telephone call sheet relevé des appels téléphoniques *m*, relevé de communications téléphoniques *m*

telephone directory annuaire téléphonique *m*

telephone message message téléphonique *m*

telephone operator standardiste *mf*

telephone reservation réservation par téléphone *f*, réservation téléphonique *f*

telephone selling télévente *f*

telephone switchboard standard téléphonique *m*

telesales télévente *f*

television télévision *f*

television room salle de télévision *f*

telex télex *m*

telex operator télexiste *mf*

temperate tempéré

temperature température *f*

temple temple *m*

temporary contract contrat temporaire *m*

tender [*boat*] chaloupe *f*

tenderloin contre-filet *m*, faux-filet *m*

tennis tennis *m*

tennis court court de tennis *m*

tent tente *f*

terminal gare maritime *f*; [*in airport*] aérogare *f*; [*screen*] terminal *m*

terminal building aérogare *f*

to **terminate** se terminer

terminus hotel [*in railway*] hôtel de gare *m*

terrace terrasse *f*

tertiary sector secteur tertiaire *m*

tetanus tétanos *m*

TGC = Travel Group Charter

thalassotherapy thalassothérapie *f*

thalassotherapy centre centre de thalassothérapie *m*

thatched cottage maison au toit de chaume *f*

theatre théâtre *m*

theft vol *m*

theme evening soirée à thème *f*

theme park parc à thème *m*

theme restaurant restaurant à thème *m*

theme weekend week-end à thème *m*

thermal insulation isolation thermique *f*

thigh [*of chicken*] cuisse *f*

Third Age troisième âge *m*

three-course meal repas avec trois plats (entrée, plat de résistance, dessert) *m*

through carriage transport direct *m*

through fare tarif direct *m*

through passenger [*on same vehicle to final destination*] passager "direct" *m*

through train train direct *m*

throwaway [*item in IT not used*] élément non utilisé d'un forfait *m*

TIC = Tourist Information Centre

ticket billet *m*; [*train, underground*] titre de transport *m*; [*bus, underground, cloakroom*] ticket *m*

ticket desk guichet *m*

ticket machine billetterie

automatique *f*, distributeur automatique de billets *m*

ticket office guichet *m*, billetterie *f*

Ticketed Point Mileages [*total flown mileage*] total de kilomètres de vol *m*

ticketing billetterie *f*

ticketing code code de billetterie *m*

ticketing time limits date limite d'émission de billet *f*

tied house pub qui ne vend qu'une marque de bière *m*

TIM (= Travel Information Manual) TIM *m*

time charter affrètement total *m*

time difference décalage horaire *m*

time release [*for accommodation*] location après désistement *f*

time series analysis analyse statistique tenant compte des données déjà enregistrées et des variations annuelles

timeshare appartement en multipropriété *m*, time propriété *f*

Timeshare Council conseil de multipropriété *m*

timesharing multipropriété *f*

time sheet feuille de présence *f*

timetable horaires *mpl*, indicateur horaire *m*

time-zone fuseau horaire *m*

TIMG = Travel Industry Marketing Group

tip pourboire *m*

tkt (= ticket) billet *f*

to à

toast [*bread*] toast *m*

toast master animateur de réception *m*

tobacco tabac *m*

today's special plat du jour *m*

toilet toilettes *fpl*, cabinet de

toilettes *m*; [*actual bowl*] cuvette *f*

toilet block bloc sanitaire *m*

toilet tissue papier hygiénique *m*

toilet water eau de toilette *f*

toll péage *m*

toll-free number *Am* numéro vert *m*

tomato tomate *f*

tomato ketchup ketchup *m*

tonic schweppes® *m*, tonique *f*

tonnage tonnage *m*

tooth glass verre à dents *m*

toothpaste dentifrice *m*

TOSG = Tour Operators' Study Group

total staying visitor expenditure dépenses totales des touristes sur leur lieu de vacances *fpl*

tour circuit *m*, circuit touristique *m*

tour brochure brochure de voyages *f*, catalogue de voyages *m*

tour code number numéro de code de voyage *m*

tour conductor [*Am, courier*] accompagnateur *m*; accompagnatrice *f*

tour director [*Am, courier*] accompagnateur *m*; accompagnatrice *f*

tour escort accompagnateur de voyage *m*

tour group groupe (de touristes) *m*

tour guide guide *mf*

tour leader *or* **manager** *Am* accompagnateur *m*; accompagnatrice *f*

tour of inspection inspection *f*

tour operator tour opérateur *m*, voyagiste *m*

Tour Operators' Study Group groupe d'étude de voyagistes *m*

tour organizer organisateur de
voyages *m*

tour package forfait voyage *m*

tour ticket billet (de voyage) *m*

tour voucher bon de voyage *m*

tour wholesaler voyagiste
(grossiste) *m*

touring: to do some touring faire
un circuit

touring caravan caravane de
tourisme *f*

touring holiday circuit *m*

touring site [*caravan site*] terrain
de caravaning *m*

tourism tourisme *m*

tourism administration gestion
du tourisme *f*

tourism balance balance
touristique *f*

**Tourism Committee of the
Organisation for Economic
Cooperation and Development**
Comité du tourisme de
l'Organisation de coopération et
de développement
économiques *m*

tourism destination destination
touristique *f*

tourism development
développement du tourisme *m*

tourism flow mouvement
touristique *m*

tourism-generated employment
emploi généré par le tourisme *m*

tourism-generating country pays
d'outgoing *m*, pays émetteur de
tourisme *m*

tourism growth croissance du
tourisme *f*

Tourism Intergroup Intergroupe
Tourisme *m*

tourism multiplier multiplicateur
du tourisme *m*

tourism policy politique
touristique *f*, politique du
tourisme *f*

tourism-receiving country pays
d'incoming *m*

tourism-related employment
emploi lié au tourisme *m*

tourism-related industry
industrie liée au tourisme *f*

tourism sector secteur du
tourisme *m*

Tourism Society syndicat
professionnel des cadres de
l'industrie touristique *m*

tourist touriste *mf*

tourist *adj* touristique

tourist appeal attrait touristique *m*

tourist area zone touristique *f*

tourist arrival arrivée de
touristes *f*

tourist attraction attrait
touristique *m*, attraction
touristique *f*, site touristique *m*

tourist board comité du
tourisme *m*

tourist class classe touriste *f*

tourist class hotel hôtel classe
touriste *m*

tourist day journée-vacance *f*

tourist destination destination
touristique *f*

tourist enclave enclave
touristique *f*

tourist environment
environnement touristique *m*

tourist expenditure impact impact
des dépenses des touristes *m*

tourist facilities installations
touristiques *fpl*

tourist-generating [*country*]
émetteur de touristes

tourist guide [*book*] guide
touristique *m*; [*person*] guide

(touristique) *mf*
tourist industry industrie touristique *f*
tourist information centre syndicat d'initiative *m*, office du tourisme *m*
tourist literature littérature du tourisme *f*
tourist market marché touristique *m*
tourist night nuitée *f*
tourist office syndicat d'initiative *m*, office du tourisme *m*
tourist product produit touristique *m*
tourist profession profession touristique *f*
tourist qualities qualités touristiques *fpl*
tourist route itinéraire touristique *m*
tourist traffic trafic touristique *m*
tourist trail sentier touristique *m*
touristic touristique
touristy trop touristique
tournedos tournedos *m*
towel serviette (de toilette) *f*
town ville *f*
town hall hôtel de ville *m*
town hotel hôtel en ville *m*
town house hotel grande maison en ville aménagée en hôtel *f*
town twinning jumelage *m*
TPM = Ticketed Point Mileages
trade association association commerciale *f*
trade fair foire commerciale *f*, salon professionnel *m*
traffic conference area zone de trafic aérien *f*
traffic rights droits de trafic *mpl*
trail sentier *m*, chemin de

randonnée *m*
trailer *Am* caravane *f*; *Br* remorque *f*
train train *m*
train station gare *f*
trainee apprenti *m*
trainee chef de rang commis de rang *m*
training formation *f*
transatlantic carrier transporteur transatlantique *m*
transfer transfert *m*
to **transfer** [*call*] transférer
transfer bus navette de transfert *f*
transfer debit voucher bon de transfert débit *m*
transfer from main airport post-acheminement *m*
transfer passenger passager en correspondance *m*
transfer to main airport pré-acheminement *m*
transfer transport transport d'acheminement *m*
transient *Am* client de passage *m*
transient de passage
transit: in transit en transit
transit accommodation hébergement de transit *m*
transit hotel hôtel de passage *m*, hôtel de transit *m*
transit passenger passager en transit *m*
transit traveller voyageur en transit *m*
transport company compagnie de transport *f*
transport museum musée des transports *m*
transportation desk *Am* bureau de voyages *m*
travel voyages *mpl*; [*professional, business also*] déplacements *mpl*

travel agent agent de voyages *m*

travel agent's licence licence d'agent des voyages *f*

travel agent's voucher bon d'agence *m*, bon d'échange *m*, voucher *m*

travel bag sac de voyage *m*

travel directory guide de voyages *m*

travel documents dossier de voyage *m*

travel group charter *Am* achat de bloc-sièges *m*

travel guide guide touristique *m*

Travel Industry Marketing Group société de marketing spécialisée dans l'industrie du tourisme *f*

Travel Information Manual Travel Information Manual *m*

travel literature documentation touristique *f*

travel market marché du tourisme *m*

travel medical insurance assurance médicale de voyage *f*

Travelpass [*British Rail*] carte qui permet de voyager sur tout le réseau ferroviaire écossais

travel receipts recettes générées par le tourisme *fpl*

travel-size [*shampoo etc*] de voyage

travel trade industrie du voyage *f*

travel trade manual manuel de l'industrie du voyage *m*

traveler's check *Am* chèque de voyage *m*, traveller-chèque *m*

traveller voyageur *m*

traveller's cheque chèque de voyage *m*, traveller-chèque *m*

travelling salesman voyageur de commerce *m*

travelogue documentaire de voyage *m*, documentaire touristique *m*

tray plateau *m*

to **trek** faire du trekking

trekking trekking *m*

trip voyage *m*

tripe tripes *fpl*

triple room chambre triple *f*

trolley chariot *m*, desserte *f*, table roulante *f*

tronc [*pooled tips*] bourse commune des pourboires dans un restaurant *f*

tropics tropiques *mpl*

trouser-press presse à pantalon *f*

trout truite *f*

trunk malle *f*

trunk call appel interurbain *m*

trunk road axe routier *m*

tub *Am* bain *m*

tube [*London*] métro *m*

tube station station de métro *f*

tuberculosis tuberculose *f*

tumbler verre *m*

tuna thon *m*

turbot turbot *m*

turkey dinde *f*

turndown housekeeper gouvernante du soir *f*

turnip navet *m*

turnover chiffre d'affaires *m*

TV lounge salle de télévision *f*

twin-bedded room chambre à lits jumeaux *f*

twin beds lits jumeaux *mpl*

twin room chambre à deux lits simples *f*

twinning [*of towns*] jumelage *m*

two-star deux étoiles *f*

two-week block deux semaines bloquées *fpl*

typist dactylo *mf*

U

UFTAA (= Universal Federation of Travel Agents' Associations) FUAAV *f*
UKTS = United Kingdom Tourism Survey
unaccompanied baggage bagages non-accompagnés *mpl*
unchecked baggage bagages non-enregistrés *mpl*
unconfirmed [*reservation*] non-confirmé
uncooked cru
to **undercharge: I undercharged you** je ne vous ai pas fait payer assez
undercloth sous-nappe *f*
underdone pas assez cuit
underground métro *m*
underground station station de métro *f*
undersheet alèse *f*
uniform uniforme *m*, tenue *f*
Uniform System of Accounts for Hotels système de comptabilité hôtelière uniformisé *m*
unit manager directeur de service *m*
United Kingdom Tourism Survey étude sur les déplacements des résidents du Royaume-Uni *f*
Universal Federation of Travel Agents' Associations Fédération universelle des associations d'agences de voyage *f*
unlimited buffet buffet à volonté *m*
unlimited travel nombre de voyages illimité *m*
unlimited value coupon *or* **voucher** voucher "crédit illimité" *m*, bon d'échange "crédit illimité" *m*
to **unpack** défaire ses bagages
upgrade [*of booking*] surclassement *m*
to **upgrade** surclasser, améliorer

V

vacancies chambres libres *fpl*
vacancy chambre libre *f*
vacant libre
to **vacate** [*room*] libérer, quitter
vacation *Am* vacances *fpl*
vacation bond [*Am, form of timeshare*] obligation "vacances" *f*
vacation center *Am* club de vacances *m*
vacation farm tourism *Am* tourisme à la ferme *m*
vacation frequency *Am* fréquence touristique *f*
vacation home *Am* résidence secondaire *f*
vacation propensity *Am* tendance touristique *f*
vacationer *Am* vacancier *m*
to **vaccinate** vacciner
vaccination vaccination *f*
vaccination certificate certificat de vaccination *m*
vaccine vaccin *m*
vaccine booster rappel (de vaccin) *m*
valet parking service de voiturier *m*
valid [*tickets etc*] valable
validated [*coach card etc*] validé
validation [*of ticket*] validation *f*
validation stamp cachet de validation des billets émis par l'agence de voyages *m*

validator cachet *m*
valuables objets de valeur *mpl*
value added tax taxe sur la valeur ajoutée *f*
valued customer card carte de fidélité *f*
vanity case vanity case *m*
VAT (= Value Added Tax) TVA *f*
VDU = Visual Display Unit
veal veau *m*
vegan végétalien
vegetable cook responsable des légumes *m*
vegetables légumes *mpl*; [*as accompaniment to dish*] garniture *f*
vegetarian végétarien
vending machine distributeur automatique *m*
venison chevreuil *m*
ventilation ventilation *f*
venue lieu (de rendez-vous) *m*
vertical backward integration intégration verticale en amont *f*
vertical forward integration intégration verticale en aval *f*
vertical integration intégration verticale *f*
Very Important Person VIP *mf*
VFR = Visiting Friends and Relatives
via via
video vidéo *f*
video playback system système

de lecture de cassettes vidéo *m*
video recorder magnétoscope *m*
videotex vidéotex *m*
view vue *f*
viewdata system vidéotex *m*
villa villa *f*
village village *m*
vinegar vinaigre *m*
vintage cru *m*, millésime *m*
VIP (= Very Important Person) VIP *mf*
VIP guest hôte de marque *m*
VIP list liste des VIP *f*
VIP lounge salon VIP *m*
visa visa *m*
Visa (card) Carte Bleue *f*, carte Visa *f*
Visiting Friends and Relatives hébergement à titre gracieux *m*, hébergement non-marchand *m*
visitor visiteur *m*
Visitor and Convention Bureau office du tourisme et des congrès *m*
visitor attraction attraction

touristique *f*, centre d'intérêt touristique *m*
visitor centre centre d'accueil *m*
visitor facilities installations touristiques *fpl*
visitor interview survey enquête auprès des touristes *f*
visitor profile characteristics caractéristiques des touristes *fpl*
visitor survey étude sur les touristes *f*
visitor tax taxe de séjour *f*
visitors paid out voucher bon de débours *m*
visual display unit afficheur *m*
vocational qualification brevet professionnel *m*
vocational travel voyages professionnels *mpl*
voltage courant électrique *m*
volume [*of tourism*] volume *m*
voucher bon *m*, bon d'échange *m*, voucher *m*
VPO = Visitors Paid Out
VPO voucher bon de débours *m*

waiter serveur *m*, garçon *m*, commis de salle *m*
waiter service service à table *m*
waiting chef chef serveur *m*

waiting list liste d'attente *f*
waiting room salle d'attente *f*
waitlist liste d'attente *f*
waitress serveuse *f*

waitress service service à table *m*
wake-up call appel de réveil *m*,
  réveil par la réception *m*
Wales Tourist Board ≈ comité du
  tourisme du pays de Galles *m*
walk-in client sans réservation *m*
walk-out client qui part sans
  payer *m*
to **walk out** [*leave without paying*]
  partir sans payer, filer à
  l'anglaise
walking marche *f*
walking tour randonné *f*; [*in
  town*] visite à pied *f*
wallpaper papier peint *m*
walls [*of city*] remparts *mpl*
Warsaw Convention Convention
  de Varsovie *f*
washbasin lavabo *m*
washhand basin lavabo *m*
washroom *Am* cabinet de toilette *m*
wastebasket *Am* corbeille à
  papier *f*
waste disposal broyage des
  ordures *m*
waste disposal unit broyeur
  d'ordures *m*
wastepaper basket corbeille à
  papier *f*
**WATA = World Association of
  Travel Agencies**
water eau *f*
water cures thermalisme *m*, cures
  thermales *fpl*
waterfall cascade *f*
water glass verre à eau *m*
water park parc aquatique *m*
water skiing ski nautique *m*
water sports sports nautiques *mpl*
water sterilizing tablet pastille
  pour purifier l'eau *f*
waterway voie navigable *f*

WC W.-C. *mpl*
weather temps *m*
weather conditions conditions
  météorologiques *fpl*
weather forecast météo *f*,
  prévisions météorologiques *fpl*
week semaine *f*
weekend week-end *m*
weekend bargain break week-end
  promotionnel *m*
weekend break séjour de week-
  end *m*
weekend rate tarif week-end *m*
weekly [*flight, sailing etc*]
  hebdomadaire
weight poids *m*
weight limit limitation de poids *f*
weight system [*to charge for
  baggage*] système de facturation
  au poids des bagages *m*
welcome: *welcome to Scotland*
  bienvenue en Écosse; *welcome
  to Paris* bienvenue à Paris
welcome bouquet bouquet
  d'accueil *m*
welcome drink cocktail
  d'accueil *m*, pot d'accueil *m*
welcome pack produits
  d'accueil *mpl*
welcome reception réception de
  bienvenue *f*
well-appointed bien aménagé
well chilled frappé
well done bien cuit
wet [*weather*] pluvieux
wet lease [*for aircraft*] location
  d'avion avec équipage *f*
wheelchair fauteuil roulant *m*
wheelchair access facilité d'accès
  pour fauteuils roulants *f*
whiskey [*Am, Ireland*] whisky *m*
whisky whisky *m*
whisky glass verre à whisky *m*

white blanc

white coffee (café) crème *m*, café au lait *m*

Whitney advance booking rack planning de réservation de type Whitney *m*

Whitney card fiche Whitney *f*, fiche client *f*

Whitney system planning Whitney *m*

wide-bodied aircraft avion gros porteur *m*

window seat place côté fenêtre *f*

windsurfing planche à voile *f*

wine vin *m*

wine bar bar à vin *m*

wine cellar cave *f*, cave à vin *f*

wine glass verre à vin *m*, ballon *m*

wine list carte des vins *f*

wine route route des vins *f*

wine steward *Am* sommelier *m*

wine waiter sommelier *m*

wing aile *f*

winter hiver *m*

winter break (petites) vacances d'hiver *fpl*

winter holiday vacances d'hiver *fpl*

winter resort station de sports d'hiver *f*

winter season saison d'hiver *f*

winter sports sports d'hiver *mpl*

winter sports holiday vacances aux sports d'hiver *fpl*

winter sports resort station de sports d'hiver *f*

winter sports tourism tourisme blanc *m*

winter tourism tourisme hivernal *m*

wire câble *m*

wood bois *m*

word processor traitement de texte *m*

to **work in shifts** travailler en équipe de roulement

work schedule planning de travail *m*

workshop atelier *m*

World Association of Travel Agencies association mondiale des agences de voyages *f*

World Heritage Site site du patrimoine mondial *m*

Worldspan [*US airline reservation system*] Worldspan *m*

World Tourism Organization Organisation mondiale du tourisme *f*

world travel voyages internationaux *mpl*

World Travel and Tourism Council Conseil des voyages et du tourisme mondial *m*

World Travel Market salon du tourisme mondial *m*

writing desk table à écrire *f*

writing room salon d'écriture *m*

written confirmation confirmation écrite *f*, confirmation par écrit *f*

WTB = Wales Tourist Board

WTM = World Travel Market

WTO (= World Tourism Organization) OMT *f*

WTTC = World Travel and Tourism Council

XYZ

X-ray machine machine à
rayon X *f*
yacht voilier *m*
yachting navigation de plaisance *f*
YHA = Youth Hostels Association
yoghurt yaourt *m*
Young Persons' Railcard carte de
réduction pour les jeunes âgés
de 16 à 23 ans sur le réseau
BR *f*, ≈ Carte Jeune *f*

youth fare tarif jeune *m*
youth hostel auberge de jeunesse *f*
Youth Hostels Association
association des auberges de
jeunesse *f*
zero-rated exempt de TVA
zoning répartition en zones *f*
zoo zoo *m*
zoo park parc zoologique *m*
zucchini *Am* courgette *f*

Annexes
Appendices

NOMS GEOGRAPHIQUES

Afghanistan *m* Afghanistan
Afrique *f* Africa
Afrique du Sud *f* South Africa
Algérie *f* Algeria
Allemagne *f* Germany
Amérique *f* America
Amérique du Nord *f* North America
Amérique du Sud *f* South America
Andorre *f* Andorra
Angleterre *f* England
Angola *m* Angola
Antilles *fpl* West Indies
Arabie Saoudite *f* Saudi Arabia
Argentine *f* Argentina
Arménie *f* Armenia
Asie *f* Asia
Australie *f* Australia
Autriche *f* Austria
Azerbaïdjan *m* Azerbaijan
Bahreïn *m* Bahrain
Bangladesh *m* Bangladesh
Barbade *f* Barbados
Belgique *f* Belgium
Bélize *m* Belize
Bhoutan *m* Bhutan
Biélorussie *f* Byelorussia
Bolivie *f* Bolivia
Botswana *m* Botswana
Brésil *m* Brazil
Brunei *m* Brunei
Bulgarie *f* Bulgaria
Cambodge *m* Cambodia
Cameroun *m* Cameroon
Canada *m* Canada
CEI (Communauté des États Indépendants) *f* CIS (Commonwealth of Independent States)
Chili *m* Chile
Chine *f* China
Colombie *f* Colombia

Congo *m* Congo
Corée du Nord *f* North Korea
Corée du Sud *f* South Korea
Corse *f* Corsica
Costa Rica *m* Costa Rica
Côte d'Ivoire *f* Ivory Coast
Danemark *m* Denmark
Écosse *f* Scotland
Égypte *f* Egypt
Eire *f* Eire
Émirats arabes unis *mpl* United Arab Emirates
Espagne *f* Spain
Estonie *f* Estonia
États-Unis *mpl* United States
Europe *f* Europe
Finlande *f* Finland
France *f* France
Gabon *m* Gabon
Gambie *f* Gambia
Géorgie *f* Georgia
Ghana *m* Ghana
Grande-Bretagne *f* Great Britain
Grèce *f* Greece
Groenland *m* Greenland
Guadeloupe *f* Guadeloupe
Guatemala *m* Guatemala
Guinée *f* Guinea
Guyana *f* Guyana
Guyane française *f* French Guiana
Hollande *f* Holland
Honduras *m* Honduras
Hong Kong Hong Kong
Hongrie *f* Hungary
îles de la Manche *fpl* Channel Islands
Inde *f* India
Indonésie *f* Indonesia
Irak *m* Iraq
Iran *m* Iran
Irlande *f* Ireland
Irlande du Nord *f* Northern Ireland

Islande f Iceland
Israël m Israel
Italie f Italy
Jamaïque f Jamaica
Japon m Japan
Jordanie f Jordan
Kenya m Kenya
Koweït m Kuwait
Laos m Laos
Lettonie f Latvia
Liban m Lebanon
Liberia m Liberia
Libye f Libya
Liechtenstein m Liechtenstein
Lituanie f Lithuania
Luxembourg m Luxemburg
Madagascar m Madagascar
Maghreb m countries of North
  Africa
Malawi m Malawi
Malaysia f Malaysia
Mali m Mali
Maroc m Morocco
Mauritanie f Mauritania
Mexique m Mexico
Moldavie f Moldavia
Moyen-Orient m Middle East
Mozambique m Mozambique
Namibie f Namibia
Népal m Nepal
Nicaragua m Nicaragua
Niger m Niger
Nigeria m Nigeria
Norvège f Norway
Nouvelle-Zélande f New Zealand
Oman m Oman
Ouganda m Uganda
Pakistan m Pakistan
Palestine f Palestine
Papouasie-Nouvelle-Guinée f
  Papua New Guinea
Paraguay m Paraguay
Pays-Bas mpl Netherlands

Pays de Galles m Wales
Pérou m Peru
Philippines fpl Philippines
Pologne f Poland
Portugal m Portugal
République dominicaine f Domini-
  can Republic
République tchèque f Czech
  Republic
Roumanie f Romania
Royaume-Uni m United Kingdom
Russie f Russia
Scandinavie f Scandinavia
Sénégal m Senegal
Sierra Leone f Sierra Leone
Singapour m Singapore
Slovaquie f Slovakia
Somalie f Somalia
Soudan m Sudan
Sri Lanka m Sri Lanka
Suède f Sweden
Suisse f Switzerland
Syrie f Syria
Taiwan Taiwan
Tanzanie f Tanzania
Tasmanie f Tasmania
Tchad m Chad
Thaïlande f Thailand
Tiers Monde m Third World
Tobago Tobago
Togo m Togo
Trinidad f Trinidad
Tunisie f Tunisia
Turquie f Turkey
Ukraine f Ukraine
Uruguay m Uruguay
Venezuela m Venezuela
Viêt-nam m Vietnam
Yémen du Nord m North Yemen
Yémen du Sud m South Yemen
Zaïre m Zaire
Zambie f Zambia
Zimbabwe m Zimbabwe

GEOGRAPHICAL NAMES

* *employé sans article*

* used without any article

Afghanistan Afghanistan *m*
Africa Afrique *f*
Algeria Algérie *f*
America Amérique *f*
Andorra Andorre *f* *
Angola Angola *m*
Argentina Argentine *f*
Armenia Arménie *f*
Asia Asie *f*
Australia Australie *f*
Austria Autriche *f*
Azerbaijan Azerbaïdjan *m*
Bahrain Bahreïn *m*
Bangladesh Bangladesh *m*
Barbados Barbade *f*
Belgium Belgique *f*
Belize Bélize *m*
Bhutan Bhoutan *m*
Bolivia Bolivie *f*
Botswana Botswana *m*
Brazil Brésil *m*
Brunei Brunei *m*
Bulgaria Bulgarie *f*
Byelorussia Biélorussie *f*
Cambodia Cambodge *m*
Cameroon Cameroun *m*
Canada Canada *m*
Chad Tchad *m*
Channel Islands îles de la
   Manche *fpl*
Chile Chili *m*
China Chine *f*
**CIS (Commonwealth of
   Independent States)** CEI
   (Communauté des États
   Indépendants) *f*
Colombia Colombie *f*
Congo Congo *m*
Corsica Corse *f*
Costa Rica Costa Rica *m*

Czech Republic République
   tchèque *f*
Denmark Danemark *m*
Dominican Republic République
   dominicaine *f*
Egypt Égypte *f*
Eire Eire *f*
England Angleterre *f*
Estonia Estonie *f*
Ethiopia Éthiopie *f*
Europe Europe *f*
Finland Finlande *f*
France France *f*
French Guiana Guyane française *f*
Gabon Gabon *m*
Gambia Gambie *f*
Georgia Géorgie *f*
Germany Allemagne *f*
Ghana Ghana *m*
Great Britain Grande-Bretagne *f*
Greece Grèce *f*
Greenland Groenland *m*
Guadeloupe Guadeloupe *f*
Guatemala Guatemala *m*
Guinea Guinée *f*
Guyana Guyana *f*
Holland Hollande *f*
Honduras Honduras *m*
Hong Kong * Hong Kong
Hungary Hongrie *f*
Iceland Islande *f*
India Inde *f*
Indonesia Indonésie *f*
Iran Iran *m*
Iraq Irak *m*
Ireland Irlande *f*
Israel Israël *m* *
Italy Italie *f*
Ivory Coast Côte d'Ivoire *f*
Jamaica Jamaïque *f*

Japan Japon *m*
Jordan Jordanie *f*
Kenya Kenya *m*
Kuwait Koweït *m*
Laos Laos *m*
Latvia Lettonie *f*
Lebanon Liban *m*
Liberia Liberia *m*
Libya Libye *f*
Liechtenstein Liechtenstein *m*
Lithuania Lituanie *f*
Luxemburg Luxembourg *m*
Madagascar Madagascar *m* *
Malawi Malawi *m*
Malaysia Malaysia *f*
Mali Mali *m*
Mauritania Mauritanie *f*
Mexico Mexique *m*
Middle East Moyen-Orient *m*
Moldavia Moldavie *f*
Morocco Maroc *m*
Mozambique Mozambique *m*
Namibia Namibie *f*
Nepal Népal *m*
Netherlands Pays-Bas *mpl*
New Zealand Nouvelle-Zélande *f*
Nicaragua Nicaragua *m*
Niger Niger *m*
Nigeria Nigeria *m*
North America Amérique du Nord *f*
North Korea Corée du Nord *f*
North Yemen Yémen du Nord *m*
Northern Ireland Irlande du Nord *f*
Norway Norvège *f*
Oman Oman *m* *
Pakistan Pakistan *m*
Palestine Palestine *f*
Papua New Guinea Papouasie-Nouvelle-Guinée *f*
Paraguay Paraguay *m*
Peru Pérou *m*
Philippines Philippines *fpl*
Poland Pologne *f*
Portugal Portugal *m*

Romania Roumanie *f*
Russia Russie *f*
Saudi Arabia Arabie Saoudite *f*
Scandinavia Scandinavie *f*
Scotland Écosse *f*
Senegal Sénégal *m*
Sierra Leone Sierra Leone *f*
Singapore Singapour *m* *
Slovakia Slovaquie *f*
Somalia Somalie *f*
South Africa Afrique du Sud *f*
South America Amérique du Sud *f*
South Korea Corée du Sud *f*
South Yemen Yémen du Sud *m*
Spain Espagne *f*
Sri Lanka Sri Lanka *m*
Sudan Soudan *m*
Sweden Suède *f*
Switzerland Suisse *f*
Syria Syrie *f*
Taiwan Taiwan *
Tanzania Tanzanie *f*
Tasmania Tasmanie *f*
Thailand Thaïlande *f*
Third World Tiers Monde *m*
Tobago Tobago *
Togo Togo *m*
Trinidad Trinidad *f*
Tunisia Tunisie *f*
Turkey Turquie *f*
Uganda Ouganda *m*
Ukraine Ukraine *f*
United Arab Emirates Émirats arabes unis *mpl*
United Kingdom Royaume-Uni *m*
United States États-Unis *mpl*
Uruguay Uruguay *m*
USA États-Unis *mpl*
Venezuela Venezuela *m*
Vietnam Viêt-nam *m*
Wales Pays de Galles *m*
West Indies Antilles *fpl*
Zaire Zaïre *m*
Zambia Zambie *f*
Zimbabwe Zimbabwe *m*

VILLES

Alger Algiers
Athènes Athens
Barcelone Barcelona
Bruxelles Brussels
Le Caire Cairo
Copenhague Copenhagen
Douvres Dover
Édimbourg Edinburgh
Francfort Frankfurt
Gênes Genoa
Genève Geneva
Hambourg Hamburg
La Haye The Hague
Lisbonne Lisbon
Londres London
Lyon Lyons
Marseille Marseilles
Montréal Montreal
Moscou Moscow
Québec Quebec City
Téhéran Tehran
Varsovie Warsaw
Venise Venice
Vienne Vienna

CITIES

Algiers Alger
Athens Athènes
Barcelona Barcelone
Brussels Bruxelles
Cairo Le Caire
Copenhagen Copenhague
Dover Douvres
Edinburgh Édimbourg
Frankfurt Francfort
Geneva Genève
Genoa Gênes
The Hague La Haye
Hamburg Hambourg
Lisbon Lisbonne
London Londres
Lyons Lyon
Marseilles Marseille
Montreal Montréal
Moscow Moscou
Quebec City Québec
Tehran Téhéran
Venice Venise
Vienna Vienne
Warsaw Varsovie

MONNAIES

couronne *f* crown
dinar *m* dinar
dollar *m* dollar
dollar australien *m* Australian dollar
dollar canadien *m* Canadian dollar
dollar de Hong Kong *m* Hong Kong dollar
drachme *f* drachma
escudo *m* escudo
florin *m* florin
franc *m* franc
franc belge *m* Belgian franc
franc français *m* French franc
franc suisse *m* Swiss franc
lire *f* lira
livre *f* pound
livre irlandaise *f* punt
livre sterling *f* pound sterling
mark *m* mark
peseta *f* peseta
peso *m* peso
rand *m* rand
rial *m* rial
rouble *m* rouble
roupie *f* rupee
schilling *m* schilling
shilling *m* shilling
yen *m* yen

CURRENCIES

Australian dollar dollar australien *m*
Belgian franc franc belge *m*
Canadian dollar dollar canadien *m*
crown couronne *f*
dinar dinar *m*
dollar dollar *m*
drachma drachme *f*
escudo escudo *m*
florin florin *m*
franc franc *m*
French franc franc français *m*
Hong Kong dollar dollar de Hong-Kong *m*
lira lire *f*
mark mark *m*
peseta peseta *f*
peso peso *m*
pound livre sterling *f*
pound livre *f*
punt livre irlandaise *f*
rand rand *m*
rial rial *m*
rouble rouble *m*
rupee roupie *f*
schilling schilling *m*
shilling shilling *m*
Swiss franc franc suisse *f*
yen yen *m*

CONFIRMER UNE RÉSERVATION

Grand Central Hotel
121 Cedar Crescent
Guildford
GU5 8HD
ENGLAND

Guildford, le 19 février 1993

M. Mathieu Sorel
Directeur du Personnel
145, avenue des Anglais
92210 St Cloud
FRANCE

Monsieur,

Nous accusons réception de votre courrier du 14 février 1993 au sujet de l'hébergement de votre Directeur général, M. Jean-Luc Delatte, et nous vous en remercions.

Nous avons le plaisir de vous informer que nous avons une chambre disponible aux dates demandées qui vous conviendra parfaitement. J'ai donc réservé cette chambre avec bain pour les nuits du 15, 16 et 17 mars, au nom de M. J.-L. Delatte.

La chambre sera à sa disposition à partir de 18h00 le 15 mars et devra être libérée avant 11h00 le jour du départ. S'il devait arriver ou partir plus tard, nous vous serions reconnaissants de nous le préciser afin de prendre les disposi ns nécessaires.

Si vous ave besoin d'autres informations sur le Grand Central Hotel ou sur Guildford, n'hésitez pas à nous les demander.

Dans l'attente de recevoir M. Delatte et en vous assurant que nous ferons notre possible pour lui rendre son séjour agréable, nous vous prions d'agréer, Monsieur, l'assurance de nos sentiments les meilleurs.

Stephen Plunkett
Directeur des réservations

CONFIRMING A RESERVATION

19th February 1993

M. Mathieu Sorel
Directeur du Personnel
145, avenue des Anglais
92210 St Cloud
FRANCE

Dear M. Sorel

Thank you for your letter of 14 February 1993 requesting accommodation for your Managing Director, Mr Jean-Luc Delatte.

I am pleased to inform you that we have a suitable room available for the required dates. I have therefore reserved a single room with bathroom for the nights of 15, 16 and 17 of March under the name of Mr J.-L. Delatte.

The room will be kept until 6pm on the 15th of March and should be vacated by 11am on the day of departure. Please notify us of a late arrival or departure in order that suitable arrangements can be made.

If you require any further information concerning the Grand Central Hotel or Guildford, please do not hesitate to contact us.

We look forward to meeting Mr Delatte and trust that his stay with us will be a very pleasant experience.

Yours sincerely

Stephen Plunkett
Reservations Manager

DONNER DES INFORMATIONS

Scottish Tourist Board
23, Ravelston Terrace
EDINBURGH EH4 3EU
SCOTLAND

Édimbourg, le 13 juillet 1993

Mme J. Vermeil
34, avenue Jean-Jaurès
75019 PARIS
FRANCE

Chère Madame,

Nous vous remercions pour votre lettre du 21 juin 1994 dans laquelle vous exprimiez votre désir d'être informée sur les différents types d'hébergement qu'offre notre ville.

Dans la gamme de prix qui vous convient, nous vous recommandons le City Hotel, central, bien desservi et proche des principaux centres d'intérêt touristiques. Le prix d'une chambre double avec salle de bain est de 34 £ par nuit et par personne, petit déjeuner compris. Pour dîner à l'hôtel, il faut compter un supplément de 15 £ par personne.

Cependant, si vous préférez loger dans un quartier plus calme, vous apprécierez sûrement le Riverside Inn. Il se situe à 10 minutes seulement du centre ville et propose des chambres doubles avec bain pour 36 £ par nuit et par personne, petit déjeuner compris. Mais il n'est pas possible d'y prendre le repas du soir.

Nous vous envoyons ci-joint les brochures de ces deux hôtels, et nous nous tenons à votre entière disposition pour vous communiquer de plus amples informations. Nous serons heureux de vous réserver une chambre dans l'un de ces hôtels ou tout autre hôtel de votre choix.

En espérant vous voir bientôt à Édimbourg, nous vous prions de croire, Madame, à nos sentiments dévoués.

Kevin McManus
Conseiller commercial

REPLYING TO AN ENQUIRY

13 July 1993

Mme. J. Vermeil
34, avenue Jean-Jaurès
75019 Paris
FRANCE

Dear Mme. Vermeil

Thank you for your letter of the 21st of June in which you expressed an interest in the accommodation available in our city.

Within your price range, I can recommend the City Hotel which is central and close to all amenities and the major tourist attractions. A double room with private facilities costs £34 per person per night. Breakfast is included, but there is an additional charge of £15 per person for an evening meal.

However, if you prefer a quieter location, I am sure you would like the Riverside Inn. It is only 10 minutes away from the city centre and a double room with bathroom costs £36 per person per night. Breakfast is included but no evening meals are served.

I have enclosed leaflets on both hotels, but if you require any more information please do not hesitate to contact us. If you wish us to make a reservation in your name at either of these hotels or at any hotel of your choice, we will be very happy to do so.

I hope we will see you in Edinburgh very soon.

Yours sincerely

Kevin McManus
Sales Consultant

DONNER DES INFORMATIONS

Tourist Information Centre
3 Queen's Gate
DERRY BT48 3NP
N. IRELAND

Derry, le 7 septembre 1993

Miss Charlotte Evans
20 St Stephen's Avenue
LEEDS L23 9HT

Mademoiselle,

Nous avons pris note de votre lettre du 21 août 1993, et nous vous remercions de l'intérêt que vous manifestez pour les nombreuses attractions touristiques et les infrastructures de notre cité historique.

Derry est une ville fortifiée dont les murailles ont été fort bien conservées. Une promenade autour de celles-ci vous permettra de jouir des panoramas les plus intéressants de notre ville. Vous pourrez en effet admirer la cathédrale St Columb, le Guildhall et le Fort O'Doherty.

Plusieurs musées, également, témoignent du fascinant passé de notre ville, et un musée d'art expose régulièrement les œuvres de talentueux artistes locaux. Et bien sûr, nous avons un théâtre, des cinémas et des restaurants pour tous les goûts.

Si vous aimez la campagne, les sports nautiques ou la pêche, Donegal est à quelques minutes en bus. Là, un paysage typique et de nombreuses plages vous attendent.

Veuillez trouver ci-joint des dépliants qui vous présenteront ces attractions dans le moindre détail. N'hésitez pas à nous contacter si vous désirez en savoir plus sur ces sites et les services qui y sont offerts.

Bien cordialement,

Catherine Phillips
Responsable des relations publiques

REPLYING TO AN ENQUIRY

7 September 1993

Miss Charlotte Evans
20 St Stephen's Avenue
Leeds L23 9HT

Dear Miss Evans

Thank you for your letter of the 21st August in which you expressed an interest in the many tourist attractions and facilities of our historic town.

Derry is a walled city, and the walls have remained very well preserved. A walk around them brings you past the most interesting sights of our city, including St Columb's Cathedral, the Guildhall and the O'Doherty Fort.

There are also several museums which chart the fascinating past of our city, and an art gallery which regularly displays work by talented local artists. And of course we have a theatre, cinemas and restaurants catering to a wide variety of tastes.

If you enjoy the countryside and watersports or fishing, Donegal is only a bus-ride away. There you will find unspoilt countryside and dozens of beaches.

I am enclosing leaflets which explain all these attractions in greater detail. Please feel free to contact us if you would like to know more about the many attractions and facilities on offer.

Yours sincerely

Catherine Phillips
Public Relations Manager

CONSEILS PRATIQUES

LES POURBOIRES *(Royaume-Uni)*

Lorsque vous allez au restaurant, vérifiez si le service est compris dans l'addition. S'il ne l'est pas, vous pouvez laisser, en règle générale, un pourboire de 10% du montant de l'addition. Il est courant de laisser un pourboire au chauffeurs de taxi et aux coiffeurs. En revanche, on ne laisse généralement pas de pourboire dans les bars et les magasins, au cinéma ou au théâtre.

LA CONDUITE *(Royaume-Uni)*

En Grande-Bretagne et en Irlande, on conduit sur le côté gauche de la route. Sur l'autoroute et les routes à deux voies on ne peut dépasser que par la droite.

À l'approche d'un rond-point, on doit laisser la priorité aux véhicules déjà engagés.

Limitations de vitesse:

* sur autoroute - 70 mph (110km/h)
* sur route à double voie - 70 mph (110 km/h)
* sur route à voie unique - 60mph (95km/h) sauf indication contraire
* en agglomération - 30 mph (50km/h)

Le taux maximal d'alcoolémie autorisé est de 0,8 g/ml de sang.

ASSURANCE *(auto)*

Pour conduire au Royaume-Uni, vous devez avoir sur vous votre attestation d'assurance et la carte grise du véhicule.

ASSURANCE MALADIE

Les Français qui se rendent au Royaume Uni peuvent se procurer une fiche E111 auprès de leur CPAM ou de leur mutuelle afin de bénéficier de soins médicaux gratuits.

QUARANTAINE

L'importation au Royaume Uni d'animaux sans licence est sujette à de sévères pénalités, et tout animal introduit illégalement est passible d'être abattu.

PRACTICAL TIPS

TIPPING (France)

In restaurants, cafés and at the hairdresser's a service charge of 15% is included by law. Therefore tipping is entirely optional. A small tip is normally given to usherettes in cinemas and theatres.

DRIVING (France)

To drive in France, a UK citizen must be 18 or over.

It is compulsory to carry a warning triangle and/or have hazard warning lights.

When driving in France, you must give way to any vehicle coming from the right unless the signposts indicate that you have priority. You must give way to traffic already on a roundabout.

Speed limits:

* towns - 50km/h (30mph)
* rural - 90km/h (56mph)
* dual carriageway - 110km/h (70mph) (Belgium 120km/h (75mph))
* motorway - 130km/h (80mph) unless otherwise indicated (Belgium 120km/h (75mph))

Unless your headlights have manual adjustment, you will need clip-on beam deflectors or PVC strips for night driving.

The legal limit for alcohol when driving is 70mg/100ml of blood.

INSURANCE (driving)

France: minimum third party insurance is required, and a "green card" is recommended. This can be obtained from your insurance company. Further insurance is needed to cover breakdown and recovery costs.

INSURANCE (health)

Visitors to France can obtain an E111 to cover medical expenses by filling out form DoT T1 at the Post Office. This can be obtained by filling out a DoT T1 form at the Post Office. However, personal insurance is required to cover the cost of private hospitals and transport home. Furthermore, in France you will have to pay approximately 20% of medical expenses.

TAKING ANIMALS TO FRANCE

Any pet being taken into France must have an Export Health Certificate. On return to the U.K., it will have to remain in quarantine for 6 months.

GREETING AND CHECKING IN/OUT

SALUER, ACCUEILLIR ET PRENDRE CONGÉ

Hello, (how) can I help you?	Bonjour, puis-je vous aider ? *OU* Bonjour, que puis-je faire pour vous ?
I'm afraid we're fully booked at the moment.	Je regrette, nous sommes 'complet' en ce moment.
Would you like me to reserve you a room in another hotel?	Voulez-vous que je vous réserve une chambre dans un autre hôtel ?
Did you have a pleasant trip?	Vous avez fait bon voyage?
Can I have your name please?	Votre nom, s'il vous plaît ?
Have you made a reservation?	Avez-vous une réservation ?
How many people are with you?	Combien de personnes vous accompagnent ?
Would you like separate rooms or a family room?	Vous préférez des chambres séparées ou une grande chambre (pour toute la famille) ?
Would you prefer a double bed or twin beds?	Préférez-vous un grand lit ou deux lits simples ?
A double room costs 300FF per person per night.	Le tarif en chambre double est de 300 FF par nuit et par personne.
Would you prefer a sea view or a room overlooking the garden?	Vous préférez une chambre avec vue sur mer ou sur jardin ?
I can give you a double room on the fourth floor.	Je peux vous donner une chambre double au quatrième étage.
Would you prefer a room with a bath or a shower?	Vous préférez une chambre avec bain ou avec douche ?
Would you like a room with private facilities?	Voulez-vous une chambre avec salle de bain ?
Can you fill out this form please?	Pourriez-vous remplir ce formulaire, s'il vous plaît ?
May I see your passport or some other form of identification?	Puis-je voir votre passeport ou une autre pièce d'identité ?
Breakfast is included in the price.	Le prix comprend le petit déjeuner.

Will you require an evening meal as well?	Vous dînerez aussi à l'hôtel ?
Breakfast is served between 7am and 9am.	Le petit déjeuner est servi entre 7h00 et 9h00.
How many nights do you plan to stay with us?	Combien de nuits comptez-vous passer dans notre établissement ?
Your room is number 34, on the second floor.	Vous avez la chambre 34, au deuxième étage.
The porter will carry up your luggage.	Le porteur va s'occuper de vos bagages.
Would you like a wake-up call in the morning?	Souhaitez-vous être réveillé (par téléphone) demain matin ?
Please leave your key at reception before you go out.	Veuillez laisser votre clé à la réception avant de sortir.
Can you vacate the room by 11am tomorrow please?	Pouvez-vous libérer la chambre avant 11h00 demain matin, s'il vous plaît ?
Can you pay in advance please?	Pouvez-vous régler à l'avance, s'il vous plaît ?
We accept cash, cheques or credit cards.	Nous acceptons les espèces, les chèques et les cartes de crédit.
How would you like to pay?	Comment souhaitez-vous payer / régler ?
Make the cheque payable to "Grand Central Hotel" please.	Veuillez libeller votre chèque à l'ordre du "Grand Cental Hotel".
Would you like a receipt?	Voulez-vous un reçu ?
Here is your bill.	Voilà votre note.
I hope you enjoyed your stay.	J'espère que vous avez passé un agréable séjour chez nous.
Have a pleasant journey home.	Bon voyage. *OU* Bon retour.

INFORMATION (in the Tourist Office or at reception)

Informations (à l'Office du tourisme ou à la réception)

The church is two minutes' walk from the hotel.

L'église est à deux minutes à pied de l'hôtel.

Turn right at the traffic lights, and then go straight ahead. You will see the post office on your left.

Tournez à droite au feu rouge, puis continuez tout droit. Vous verrez la poste sur votre gauche.

The shops close at 5.30pm (half past five) and the banks close at 3pm (three).

Les magasins ferment à 17h30 (dix-sept heures trente) et les banques à 15h00 (quinze heures).

There are several museums in the city, and a wonderful art gallery.

Vous trouverez plusieurs musées en ville, dont un magnifique musée d'art.

There is a taxi rank outside the main entrance.

Il y a une station de taxis juste devant l'entrée principale.

I can recommend the pizzeria in Victoria Street.

Je vous recommande la pizzeria de Victoria Street.

You'll find a baker's in the rue de Vienne.

Vous trouverez une boulangerie dans la rue de Vienne.

You can change your money and traveller's cheques here in the hotel.

Vous pouvez changer votre argent et vos travellers-chèques à l'hôtel.

Take the number 25 bus.

Prenez le bus numéro 25.

There is a tube station at the corner.

Il y a une station de métro au coin de la rue.

What sort of accommodation do you require?

Quel type d'hébergement recherchez-vous ?

Here is a map of the town with the bus routes and tourist attractions.

Voici un plan de la ville avec les lignes de bus et les centres d'intérêt.

There are several banks and bureaux de change in the town centre.

Vous trouverez plusieurs banques et bureaux de change dans le centre ville.

There's a train for London every hour.

Il y a des trains pour Londres toutes les heures.

There are three sightseeing tours per day.

Il y a trois visites guidées par jour.

I can reserve you three places for the sightseeing tour if you wish.	Je puis vous réserver trois places pour la visite guidée, si vous le désirez.

TAKING CALLS

RÉPONDRE AU TÉLÉPHONE

Hello, the Grand Central Hotel. How can I help you?	Grand Central Hotel, bonjour. Que puis-je faire pour vous ? *OU* Bonjour, Grand Central Hotel à votre service.
What room number please?	Quel numéro de chambre, s'il vous plaît ?
I'm afraid he's not in at the moment. Can I take a message?	Je regrette, il n'est pas là. Puis-je prendre un message ?
I'll put you through to the reservations department.	Je vous passe le service des réservations.
Hold the line please.	Ne quittez pas.

RESTAURANT

RESTAURANT

Good evening, Sir/Madam.	Bonsoir monsieur/madame.
Have you reserved a table?	Avez-vous réservé ?
Can I take your coat?	Puis-je prendre votre manteau ?
Would you like a table near the window?	Vous préférez une table près de la fenêtre ?
Smoking or non-smoking?	Fumeur ou non-fumeur ?
A table for four?	Une table pour quatre ?
Would you like to come this way please.	Veuillez me suivre, s'il vous plaît.
Can I get you a drink?	Désirez-vous un apéritif ?
I can recommend the sole.	Je vous recommande la sole.
Today's special is roast veal.	Comme plat du jour, nous vous proposons un rôti de veau.
Would you like to see the dessert menu?	Voulez-vous consulter la carte des desserts ?

179

COMPLAINTS

RÉCLAMATIONS

What seems to be the matter? *OR* What seems to be the problem?	Y a-t-il un problème ? *OU* Que puis-je faire pour vous ?
I'm very sorry, but we are rather short-staffed at the moment.	Je suis vraiment désolé(e), mais nous manquons de personnel en ce moment.
I shall see to the matter immediately.	Je m'en occupe immédiatement.
The management cannot be held responsible.	La direction décline toute responsabilité. *OU* La direction ne peut être tenue pour responsable.
I apologize for any inconvenience caused.	Je m'excuse pour tout désagrément occasionné. *OU* Je m'excuse pour les désagréments occasionnés.
This is due to circumstances beyond our control.	Cela est dû à des circonstances indépendantes de notre volonté.
Please accept our apologies.	Veuillez nous excuser. *OU* Nous vous prions de bien vouloir nous excuser.
There must have been a misunderstanding.	Il y a sûrement (eu) un malentendu.
I am very sorry for the delay.	Je m'excuse pour ce retard.
A mistake has been made.	Il y a (une) erreur.
I'm afraid a double-booking has been made.	Je crains qu'il (n')y ait eu surlocation.
I will call the manager.	Je vais chercher le directeur.
I shall make sure that this does not happen again.	Je veillerai à ce que cela ne se reproduise plus.
Would you like to move room?	Souhaitez-vous changer de chambre ?
I shall have your shower repaired immediately.	Je fais réparer votre douche immédiatement.
I will call the police at once.	J'appelle la police.

TABLES DE CONVERSION/
CONVERSION TABLES

Longueur/Length

A mile is 1.6km. To convert kilometres to miles, divide the kilometres by 8 and multiply by 5. To convert miles to kilometres, divide the miles by five and multiply by 8.

cm	2,54	5,08	7,62	10,16	12,70	15,24	17,78	20,32	22,86	25,40
cm/ins	1	2	3	4	5	6	7	8	9	10
ins	0.39	0.79	1.18	1.58	1.97	2.36	2.76	3.15	3.54	3.94

km	1,61	3,22	4,83	6,44	8,05	9,66	11,27	12,88	14,48	16,09
km/miles	1	2	3	4	5	6	7	8	9	10
miles	0.62	1.24	1.86	2.49	3.11	3.73	4.35	4.97	5.59	6.21

Poids/Weight

To convert kilos to pounds, divide by 5 and multiply by 11. To convert pounds to kilos, divide by 11 and multiply by 5.

kg	0,45	0,91	1,36	1,81	2,27	2,72	3,18	3,63	4,08	4,54
kg/lb	1	2	3	4	5	6	7	8	9	10
pounds	2.20	4.41	6.61	8.82	11.02	13.23	15.43	17.64	19.84	22.05

tonnes	1,02	2,03	3,05	4,06	5,08	6,10	7,11	8,13	9,14	10,16
tonnes/ tons	1	2	3	4	5	6	7	8	9	10
tons	0.98	1.97	2.95	3.94	4.92	5.91	6.89	7.87	8.86	9.84

Volume/Volume

1 litre = approximately 1¾ pints or 0.22 gallons

litres	4,55	9,09	13,64	18,18	22,73	27,28	31,82	36,37	40,91	45,46
litres/ gallons	1	2	3	4	5	6	7	8	9	10
gallons	0.22	0.44	0.66	0.88	1.10	1.32	1.54	1.76	1.98	2.20

N.B. : *les anglophones indiquent la décimale en utilisant un point.*
In France the decimal point is indicated by a comma.

Surface/Area

hectares	0,41	0,81	1,21	1,62	2,02	2,43	2,83	3,24	3,64	4,05
hectares/ acres	1	2	3	4	5	6	7	8	9	10
acres	2.47	4.94	7.41	9.88	12.36	14.83	17.30	19.77	22.24	24.71

Température/Temperature

To convert Celsius into Fahrenheit, multiply the °C figure by 1.8 and add 32. To convert °F to °C, subtract 32 from the F° figure and divide by 1.8.

°C	-10	0	5	10	20	30	36.9	40	100
°F	14	32	41	50	68	77	98.4	104	212

POIDS ET MESURES
WEIGHTS AND MEASURES

MESURES
METRIC MEASURES

Longueur/**Length**

1 millimètre (mm)		=0.0394 inch (in)
1 centimètre (cm)	= 10 mm	=0.3937 in
1 mètre (m)	= 100 cm	=1.0936 yards (yds)
1 kilomètre (km)	= 1000 m	=0.6214 mile

Poids/**Weight**

1 milligramme (mg)		=0.0154 grain
1 gramme (g)	= 1000 mg	=0.0353 ounce (oz)
1 kilogramme (kg)	= 1000 g	=2.2046 pounds (lbs)
i tonne (t)	= 1000 kg	=0.984 ton

Surface/**Area**

1 cm²	= 100 mm²	=0.1550 square (sq.) in
1 m²	= 10000 cm²	=1.1960 sq. yds
1 are (a)	= 100 m²	=119.60 sq. yds
1 hectare (ha)	= 100 ares	=2.4711 acres

Capacité/**Capacity**

1 cm³		=0.0610 cubic (cu.) in
1 dm³	= 1000 cm³	=0.0353 cu. ft
1 m³	= 1000 dm³	=1.3080 cu. yds
1 litre	= 1 dm³	=0.2200 gallon

MESURES BRITANNIQUES
IMPERIAL MEASURES

Longueur/**Length**

1 inch		= 2,54 cm
1 foot	=12 inches	= 0,3048 m
1 yard	=3 feet	= 0,9144 m
1 mile	=1760 yards	= 1,6093 km

Poids/Weight

1 ounce	=16 drams	= 28,35 g
1 pound	=16 ounces	= 0,4536 kg
1 stone	=14 pounds	= 6,3503 kg
1 hundredweight (cwt)	=112 pounds	= 50,802 kg
1 ton	=20 cwt	= 1,0161 tonnes

Surface/Area

1 sq. inch		= 6,4516 cm²
1 sq. foot	=144 sq. ins	= 0,0929 m²
1 sq. yard	=9 sq. ft.	= 0,8361 m²
1 acre	=4840 sq. yds	= 4046,9 m²
1 sq. mile	=640 acres	= 259 hectares

Capacité/Capacity

1 cu. inch		= 16,387 cm³
1 cu. foot	=1728 cu. inches	= 0,0283 m³
1 cu. yard	=27 cu. ft.	= 0,7646 m³
1 pint	=4 gills	= 0,5683 litre
1 quart	=2 pints	= 1,1365 litres
1 gallon	=8 pints	= 4,5461 litres

MESURES US: MATIÈRES SÈCHES
US: DRY MEASURES

1 pint	=0.9689 UK pint	= 0,5506 litre

MESURES US: LIQUIDES
US: LIQUID MEASURES

1 fluid ounce	=1.0408 UK fl oz	= 0,0296 litre
1 pint (16 oz)	=0.8327 UK pint	= 0,4732 litre
1 gallon	=0.8327 UK gal	= 3,7853 litres

GUESTS REGISTRATION

SURNAME (NOM) BLOCK CAPITALS PLEASE	**FOR OFFICE USE ONLY**
FIRST NAMES (PRÉNOMS)	**Arrival Date**
HOME ADDRESS (ADRESSE DU DOMICILE)	**Departure Date**

FOR OFFICE USE ONLY

Arrival Date	
Departure Date	
No. of nights	No. of persons
Room No.	
Rate	
Deposit taken £	
Checked in by	

SURNAME (NOM) BLOCK CAPITALS PLEASE ....

FIRST NAMES (PRÉNOMS) ....

HOME ADDRESS
(ADRESSE DU DOMICILE) ....

.... PHONE No. ....

COMPANY (where applicable) ....

NATIONALITY (NATIONALITÉ)

PASSPORT No. (No. DU PASSEPORT) ....

PAYMENT TO BE MADE BY (please tick)

CAR No. (No. D'AUTO) ....

CASH ☐

NEXT DESTINATION ....

PERSONAL CHEQUE ☐ (with cheque card only)

A/C to be sent to: ....

CREDIT CARD ☐

....

PHONE No. ....

A/C TO BE SENT ☐ (by prior arrangement only)

Signature

YOUR ATTENTION IS DRAWN TO THE DISPLAYED
HOTEL PROPRIETORS LIABILITY NOTICE

(RESERVATION) THIS SIDE FOR OFFICE USE ONLY

NAME ....

ADDRESS ....

.... PHONE No. ....

COMPANY ....

ADDRESS ....

.... PHONE No. ....

A/C (TO BE CONFIRMED ON COMPANY LETTERHEAD)

....

ARRIVAL	
No. of nights	Conf. sent and sig.
Accom. reqd.	Deposit reqd.
Rates	
Booked by	

EXPECTED ARRIVAL TIME			Remarks and special requirements	A/C to be settled OWN ☐ COMPANY ☐ VOUCHER ☐
6pm Release	Credit Card Co.	Deposit Received		**Dated booked**
	Name No.	£		
		No.		

185

FICHE DE RÉSERVATION

RÉSERVATION **MODIFICATION** **ANNULATION**

DATE D'ARRIVÉE : DURÉE DU SÉJOUR :
DATE DE DÉPART :

HEURE D'ARRIVÉE :

CATÉGORIE DE CHAMBRE : NOMBRE DE PERSONNES :
OU NUMÉRO DE CHAMBRE :

OPTION ☐ RÉSERVATION FERME ☐ DATE DE RÉTROCESSION :

NOM ET PRÉNOM :
ADRESSE : N° TÉLÉPHONE :

SOURCE DE RÉSERVATION :
ADRESSE : TÉLÉPHONE :

FACTURE RÉGLÉE PAR :
CONDITIONS / PRIX :
ARRHES ☐ DATE DE VERSEMENT :
MONTANT : MODE DE RÈGLEMENT
OBSERVATIONS :

RÉSERVATION ACCEPTÉE PAR : ATTENTIONS SPÉCIALES :

DATE :
MODE DE RÉSERVATION :